Teacher's resource

150
Numeracy Hour
Lessons

YEAR 1

Contents	Page
Summary of objectives	3
Mental maths starters	6
Autumn term lesson plans	8
Spring term lesson plans	28
Summer term lesson plans	48
Copymasters	68
Homework copymasters	128

First published 2001
exclusively for WHSmith by

Hodder & Stoughton Educational,
a division of Hodder Headline Ltd
338 Euston Road
London NW1 3BH

Text and illustrations © Hodder & Stoughton Educational 2001

All rights reserved. This work is copyright. Permission is given for copies to be made of pages provided they are used exclusively within the institution for which this work has been purchased. For reproduction for any other purpose, permission must first be obtained in writing from the publishers.

A CIP record for this book is available from the British Library.

Authors: Sarah Carvill and Simon Greaves
Series editor: Paul Broadbent

ISBN 0340 79003 2

Typeset by Servis Filmsetting Ltd
Printed and bound in Spain by Graphycems

Year 1
Summary of objectives

	Theme	Topics	Objectives – children will be taught to:
Autumn Term			
1	Place value	Place value and ordering	Read numerals from 1 to at least 20. Write numerals from 1 to 10. Say the number that is one more or less than a given number to 20. Begin to know what each digit in a two-digit number represents. Partition a 'teens' number into tens and ones.
2	Adding and taking away	Understanding + and – Mental calculation strategies (+ and –)	Understand the operation of addition; recognise that addition can be done in any order. Understand the operation of subtraction (as *take away*). Begin to use + , – and = signs to record mental calculations in a number sentence. Put the larger number first. Count on in ones, including beyond 10, e.g. 7 + 5.
3	Money problems	Money and 'real life' problems Making decisions	Recognise 1p and 2p coins. Find totals up to 10p. Choose and use the appropriate number operation and mental strategy to solve problems.
4	Measuring	Measures, including problems	Understand and use the vocabulary related to length and time. Order familiar events. Compare two, then more, lengths using direct comparison. Measure lengths using uniform non-standard units or standard units, e.g. metre sticks.
5	Shapes and positions	Shape and space Reasoning about shapes	Use everyday language to describe features of familiar 2D and 3D shapes, referring to shapes with flat faces. Make and describe models, patterns and pictures using construction kits. Recognise simple patterns. Use one or more shapes to make repeating patterns. Use everyday language to describe position.
6	Counting patterns	Counting, properties of numbers and number sequences Reasoning about numbers	Know the number names and recite them in order to at least 20, from and back to zero. Count on or back in ones from any small number. Solve mathematical problems. Recognise and predict from simple patterns and relationships.
7	Place value and ordering	Place value, ordering, estimating	Read and write numerals from 0 to 20. Say the number that is 10 more than any given number to 20. Understand the vocabulary of comparing and ordering numbers, including ordinal numbers to at least 10. Use = sign. Understand the vocabulary of estimation and give a sensible estimate of up to 10 objects.
8	Finding differences	Understanding + and – Mental calculation strategies (+ and –)	Understand the operation of addition and of subtraction (as difference) and use the related vocabulary. Use patterns of similar calculations.
9	Measuring length	Measures, including problems	Suggest suitable (non) standard units and measuring equipment to estimate, then measure a length, recording estimates and measurements as '3 and a bit'. Solve simple problems involving length.
10	Sorting information	Handling data and time	Solve a problem by sorting information using objects or pictures. Solve simple problems involving time. Know days of the week. Read time to hour on analogue clocks.

Summary of objectives

	Theme	Topics	Objectives – children will be taught to:
Spring Term			
1	Two-digit numbers	Place value and ordering	Read and write numerals from 0 to at least 20. Know what each digit in a two-digit number represents. Begin to partition larger two-digit numbers into a multiple of ten and ones. Say the number that is 1 or 10 more or less than any given number to 20.
2	Doubles and near doubles	Understanding + and − Mental calculation strategies (+ and −)	Understand the operations of addition and subtraction and the related vocabulary. Identify near doubles using doubles already known.
3	Money	Money and 'real life' problems Making decisions	Recognise 1p, 2p, 5p and 10p coins and equivalent values. Find totals. Choose and use the appropriate number operation and mental strategy to solve problems.
4	Measuring mass	Measures, including problems	Understand and use the vocabulary related to mass. Compare two, then more, masses using direct comparison. Measure mass using uniform non-standard units.
5	Shapes and positions	Shape and space Reasoning about shapes	Use everyday language to describe features of familiar 2D and 3D shapes, referring to shapes with flat faces, number of faces or corners, number of sides. Make and describe models, patterns and pictures using everyday materials, plasticine. Use everyday language to describe position and direction. Talk about things that turn. Use one or more shapes to make patterns, describe repeating patterns. Predict from simple patterns, and suggest extensions.
6	Counting patterns	Counting, properties of numbers and number sequences Reasoning about numbers	Count on in twos from zero, then one, and begin to recognise odd and even numbers to 10. Count in steps of 5 from zero to 20 or more. Solve mathematical problems or puzzles. Suggest extensions 'What if?' 'What could I try next?'
7	Ordering numbers	Place value, ordering, estimating	Understand the vocabulary of comparing and ordering numbers, including ordinal numbers to at least 20. Compare two familiar numbers, say which is more or less. Understand the vocabulary of estimation, give a sensible estimate of a number of objects and check by counting (up to 30 objects).
8	Adding and subtracting	Understanding + and − Mental calculation strategies (+ and −)	Understand operation of addition, and of subtraction (as *how many more*). Partition into 5 and a bit when adding 6, 7, 8, or 9. Bridge through 10 when adding single digit numbers. Find totals, give change. Work out how to pay an amount by using smaller coins. Solve simple mathematical problems or puzzles. Explain methods orally. Choose and use the appropriate number operation and mental strategy to solve a problem.
9	Measuring	Measures, including problems	Suggest suitable (non) standard units and measuring equipment to estimate, then measure, mass recording estimates and measurement as *'about as heavy as 20 cubes'*. Know seasons of the year. Solve simple problems involving mass or time.
10	Lists and tables	Handling data and time	Solve a problem by sorting, classifying and organising information in a list or simple table.

Summary of objectives

	Theme	Topics	Objectives – children will be taught to:
Summer Term			
1	Comparing and ordering numbers	Place value and ordering	Say the number that is one or ten more or less than a given number to 30. Compare two familiar numbers, say which is more or less, and give a number that lies between them. Order numbers to at least 20 and position them on a number track.
2	Adding and taking away	Understanding + and − Mental calculation strategies (+ and −)	Use +, − and = signs to record mental calculations in a number sentence. Recognise and use □ or △ to stand for an unknown number. Use number facts to add/subtract pair of numbers in range 0 to 10.
3	Money problems	Money and 'real life' problems Making decisions	Recognise coins of different values up to 20p. Find totals, give change from up to 20p and work out how to pay using smaller coins. Choose and use the appropriate number operation and mental strategy to solve problems.
4	Capacity	Measures, including problems	Understand and use the vocabulary related to capacity. Compare two, then more, capacities using direct comparisons. Measure capacity using uniform non-standard units or standard units (litre).
5	Shapes and positions	Shape and space Reasoning about shapes	Fold shapes in half, then make them into symmetrical patterns. Begin to relate solid shapes to pictures of them. Use one or more shapes to make, describe and continue repeating patterns. Make whole turns and half turns. Use everyday language to describe position, direction and movement. Investigate general statements about shapes.
6	Counting patterns	Counting, properties of numbers and number sequences Reasoning about numbers	Begin to count on in steps of 3 from zero. Recognise and extend number sequences with differences of 1, 2 or 3. Investigate a general statement about familiar numbers by finding examples that satisfy it. Explain methods and reasoning orally.
7	Addition	Understanding + and − Mental calculation strategies (+ and −)	Add more than two numbers. Use number facts to add/subtract pair of numbers within range 0 to 20. Add 9 to a single-digit number by adding 10 then subtracting 1. Bridge through 20 when adding a single digit number.
8	Solving problems	Money and 'real life' problems Making decisions	Choose and use the appropriate number operation and mental strategies to solve simple money or 'real life' problems using counting, addition or subtraction, halving or doubling.
9	Measuring capacity	Measures, including problems	Suggest suitable uniform non-standard then standard units and measuring equipment to estimate, then measure capacity recording estimates and measurements as 'about 3 beakers full' or 'just under 5 litres'. Solve simple problems involving capacity.
10	Sorting information	Information and time	Read time to half hour on analogue clocks. Solve a problem by organising information in a list or table. Discuss and explain results.

Year 1

Mental maths starters

Numbers and the number system

1. Counting stick – Point to one end of stick and name with appropriate number. Ask children to count on from this number in various sized steps. Repeat starting with a different number, counting backwards and randomly.

2. Number sequences – Say the number sequence, 1, 2, 3 … slowly, quickly, loudly, quietly, in a silly voice.

3. Number songs and rhymes – Sing/say together 'Ten green bottles', 'One, two, three, four, five, once I caught a fish alive', 'One, two, buckle my shoe', 'Five little speckled frogs'.

4. More or less – point to a number on a number line, use digit cards to show numbers one more/less. Then try two more/less etc.

5. Counting sounds – play regular beats on a percussion instrument for the children to count in their heads. Stop and ask how many they counted up to.

6. Odds and evens – Start rhythm of slapping thighs and clapping hands. Begin counting in ones so that every odd number is a thigh slap and every even number is a hand clap. Tell the children to continue counting in their heads, stop the rhythm and ask for the finishing number.

7. Counting objects – Show a group of up to 10 objects, then up to 20, in a hoop on an OHP or flashcard. Ask the children to count them and show the answer on a digit card.

8. Bingo – Provide each child with a blank bingo card. Ask the children to fill in numbers less than 20 (or 30). Call out questions such as giving the number name, partitioning the number into tens and ones, or by pointing to a number on a number line.

Calculations

9. Doubles – Recall doubles and halves up to 5 + 5. Call out a number up to 5. Children show the double on digit card. Call out a doubled number and ask children to show the number that was doubled.

10. Number bonds – Show two numbers that total up to 10. Ask children to show the number that has to be added to the number shown to make totals up to 10.

11. Difference – Show two cards with a difference of a given number.

12. Pass on the number – Choose a starting number, pass to a child with the instruction one more or one less. Continue passing the number, giving instructions each time.

13. Calculation collection – Write a number on the board and ask for different calculations which have the number as the answer.

14. Cover ups – Provide each child with a 4 × 4 grid, showing the numbers 1–16 in random order. Ask children to cover two numbers that add to a given total with counters; two numbers with a difference of a given number.

Place value

15. Ordinal numbers – Show a row of objects and ask which is first; point to seventh and ask which it is.

16. Number names/Matching cards – Call out a number name or show a number word card and children show the corresponding number card.

Mental maths starters

17 Higher or lower – Show a number card up to 20. Ask the children to show a number higher or lower than it.

18 Show me your number – Give one 0–30 number card to each child. Ask questions such as 'Show me your card if it is one more than 20/has two tens and five ones/is between 13 and 15'.

19 Measures – Show cards with two measures or money values. Ask questions to size and value, *e.g. Tom's cat weighs 5 kg. Sarim's cat weighs 3 kg. Whose cat weighs more?*

20 Provide five children with a digit card from 0 to 20. Put the numbers in order from smallest to largest and largest to smallest. Ask what numbers could go in between.

Theme 1 Place value

Objectives
- To read numerals from 0 to at least 20
- To write numerals from 1 to 10
- To say the number that is one more or one less than a given number to 20
- To begin to know what each digit in a two-digit number represents
- To partition a teens number into tens and ones

Vocabulary
all number names to 20, ones, units, tens, digit, two-digit number, more, less

Resources
Copymasters 1 and 2, 0–20 cards, number lines, number tracks, place value cards, large cards showing numbers to 20 and number names to 20, washing line, counters, cubes, large abacus

Homework Copymaster 1
Mental maths starters 2, 16

Assessment
At the end of this theme is the pupil able to:
- Read and write numbers to 10 and read numbers to 20;
- Recognise numbers one more or less than a number less than 20;
- Say what each digit in a teens number represents;
- Partition a teens number into tens and ones?

Lesson 1

Introduction   10 mins
Provide each child with a set of 0–20 digit cards. Show a number between 0 and 20 on a large card and ask the children to show the same number and say it together. Repeat for several numbers.

Activities   25 mins
Missing numbers (whole class)
Give a child a digit card and ask them to place it on the washing line in the correct place. Continue until all numbers to 20 are on the line. Ask the children to close their eyes and remove one of the cards. Ask if they can see which number is missing. Repeat several times.

Number tracks (individual)
Provide the children with a variety of number lines and tracks starting and ending with different numbers. Leave some blank spaces for the children to fill in the missing numbers.

Differentiation
Low Attainers – Provide the children with tracks up to 10 only or with fewer numbers missing.
High Attainers – Leave more numbers blank and provide some tracks going backwards.

Plenary   5 mins
Show the washing line with some of the numbers muddled up for the children to put in the correct places.

Lesson 2

Introduction   10 mins
Provide each child with a set of 0–20 digit cards. Show a large card of a number name up to twenty. The children say it aloud and find the matching numeral card. Repeat with several numbers.

Activities   25 mins
Tracing numbers (whole class)
Show a large numeral card from 0–9 and ask a child to come and write it on the board. Everybody traces the number in the air starting at the top. Repeat and trace the number on the desk or on each other's backs.

Writing numbers (individual)
Use a set of 0–9 digit cards for each child. Ask the children to put the cards in order and trace over each number onto tracing paper. Remind them of the correct way to trace.

Differentiation
Low Attainers – Provide a number line to help put the cards in order.
High Attainers – Practise writing the numbers freehand.

Plenary   5 mins
Trace a number in the air and ask the children to show the card of the number they think it is. Repeat. Give out the homework activity.

Autumn Term

Lesson 3

Introduction   **10 mins**
Share out a set of 0–20 digit cards and 0–20 number name cards (more able children may have two). Call out a number and the two children with the numeral card and the number name card show their cards. Repeat so that all children have at least one go.

Activities   **25 mins**
More or less (whole class)
Show a numeral card and ask the children to show the number, using their 0–20 digit cards, that comes before (one less) or the number that comes after (one more). Use a range of vocabulary when asking the questions.

One more or less (individual)
Provide each child with a copy of Copymaster 1 and remind them what one more and one less means. Insert numbers in the hexagons in numerals and words. Display flash cards of the vocabulary to help.

Differentiation
Low Attainers – Write the numbers in numerals only.
High Attainers – Write some of the numbers in the one more or one less circles.

Plenary   **5 mins**
Show a number name card and ask the children to show the digit card for one more or less.

Lesson 4

Introduction   **10 mins**
Put 14 counters on the OHP and ask the children to count them quietly. Write the number on the board and show it is a two-digit number. Ask the children what they think the one means and what the four means. Find the number on a number line and ask them to show this number on their digit cards. Separate the counters into a group of ten and a group of 4. Draw the children's attention to the fact that there is one group of ten, this is what the one digit stands for, and a group of four, this is what the four digit stands for. Repeat with other teens numbers.

Activities   **25 mins**
Teens (pairs)
Show a teens number on digit cards and ask each pair to count out that number of cubes, counters or straws. They then split it into a group of ten and a group of ones. Show this in a simple tens and ones chart on the board. Repeat for other numbers with the children taking turns to take the ten or the ones.

Tens and ones (individual)
Provide each child with a copy of Copymaster 2 where they have to sort the sets into a group of tens and ones and record the number.

Differentiation
Low Attainers – Provide adult support with recording.
High Attainers – Provide a bundle of straws that have to be grouped into tens and ones. Record the number.

Plenary   **5 mins**
Ask the children to show the number that is made from: one ten and five ones, seven units and a group of ten etc.

Lesson 5

Introduction   **10 mins**
Show the number 16 on a large abacus emphasising that ten ones changes into a group of ten and there are 6 more ones. Repeat with other numbers and draw the abacus on the board.

Activities   **25 mins**
Place value (individual)
Provide each child with a ten and units place value cards. Model how to show a number using the cards and emphasise that the number is made from a ten and ones.

Splitting it up (individual)
Show 18 using large place value cards and model how to split it up, 18 → 1 ten 8 ones.
Ask the children to pick a number card from their set of 11–20 and write as demonstrated.

Differentiation
Low Attainers – Give the numbers 11–15 only.
High Attainers – Try other numbers above 20.

Plenary   **5 mins**
Ask the children to use place value cards to show what two numbers make 17, 13, 11 etc.

Theme 2 — Adding and taking away

Objectives
- To understand the operation of addition and recognise that addition can be done in any order
- To understand the operation of subtraction as taking away
- To begin to use +, − and = to record mental calculations in a number sentence
- To put the largest number first when adding
- To count on in ones, including beyond 10

Vocabulary
add, sign, equals, minus, altogether, makes, count on, order, plus, total, take away, leaves, less, is the same as

Resources
Copymasters 3 and 4, objects from around the classroom, hoops, large 0–20 cards, cards showing +, −, = signs, 1–6 dice, 5–10 dice, 1, 2, 3, 1, 2, 3 dice, counters

Homework Copymaster 2

Mental maths starters 1, 10

Assessment
At the end of this theme is the pupil able to:
- Add two numbers in any order;
- Understand subtraction as taking away;
- Record calculations using appropriate signs;
- Put the largest number first when adding;
- Count in ones beyond 10?

Lesson 1

Introduction — 10 mins
Put a number of classroom objects in a hoop and count aloud altogether. Do this for different numbers. Each time ask a child to write the number on a card.

Activities — 25 mins

Putting sets together (whole class)
Make 2 sets of different numbers of the same objects in 2 hoops. Tell the children that they are going to count how many there are altogether. They are going to add. Count how many are in each set then count the two sets together. Show this as a sentence on the board, e.g. 3 and 4 more makes 7. Do not use symbols yet. Repeat for different size sets of different objects.

Adding sets (pairs)
Provide each group with two small hoops and about 20 small objects. Each child has to make a set in their hoop and count the number in the set. The children then add together the two sets and write a sentence on a card. Draw their attention to the vocabulary cards. Repeat twice.

Differentiation
Low Attainers – Provide each pair with ten objects only.
High Attainers – Encourage the children to write their sentences in different ways.

Plenary — 5 mins
Children share some of their sentence cards while another pair show the sets that go with the sentence.

Lesson 2

Introduction — 10 mins
Remind children of the previous lesson's work of combining two sets to make one. Use a variety of vocabulary when writing the sentences.

Activities — 25 mins

Using signs (whole class)
Choose one of the number sentences and tell the children that there is a quicker way of writing than using words. Substitute the words for the + sign and then the = sign. Tell the children the correct names of the signs. Change all the sentences to ones with signs instead of words.

Adding sets, number sentences (individual)
Work as in the previous lesson's activity, making two sets and adding together. This time write a number sentence using signs for each calculation.

Differentiation
Low Attainers – Provide only 10 objects to each pair.
High Attainers – How many ways can they make the same total.

Plenary — 5 mins
Show a number sentence and ask the children to say it in different ways in order to extend their vocabulary of addition.

Autumn Term

Lesson 3

Introduction   **10 mins**
Show a set of 8 objects. Ask a child to take 5 of them away. Count together how many are left. Say this in different ways, *e.g. there were 8 apples and five were taken away which left 3. 5 from 8 leaves 3.*

Activities   **25 mins**
Taking away (whole class)
Show another set of objects and write a sentence to show what has happened. Then remind children that signs can be used instead of words and introduce them to the minus sign in the same way that the addition sign was introduced.

Take away sentences (individual)
Provide each child with a set of objects which they have to count. They then take a group away and count how many are left. They record this as a subtraction sentence. How many different subtraction sentences can they make taking away from one set. Then introduce different numbers in sets.

Differentiation
Low Attainers – Restrict the size of sets to less than 10.
High Attainers – Allow them to decide what size sets to make.

Plenary   **5 mins**
Show a group of objects on the OHP and count together. Ask a child to take some objects away and then count how many are left. Write this as a subtraction sentence using signs.

Lesson 4

Introduction   **10 mins**
Set out number squares in a large space, *e.g. a hall*, to make a 0–20 number line. Ask a child to stand on 3 then count on 2 more. Ask what number the child is on and record as an addition sentence, i.e. 3 + 2 = 5. Ask another child to stand on 2 and count on 3. Record and ask the children if they notice anything about the two sentences. Repeat with another two numbers which total less than 10 and emphasise that it does not matter which order the numbers are in when adding as the same answer is arrived at.

Activities   **25 mins**
Number lines (whole class)
Show the children a large 0–20 number line. Reinforce using it to count on when adding. Show them that the first number does not need to be counted and demonstrate that it is easier starting with the largest number as there is less to count on. Repeat with several examples.

Counting on (individual)
Provide each child with a copy of Copymaster 3 and tell them to use the number track to count on. Remind them that some addition calculations may need to be changed around to put the biggest number first.

Differentiation
Low Attainers – Work with number bonds to 10.
High Attainers – Allow children to work with larger numbers.

Plenary   **5 mins**
Review some of the number sentences and ask children to say in different ways. Give out homework activity.

Lesson 5

Introduction   **10 mins**
Show a selection of addition and subtraction calculations and ask the children to solve them using a number line or track. Draw attention to addition calculations where the smaller number is first and remind children to change the order.

Activities   **25 mins**
Add and subtract game (groups)
Provide each group with a copy of Copymaster 4, 3 counters and a 1–6 dice.

Differentiation
Low Attainers – Provide the groups with a dice numbered 1, 2, 3, 1, 2, 3.
High Attainers – Provide the groups with a dice numbered 5–10.

Plenary   **5 mins**
Discuss different strategies for adding and subtracting, *e.g. using a number line, remembering facts, one more and less.*

Theme 3 — Money problems

Objectives
- To recognise 1p and 2p coins
- To find totals up to 10p
- To choose and use the appropriate number operation and mental strategy to solve problems

Vocabulary
money, coin, penny, pence, value, amount, total, altogether, buy, spend, change, most expensive, costs the most, cheapest, costs the least,

Resources
Copymasters 5, 6, and 46, plenty of plastic 1p and 2p coins, blu-tak, trays of priced items (one tray per table/group with at least 20 different items labelled with large price tags/stickers for amounts under 10p)

Homework Copymaster 3

Mental maths starters 3, 19

Assessment
At the end of this theme is the pupil able to:
- Recognise 1p and 2p coins;
- Know that different combinations of 1p and 2p coins can have the same value;
- Mentally calculate totals up to 10p and work out change from up to 10p;
- Record calculations using +, − and = showing totals up to 10p and change from up to 10p;
- Solve simple problems involving totals and change and cheapest, most expensive?

Lesson 1

Introduction 10 mins

Show the children, and pass around and examine, 1p (one penny) and 2p (two pence) coins. Explain that two 1p coins are worth the same as one 2p coin. Go on to explain that both types of coin can be used to make up different amounts. For example, a total of 3p can be made up in two ways: either 1p and 2p or three 1p's. Stick the coins on the board to show the two methods and write the total next to them. Repeat for totals of 4p and 5p. Place a tray of 1p and 2p coins on the table. Hold up a 2p coin. Ask a pupil to exchange it for 1p coins. Repeat for totals up to 10p, e.g. hold up 5 1p coins and ask it to be exchanged for, say, 4 coins (2p and 3 1p's).

Activities 25 mins

Purses (individual)
Each pupil needs a copy of Copymaster 5. Complete by writing the total amounts contained in each purse.

Totals to ten (whole class)
Each pupil needs a set of money cards (Copymaster 46 except the last 2 rows). Call out a total up to 10p. Ask the pupils to lay out cards which make up the total. Continue this reinforcing that there are several ways of making the totals.

Differentiation
Low Attainers — Allow use of coins for Purses activity.
High Attainers — Draw around coins to make their own purses and write down the totals.

Plenary 5 mins

Hold up a number of coins with a total of 10p or less. Ask pupils to give the total value of the coins. Remove a coin and ask pupils for the new total. Repeat for different amounts.

Lesson 2

Introduction 10 mins

Have a tray of 1p and 2p coins on the table. Hold up one 1p coin and one 2p coin. Ask pupils to give the total. Explain that you want to buy a bar of chocolate that costs 6p. Ask pupils how much more money you need. Ask a pupil to give you the extra coins from the tray. Continue with other amounts.

Activities 25 mins

Prices (individual)
Provide each pupil with a pile of 1p and 2p coins. Prepare a tray of items with clearly printed price tags for each group. Ask pupils to take an item from the tray and place a pile of coins next to it to the value of the price. Repeat for several more items.

What can I buy? (individual)
Use the trays of items again. Tell the pupils that they have 10p to spend. Ask them to choose an item, or items, and work out how much it will cost and how much money they will have left. Record answers on paper by writing names of, or drawing, the item(s) chosen and the amount of money left. Continue for other amounts. Use coins to help.

Differentiation
Low Attainers — In second activity specify one item to buy at a time and work out how much will be left.
High Attainers — Aim to buy items for the exact amount allowed, with no money left over.

Plenary 5 mins

Hold up two items and ask how much it will cost to buy both. Ask a pupil to bring out the exact amount in coins. Ask another pupil to pay using a different combination of coins.

Autumn Term

Lesson 3

Introduction   **10 mins**

Stick sets of coins with different totals on to the board. Ensure that there are two sets of each total but made up of different combinations of coins. Ask pupils to come out to the board and match the sets with the same totals.

Activities   **25 mins**

Coin rubbings (individual)
Provide each pupil with a sheet of paper with a list of totals of 10p or less down one side of the sheet. Ask pupils to make rubbings on the sheet of coins totalling the amounts listed.

Mental money (whole class)
Use one of the trays of items from the previous lesson. Hold up the 'most expensive' item and explain that it is the one that 'costs the most' because it has the 'highest price'. Explain 'cheapest'. Hold up two items and ask how much they 'cost altogether' and how much 'change' will I have from 10p. Ask questions such as 'Which items can I buy for 5p or less?', 'I had 10p and bought something with it. I now have 2p left. Which item did I buy?'

Differentiation
Low Attainers – Make rubbings for fewer totals.
High Attainers – Make more than one rubbing for each total.

Plenary   **5 mins**
Reinforce vocabulary used in lesson, 'cheapest', 'altogether' etc.

Lesson 4

Introduction   **10 mins**

Hold up an item with a price tag on it, *e.g. a lollipop with a tag for 4p*. Ask a pupil to select the correct coins to pay for the item. Record the combination as a calculation on the board, *e.g. 2p + 1p + 1p = 4p*. Explain the use of + and =. Ask another pupil for a different way of paying, *e.g. 2p + 2p = 4p*. Repeat for further objects.

Activities   **25 mins**

Coin calculations (individual)
Using the trays of items, ask pupils to select an item, work out which coins they would use to pay for it and write down the calculation, *e.g.*
apple   2p + 2p + 2p = 6p
Repeat for other combinations of coins, *e.g.*
1p + 1p + 2p + 2p = 6p, and other items.

Adding prices (whole class)
Hold up two items and ask pupils for the total cost. Record the calculation on the board, *e.g. 3p + 4p = 7p*. Repeat for other items.

Differentiation
Low Attainers – Record one combination of coins for each item.
High Attainers – Choose more than one item and record the calculation for the total coins needed.

Plenary   **5 mins**
Select two items, *e.g. a pencil for 4p and a toffee for 2p*, and record the addition calculation on the board, *e.g. 4p + 2p = 6p*. Now record the possible combinations of coins as addition calculations, *e.g. 2p + 2p + 2p, 1p + 1p + 2p + 2p etc.*

Lesson 5

Introduction   **10 mins**

Explain that you have 10p to spend and you buy a ribbon for 7p. Ask pupils how much change will be left. Record this as a subtraction calculation on the board, *e.g. 10p − 7p = 3p*. Repeat for other amounts. Now explain that toffees cost 2p each and you want to buy three. Ask pupils how much this will cost. Record the calculation as an addition on the board 2p + 2p + 2p = 6p. Repeat for other amounts, possibly including giving change.

Activities   **25 mins**

Buying things (individual)
Each pupil need Copymaster 6. Write down the addition calculations and find the total cost of the items shown.

Change (whole class)
Give each pupil the set of money cards from Lesson 1. Hold up a priced object and ask 'How much change will I get from a given amount if I buy the item?' Pupils hold up cards totalling the change. Record subtraction calculations on the board.

Differentiation
Low Attainers – Use coins to help work out totals of amounts.
High Attainers – Choose items from the trays and record their own calculations.

Plenary   **5 mins**
Hold up one item and ask pupils how much change I will get from a given amount. Record calculation. Repeat, moving on to finding the total cost of two different items, three of the same items etc. and the change left from a given amount.

Theme 4 Measuring

Objectives
- To understand and use the vocabulary related to time and length
- To order familiar events
- To compare two, then more, lengths using direct comparison
- To measure lengths using uniform non-standard units

Vocabulary
before, after, next, morning, afternoon, evening, night, today, yesterday, tomorrow, weekend, early, late, now, soon, guess, estimate, measure, length, short, long, shorter than, longer than, shortest, longest, taller than, tall, tallest, length, high, low, thin, thick, narrow, wide, far, close, about the same as, nearly, almost

Resources
Copymasters 7 and 8, story showing clear succession of events, string, objects to be measures, interlocking cubes, pictures of daily events, straws, sticks, cards showing shorter than/longer than, arrows.

Homework Copymaster 4

Mental maths starters 7, 11

Assessment
At the end of this theme is the pupil able to:
- Use vocabulary related to when events happen;
- Place everyday events in the correct order;
- Use vocabulary related to comparing lengths;
- Estimate and measure lengths by direct comparison;
- Use a given non-standard unit to measure objects and compare lengths?

Lesson 1

Introduction   10 mins
Show the children 3 pictures of a child getting up, going to school and going to bed. Discuss what is happening in the pictures, the order they happen in and encourage them to talk about when these things happen. Show flash cards of vocabulary as they come into discussion.

Activities   25 mins
Storytime (whole class)
Read a short story that has events happening in a clear order and talk about this using the appropriate vocabulary as the story is read.

Ordering events (individual)
Provide the children with the name of an everyday event and a blank storyboard grid with 4 frames. Ask the children to draw what happens in the right order. Events could be getting ready to come to school, going to the supermarket, making a cake, going on a family outing, school playtime etc. Some children may be able to write a short sentence or phrase about each event.

Differentiation
Low Attainers – Choose an event that is very familiar and provide adult support to talk about it first.
High Attainers – Provide a storyboard grid with 6 frames.

Plenary   5 mins
Children share their different stories. Encourage use of appropriate vocabulary.

Lesson 2

Introduction   10 mins
Ask the children questions about their day using time vocabulary, e.g. What do you do before you come to school? What did we do yesterday? What happens every afternoon? etc.

Activities   25 mins
Washing line (whole class)
Recap on previous lesson ordering events correctly. Show the children an enlarged copy of one child's story cut into individual events. Ask the children to peg the events on the washing line in the correct order while discussing what is happening in each picture.

Which order? (pairs)
Provide each pair with a copy of Copymaster 7, a large sheet of paper, glue and a pair of scissors. Ask the children to cut the sheet into the eight pictures and look carefully at what is happening in each one. The children have to put these in the correct order. Some children may need the pictures cutting out beforehand and placing in an envelope.

Differentiation
Low Attainers – Work in small groups with adult support.
High Attainers – Write a short sentence or phrase about each event.

Plenary   5 mins
Low attainer groups can explain the story to the rest of the class. Encourage use of the correct vocabulary.

Autumn Term

Lesson 3

Introduction   **10 mins**

Tell the children that they are going to be doing some work on measuring length. Show them two pencils, flowers etc. of different lengths and colours. Ask the children to describe the two objects encouraging discussion about their relative lengths and sizes. Show the words 'shorter than' and 'less than'.

Activities   **25 mins**

How to measure (whole class)
Show the children three different length sticks, ribbons etc. Show how to compare two at a time by matching the ends together. Then put the three objects in order of length. Place them so cards can be put between them showing 'shorter than' and 'longer than' with arrow cards pointing in the right direction.

Which is longest? (pairs)
Provide each pair with sets of 3 objects of different lengths, e.g. 3 pencils, 3 straws, 3 pieces of string etc. The children have to put them in order and place the cards in between.

Differentiation
Low Attainers – Consolidate with 2 objects until they are confident with using the right vocabulary.
High Attainers – Give the children sets of up to 5 objects.

Plenary   **5 mins**
Children share their findings and show the cards and arrows. Give out and explain homework activity.

Lesson 4

Introduction   **10 mins**
Ask the children to name some objects in the classroom that are taller than, about the same height as and shorter than their teacher. Record the suggestions on a three column chart.

Activity   **25 mins**

My height (pairs)
Ask the children to find objects in the classroom that are taller than, about the same height as and shorter than themselves. Record in a chart by writing the name of the object or by drawing it. Compare results with their partner.

Differentiation
Not applicable.

Plenary   **5 mins**
Ask if everybody will have got the same results. Draw attention to the fact that some children are taller than others so they may have objects shorter than themselves that are taller than other children. Choose one child and ask the children if they can name things they estimate are taller than, shorter than or the same height as the child.

Lesson 5

Introduction   **10 mins**
Point to two objects in the classroom that cannot be moved to be measured, *e.g. window and sink*. Ask the children how they could find out which was longer if they cannot be put together to be compared. Introduce measuring with a non-standard unit, *e.g. hands, feet, cubes, straws etc*. Measure both items with the same unit and record on the board as 'the _____ is __ _____ long'. Then 'the _____ is longer/shorter than the _____'.

Activity   **25 mins**

Non-standard measuring (pairs)
Provide each child with a copy of Copymaster 8 and some non-standard units to measure with. The children choose two objects and measure the lengths using the same non-standard measure. They then choose another two pairs of objects and record their findings.

Differentiation
Low Attainers – Provide with non-standard units that are relatively long so they do not need to count too many.
High Attainers – Measure the three pairs of objects again using different non-standard units.

Plenary   **5 mins**
Ask a pair of children to share what they have found out. Write a sentence on the board about it to read together, *e.g. the _____ is longer than the _____.*

Theme 5 — Shapes and positions

Objectives
- To use everyday language to describe features of familiar 2D and 3D shapes, referring to shapes with faces, edges and corners
- To make and describe models, patterns and pictures using construction kits
- To recognise simple patterns
- To use one or more shapes to make repeating patterns
- To use everyday language to describe position

Vocabulary
triangle, square, rectangle, circle, cube, cuboid, sphere, cylinder, cone, pyramid, prism, face, side, edge, corner, pointed, curved, round, straight, flat, solid, hollow, sort, make, build, draw, repeating pattern, up, down, under, over, above, below, beside, next to, in front of, behind, on top, underneath, in the middle, on the edge, in the corner

Resources
Copymasters 9 and 10, teacher set of large coloured cardboard 2D shapes, blu-tak, pupil sets of plastic or cardboard 2D and 3D shapes, everyday 3D objects, construction kits, everyday objects with repeating patterns, gummed shapes and sheets of gummed paper

Homework Copymaster 5

Mental maths starters 5, 16

Assessment
At the end of this theme is the pupil able to:
- Name, sort and describe a variety of 2D and 3D shapes using everyday language;
- Make a picture using 2D shapes and describe which shapes have been used;
- Use a construction kit to make a 3D model and describe the shapes used;
- Make a repeating pattern using 2D shapes;
- Describe the position of objects using everyday language?

Lesson 1

Introduction 10 mins
Revise and reinforce the names and properties of 2D shapes that the pupils should already be familiar with – square, rectangle, triangle, circle.
Draw each shape on the board and ask questions about the shapes, e.g. number of corners?

Activities 25 mins
Sorting shapes (whole class)
Use blu-tak to stick the following large-size cardboard shapes on the board: circles and squares of different sizes, various rectangles and triangles, semicircle, irregular and regular pentagons and hexagons.
Ask pupils to come out and remove shapes according to given instructions. For example, all shapes which are round, or all circles, or all shapes with no straight sides, all shapes which have three points or corners or straight sides etc., until the only shapes which are left are the semicircle, pentagons and hexagons – shapes which are unfamiliar. Ask pupils to describe the remaining shapes in terms of straight or curved sides, number of sides and points.

2D shape quiz (pairs/individual)
Provide a set of small shapes as covered in the Sorting shapes activity.
Ask pupils to identify and draw around the shape which fits a given description, for example: 5 sides, 4 equal sides, 3 corners, 1 curved and 1 straight side.

Differentiation
Low Attainers – Reinforce the four main shapes, recognising different triangles and rectangles.
High Attainers – Provide a wider selection of shapes including various polygons.

Plenary 5 mins
Place a set of the small shapes used in the Shape quiz activity in a bag. Ask a pupil to hold a shape in the bag, feel it and describe it to class for them to name.

Lesson 2

Introduction 10 mins
Place a selection of everyday 3D objects on a table, e.g. cubes – dice, Rubik cube, gift box; cuboids – cereal packet, wooden block, book; cones – marker cone, party hat, sugar cone; sphere – football, marble; cylinder – Smarties tube, tin of soup. Hold up an object that is a cube. Ask pupils to describe it in their own words and to identify other objects on the table which are also cubes. Repeat this for the other four 3D shapes.

Activities 25 mins
Describing 3D shapes (whole class)
Hold up an example of an object which is a cuboid. Explain that the shape is made up of flat parts – faces. Ask a pupil to describe the shape of each face. Show and explain that the cuboid also has straight edges and corners. Ask whether it is solid or hollow. Continue in a similar way for the other shapes.

3D shape quiz (individual)
Provide each group with a set of 3D shapes and each pupil with a copy of Copymaster 9. Select each shape from the set and complete the information requested.

Differentiation
Low Attainers – Concentrate on cube, cuboid, cylinder, sphere.
High Attainers – Include other 3D shapes such as pyramids and prisms.

Plenary 5 mins
Make sure each group has a full set of 3D shapes. Ask a pupil in each group to hold up the shapes in answer to statements such as:
    Hold up a shape that has all square faces.
    Hold up a shape and point to a corner.
    Hold up a shape that has a curved edge.

Autumn Term

Lesson 3

Introduction   10 mins
Show a picture made up of 2D shapes created by drawing around flat plastic shapes, e.g. rocket, car. Ask pupils to identify the shapes which have been used to create the different parts of the picture, e.g. *circles have been used for car wheels, triangle for top of rocket.* Show a 3D model made from wooden blocks, e.g. house. Ask pupils to identify the shapes used, e.g. *cylinder for chimney, cubes for bricks.*

Activities   25 mins
Organise class into four mixed-ability groups – allow time on each of the two activities. During the activities encourage pupils to talk to each other and to teacher/helpers about their work.

Making 2D pictures (individual)
Each pupil will need a selection of flat plastic shapes to draw around, coloured pencils and a piece of paper, and use them to create a picture.

Making 3D models (pairs/individual)
Each pupil or pair will need a set of either wooden/plastic building blocks of different shapes or Duplo blocks. They should use these to create a model.

Differentiation
Low Attainers – Will need to be guided in their construction and description of their work.
High Attainers – Encourage the use of correct language and perhaps specify a picture or model to be created.

Plenary   5 mins
Select examples of work and ask pupils to describe their work and explain their choice of shapes.

Lesson 4

Introduction   10 mins
Display a collection of everyday objects which are decorated with repeating patterns made up of recognisable 2D shapes, e.g. wallpaper, borders, wrapping paper, fabric, ornaments such as mugs, vases, plates. Hold up items and ask pupils to describe the patterns referring to shapes, sizes, colours, spacing.

Activities   25 mins
Creating repeating patterns (whole class)
Stick blu-tak on the backs of a set of flat plastic or coloured cardboard shapes. Ask pupils to stick the shapes on the board and create a repeating pattern. Encourage pupils to think about the colours used, the sizes of the shapes and the spacing between them. Repeat as necessary.

Designing a T-shirt (individual)
Provide each pupil with sufficient gummed paper shapes and the outline or cut-out of a simple T-shirt shape. Explain that they should create a repeating pattern on the T-shirt using the gummed shapes.

Differentiation
Low Attainers – Encourage the pupils to use a limited variety of shapes and colours so that they concentrate more on producing a simple but repeating pattern.
High Attainers – Use sheets of gummed paper to create their own shapes for use in their pattern.

Plenary   5 mins
Select examples of pupils T-shirt designs and ask them to describe their pattern to the class

---

Lesson 5

Introduction   10 mins
Prepare a set of flashcards with the following words on them: up, down, under, over, above, below, beside, next to, in front of, behind, on top, underneath, in the middle, on the edge, in the corner.
Each pupil needs a coloured building block/Duplo brick. Ask pupils to place the block in a given position, e.g. *put your block underneath the table, hold your block up, place your block beside your ear.*
Check that pupils are following instructions correctly and repeat and demonstrate any that pose problems.

Activities   25 mins
Busy street (individual)
Each pupil needs a copy of Copymaster 10 which shows a picture of a busy street. Complete the sentences using the position words provided.

Shape positions (whole class)
Place large different coloured 2D and 3D shapes around the classroom. Ask all pupils to look for and point to a specified shape. Then ask a pupil to describe its position using the vocabulary covered in the introduction.

Differentiation
Low Attainers – Work with them to complete the Busy street sheet orally.
High Attainers – Extend the Busy street sheet by asking them to choose one object and describe its position relative to another.

Plenary   5 mins
Stick blu-tak on the backs of a set of flat plastic or coloured cardboard shapes. Ask a pupil to position the shape on the whiteboard/flipchart according to intstructions, e.g. *put the red triangle at an edge of the board*
    place the blue square in the middle of the board
    put the yellow circle next to the blue square

Theme 6 — Counting patterns

Objectives
- To know the number names and recite them in order to at least 20 from and back to zero
- To count on or back in ones from any small number
- To solve mathematical problems
- To recognise and predict from simple patterns and relationships

Vocabulary
number, zero, nought, one, two, ... twenty, count, forwards, backwards, count on, count back, share, pattern, before, after, between, add, plus, equal to, is the same as

Resources
Copymasters 11 and 12, set of teacher's number cards from 0 to 20, blu-tak, pegs, clothes line, variety of classroom objects, four small trays, sweets, buttons, counters, toy cars, multilink cubes, sets of number cards from 0 to 20 – sufficient for half the class, number lines, 10 identical wooden blocks, 1–30 grids made from first three rows of 100 square – enlarged, dice

Homework Copymaster 6

Mental maths starters 1, 20

Assessment
At the end of this theme is the pupil able to:
- Know the names of numbers from zero to twenty;
- Count on in ones from zero to twenty and back from twenty to zero;
- Count on/back in ones from any number between 0 and 20;
- Count up to 20 objects;
- Use a number line to count on and back from a given number;
- Use a number line to count between two numbers;
- Explore number patterns by sharing and counting objects?

Lesson 1

Introduction 10 mins
Stick cards with the numbers 0 to 20 in random order on the board. Ask the pupils to help you put the numbers into a row in the correct order. Ask the pupils questions such as 'Which number comes before 12, after 7, between 15 and 17, ...?'. Now remove the cards from the board and ask the pupils to recite the numbers from 0 to 20 then backwards from 20 to 0. Repeat as necessary.

Activities 25 mins
Join dots (individual)
Each pupil needs Copymaster 11. Join the dots in order to make pictures of numbers.

Washing line (whole class)
Peg out number cards from 0 to 20 on a washing line. Ask pupils to turn away while you swap two numbers. Ask the pupils to identify which numbers are in the wrong places then place them back in the correct order.

Differentiation
Low Attainers – Provide them with a list of the numbers in order from 0 to 20.
High Attainers – Include counting past 20.

Plenary 5 mins
Use the numbers from 0 to 20 on the washing line. Ask the pupils questions such as 'Which number comes between 4 and 6, is after 13, ...?'

Lesson 2

Introduction 10 mins
Place twelve different classroom objects on the floor. Show the pupils how to count the number of objects by pointing or touching each one. Count 1, 2, ..., 12. Tell the pupils that the last number is 12 and that this tells us that there are 12 objects. Show the pupils how to count the number of objects by moving each counted object to one side. Explain that sometimes it is easier if the objects are placed in a line before they are counted. Show this. Emphasise that the number of objects counted each time was the same.
Repeat for other numbers.

Activities 25 mins
Counting objects (whole class)
Arrange a collection of different objects in a pile on a table. Ask a pupil to come and count them using their own method. Place the objects in a line and ask another pupil to count them. Explain that the number of objects stays the same regardless of the way in which they are counted or arranged. Repeat for other numbers of objects.

Fruit boxes (individual)
Each pupil needs Copymaster 12. Pupils should count the number of fruit in each box and write the number in the box provided and draw the number of pieces of fruit where the number is given.

Differentiation
Low Attainers – Count up to 10 objects.
High Attainers – Count more than 20 objects.

Plenary 5 mins
Have four trays containing the following – sweets, buttons, counters, toy cars. Ask a pupil to come out and give you 6 sweets, 16 buttons, 8 toy cars etc.

Autumn Term

Lesson 3

Introduction   10 mins
Write a number on the board and ask pupils to count on up to 20 from that number then count back to zero from that number. Repeat for other numbers.

Activities   25 mins

Forwards and backwards (pairs)
Each pair of pupils needs a set of cards numbered 0 to 20. One pupil says 'forwards' or 'backwards'. The other pupil selects a card from the pile and must start with that number and recite the numbers either forwards to 20, or backwards to zero.

Multilink sticks (pairs)
Each pair of pupils needs a set of number cards from 0 to 20 and forty multilink cubes. One pupil draws the first card, e.g. *5*, and links 5 multilink cubes together, then the second pupil draws a card and links cubes together. The first pupil draws his/her second card and must add on/remove cubes to extend/shorten the rod so that it has the number of cubes given on the card.

Differentiation
Low Attainers – Just count forwards or work with numbers from 0 to 10 only.
High Attainers – Include some numbers of more than 20.

Plenary   5 mins
Write a number on the board and ask pupils to count on up to 20 from that number then count back to zero from that number.

Lesson 4

Introduction   10 mins
Draw a number line from 0 to 20 on the board. Explain how it is used to help to count on forwards and backwards. Point to a number and count on one, two, three, ... and count back one, two, ...

Activities   25 mins

Counting on number lines (whole class)
Each pupil needs a number line. Ask pupils to point to a number, e.g. *11*, then count on two. Ask pupils 'What number are you pointing to now?', 'Now count back four. What number is this?'. Repeat then go on to 'Point to 8. How many numbers will it take to count back to 4?'

Board game (pairs)
Each pair of pupils needs an enlarged 1 to 30 grid and a dice. Ask the pupils to colour any three squares red and any other three squares green. Pupils take turns to roll the dice and move their counters the number of squares given on the dice. If a pupil lands on a red square they must roll the dice again and move back that number of squares. If the pupil lands on a green square, roll the dice and move forward that number.

Differentiation
Low Attainers – Target questions which involve only counting on/back by one or two.
High Attainers – Target questions on counting between two given numbers.

Plenary   5 mins
Draw a number line from 0 to 20 on the board and use it to reinforce counting forwards and backwards by a given number or counting the number between two given numbers.

Lesson 5

Introduction   10 mins
Place 10 identical wooden blocks on the table. Give two pupils a small tray each. Explain that you are going to share the blocks between the two pupils. Give one pupil 10 and the other none. Record this way of sharing the blocks on the board as 10 + 0 = 10. Go on to share the blocks in another way, e.g. *9 + 1 = 10*. Record results neatly so that the pupils can see a pattern starting to emerge. Continue until 0 + 10 = 10 is reached. Notice that each pair of numbers is repeated in a different order and as one number goes up by one, the other goes down.

Activity   25 mins

Sharing cubes (individual)
Give each pupil a set of 8 multilink cubes and ask the pupils to share them into two piles and record their results as in the introduction. Repeat for other amounts up to 10.

Differentiation
Low Attainers – Focus effort on sorting and counting rather than recording.
High Attainers – Amounts up to 20.

Plenary   5 mins
Explain that we have shared out objects into two piles. We can share out into three piles. Use 5 blocks and ask the class to share the blocks between three pupils. Record the different results on the board, e.g. *5 + 0 + 0 = 5; 2 + 2 + 1 = 5.*

Theme 7 — Place value and ordering

Objectives
- To read and write numerals from 1 to 20
- To say the number that is 10 more than any given number to 20
- To understand the vocabulary of comparing and ordering numbers, including ordinal numbers to at least 10
- To use the = sign
- To understand the vocabulary of estimation and give a sensible estimate of up to 10 objects

Vocabulary
zero … twenty, next, before, between, first … tenth, last, numeral, more than, about, guess, roughly, nearly, close to, too many, too few, enough, not enough, exactly, estimate

Resources
Copymasters 13 and 14, number lines, 100 square, 0–20 digit cards, place value cards, washing line and pegs, objects to be put in order, cubes, conkers, counters, counting teddies etc.

Homework Copymaster 7

Mental maths starters 7, 18

Assessment
At the end of this theme is the pupil able to:
- Read and form correctly all numbers to 20;
- Add 10 to any number to 20;
- Use the vocabulary of comparing and ordering including using first, second etc …;
- Use the = sign;
- Give a sensible estimate of up to 10 objects?

Lesson 1

Introduction — 10 mins
Share out the cards showing the numbers 0–20 and ask the children in turn to peg them on the washing line in order. Remove them and shuffle so all children can have a go.

Activities — 25 mins

Time to order (pairs)
Provide each pair of children with a set of 0–20 digit cards. One child shuffles them and removes one. The other child has to put the remaining cards in order and spot which one is missing. They then take turns, repeating the activity about 4 times each.

Forming numbers (individual)
Provide children with number tracks and lines with some numbers missing for them to fill in the blanks.

Differentiation
Low Attainers — Work up to 20 with fewer blanks.
High Attainers — Provide number lines beyond 20, with some going backwards.

Plenary — 5 mins
Ask children to volunteer to write numerals on the board to match the number on the card shown.

Lesson 2

Introduction — 10 mins
Use the number line to remind the children how to add by counting on. Start on 4 and add on 6. Can they remember that the order of adding does not matter and it is best to start with the largest number first. Repeat a few more additions.

Activities — 25 mins

Adding ten (whole class)
Remind the children when they found one more than a number. Tell the children they are going to find ten more than a given number. Choose a number less than ten and show how to count on ten on the number line. Write the sentence, *e.g. 7 and ten more is 17*. Then write as a number sentence and draw attention to the = sign. Repeat with other numbers.

Ten more (individual)
Provide each child with a copy of Copymaster 13. Fill in the first hexagon of each set of three with a number less than 10.

Differentiation
Low Attainers — Give the top half of the sheet only.
High Attainers — Complete the last part with teens numbers in the first hexagon.

Plenary — 5 mins
Show number sentences with missing numbers, e.g. 10 + __ = 14, __ + 3 = 13 etc.

Autumn Term

Lesson 3

Introduction   **10 mins**
Show the children a 100 square and concentrate on the first 20 numbers. Count along and draw the children's attention to moving to a new row. Point to a number and ask them to say it together.

Activities   **25 mins**
100 square (whole class)
Point to 8. Ask the children to count on ten more. When they reach 18 show the number sentence on the board, 8 + 10 = 18. What do they notice about the position of 8 and 18? (The 18 is underneath the 8.) Repeat for other numbers less than 10. Ask if the number sentences can be written in another way, i.e. with the larger number (10) first.

10 more on a 100 square (individual)
Provide each child with a copy of the first two rows of a 1–100 square and some adding 10 calculations. Ensure the order of the numbers varies in the sentences and provide some with missing numbers as shown in the previous lesson's plenary.

Differentiation
Low Attainers – Provide a number line to double check answers.
High Attainers – Extend to adding ten onto teens numbers, providing part of the 100 square to 30.

Plenary   **5 mins**
Write a series of calcualtions on the board starting at 1 + 10 = ☐ to 9 + 10 = ☐. Ask the children to solve them. Then write ☐ = 10 + 1 etc. after each answer and show that all three are equal. What patterns do they notice?

Lesson 4

Introduction   **10 mins**
Read an abridged version of the story of Chinese New Year. Emphasise the order that the animals come in. Ask questions such as, 'What animal came after the dog?', 'Which animal came before the monkey?' etc.

Activities   **25 mins**
First and last (whole class)
Show the ordinal number words to tenth on flash cards and peg them to the number line. Peg a picture underneath each one and ask the children 'What is fourth?', 'Which picture is ninth?' etc. Show them that tenth is also last on this line because it is at the end but this is not always the case.

Queues (whole class)
Make a queue of 10 children and ask the rest of the children to give a fact about the line, e.g. *Peter is fifth, Olivia is the one before last* etc. Then make queues of objects in the classroom, lunchboxes, toys, different coloured cubes, ensuring each object in the queue is different.

Differentiation
Not applicable.

Plenary   **5 mins**
Discuss and give out the homework activity.

Lesson 5

Introduction   **10 mins**
Show the children a set of 7 drinking cups and count them. Then show 4 drinking straws and ask them if they think there are enough straws for each cup. Encourage them to guess rather than count. Repeat with different numbers of cups and straws.

Activities   **25 mins**
Estimate (whole class)
Put 8 counters on the OHP (or show a flash card with 8 objects on it). Let the children see them for a few seconds (not long enough to count) by switching it on and off and ask them how many they thought there were. Record some of the estimates and then count together. Repeat and show counters in random and regular arrays. Introduce some of the language of estimation during this activity.

What a handful! (individual)
Provide each child with a copy of Copymaster 14 and large counters, cubes, conkers, counting teddy bears etc. The children have to take a handful of the objects they have been given and estimate how many they have. They record this then count. Repeat several times.

Differentiation
Low Attainers – Provide larger objects so no more than 10 can be picked up in one handful.
High Attainers – Provide smaller objects so a handful contains more.

Plenary   **5 mins**
Repeat the activity with the OHP using different objects. Encourage children whose estimates may not be very close to the answer.

Theme 8 — Finding differences

Objectives
- To understand the operation of addition and use related vocabulary
- To understand the operation of subtraction as difference and use related vocabulary
- To use similar patterns of calculations

Vocabulary
add, sum, together, total, difference, how many more, subtract, equals, pattern

Resources
Copymasters 15 and 16, 1–6 dice, +/− dice, coloured pencils, hoops, number lines

Homework Copymaster 8

Mental maths starters 4, 11

Assessment
At the end of this theme is the pupil able to:
- Add two numbers together by counting on and begin to recall facts mentally;
- Find the difference between two numbers by subtracting;
- Identify patterns in addition and subtraction calculations and begin to use these to solve other calculations?

Lesson 1

Introduction   10 mins

Shuffle a pack of 0–9 digit cards and ask two children to pick one each. Ask the children to add the two numbers and show the answer on their digit cards. Discuss the strategies they used. Ask if they used the number line, knew the fact or put the biggest number first. Repeat the activity to ensure children are using the most efficient strategy.

Activity   25 mins
Digit card addition (pairs)
Provide each pair of children with a set of 0–9 digit cards. Turn them face down then pick two for their partner to add. The child records the addition in a sentence and the other child checks. Repeat several times.

Differentiation
Low Attainers – Provide a set of 0–5 digit cards only.
High Attainers – Ask them to identify different number sentences with the same total.

Plenary   5 mins
Ask two children to pick a card from their pack at random, show them to the class who have to find the total.

Lesson 2

Introduction   10 mins

Remind them of subtraction as taking away one number from another by doing a few examples and using the appropriate vocabulary and notation. Explain that in this lesson they are going to look at subtraction as finding the difference between two sets of numbers.

Activities   25 mins
Hoop differences (whole class)
Show a set of four identical objects in a hoop and three of the same objects in another. Ask the children to count them and put the appropriate digit card beside each hoop. Ask how many more objects are in one hoop than the other. Say that there is a difference of one and the difference tells us how many more there are in one group than another.
Repeat with different numbers of objects in the hoops. Begin to record each difference as a subtraction sentence.

Differences (pairs)
Provide each pair of children with two small hoops or sorting trays and counters or cubes. They each put some objects in their hoop/tray, count them then calculate the difference and record using a picture and/or a number sentence. This is repeated several times.

Differentiation
Low Attainers – Provide no more than 10 objects each.
High Attainers – Write their findings in a sentence also: The difference between ___ and ___ is ___.

Plenary   5 mins
Emphasise the language of difference and model again using numbers up to 20.

Autumn Term

Lesson 3

Introduction   **10 mins**
Show two sets of objects in hoops or on an OHP and ask the children to find the difference and show it on their cards. Draw their attention to counting on from the smaller to the larger number to produce the difference.

Activity   **25 mins**
Difference clowns (pairs)
Provide each pair of children with two 1–6 dice, coloured pencils and two copies of Copymaster 15. The children take turns in rolling both dice then finding the difference between the two numbers. Then they colour the corresponding part of the clown's face. If they have already coloured that part they miss a turn until one child colours the whole face. They then move on to the next face, keeping score of who won.

Differentiation
Not applicable.

Plenary   **5 mins**
Ask the children what strategies they used to find the difference between the two numbers. Can they work out the difference in their scores? Give out the homework activity.

Lesson 4

Introduction   **10 mins**
Count out 10 counters together onto the OHP. Draw two circles on the board and put all ten counters into one circle. Add the two sets, 10 + 0 = 10. Then move one counter to the other circle. Ask the children 'How many in each set?', 'How many altogether?' and record, 9 + 1 = 10. Repeat to 6 + 4 = 10. Ask the children what they notice and can they predict the next number sentence. Carry on until they are all complete. Choose a different starting number and repeat.

Activities   **25 mins**
Take away patterns (whole class)
Set out 7 counters on the OHP as before, this time subtracting so the pattern 7 − 0 = 7, 7 − 1 = 6, 7 − 2 = 5 emerges. Ask the children what will come next and repeat until complete.

Calculation patterns (individual)
Provide the children with a selection of calculation patterns to be predicted and completed.

Differentiation
Low Attainers – Work with patterns involving numbers less than 10.
High Attainers – Work with larger numbers.

Plenary   **5 mins**
Ask the children to explain some of the patterns they have been working on.

Lesson 5

Introduction   **10 mins**
Revise vocabulary associated with addition and subtraction by asking a range of questions. Show flash cards of the words as they are used.

Activity   **25 mins**
Calculating clocks (pairs)
Provide each pair of children with two copies of Copymaster 16, two 1–6 dice, a +/− dice and coloured pencils. The winner is the first to colour all sections. They then move on to the next clock.

Differentiation
Not applicable.

Plenary   **5 mins**
Ask the children which number(s) seemed to take longest to get and which numbers came up most often.

Theme 9 Measuring length

Objectives
- To suggest suitable non-standard and standard units on measuring equipment to estimate, then measure a length
- To record estimates and measurements as '3 and a bit metres'
- To solve simple problems involving length

Vocabulary
guess, estimate, measure, length, short, long, shorter than, longer than, shortest, longest, taller than, tall, tallest, length, high, low, thin, thick, narrow, wide, far, close, about the same as, nearly, almost, metre

Resources
Copymasters 17 and 18, metre rulers, interlocking cubes, objects to be measured, string, long strips of paper, ribbon, labels marked: 'more than one metre', 'less than one metre', 'about one metre'.

Homework Copymaster 9

Mental maths starters 14, 17

Assessment
At the end of this theme is the pupil able to:
- Estimate and measure objects using non-standard units and metre rulers and record these as whole and part units;
- Choose appropriate units to measure objects;
- Solve problems involving length?

Lesson 1

Introduction   10 mins
Remind the children how to compare the lengths of objects and use appropriate vocabulary by showing pairs or sets of three objects.

Activities   25 mins
Cube measuring (whole class)
Show an object on the OHP and lay out interlocking cubes along the length of it, encouraging the children to count them. Show that sometimes the length is not exactly a whole number of cubes, that it is either a bit more or a bit less. Show how to record different lengths as 'nearly 7 cubes', '4 and a bit cubes long' etc.

... and a bit! (pairs)
Provide each pair of children with some objects to be measured and interlocking cubes. One child measures then the other child measures to check. They write the name of the object and its length as shown before.

Differentiation
Low Attainers – Provide only a few objects that will be no more than 15 cubes long.
High Attainers – Put the objects in order of size when completed.

Plenary   5 mins
Choose some objects a group has measured and write the measures on the board. Ask the children if they can tell which object is the longest by looking at the measure rather than the object.

Lesson 2

Introduction   10 mins
Show a collection of items that can be used to measure. Ask the children what would be most suitable to measure named items in the classroom.

Activity   25 mins
Which measure? (pairs)
Provide each child with a copy of Copymaster 17, a selection of objects to measure and for measuring with. Work through one example, filling in the table. Ask the children to continue the measuring activity together

Differentiation
Low Attainers – Limit the choice of measuring equipment.
High Attainers – Write an estimate before measuring.

Plenary   5 mins
Draw attention to any measuring that was carried out with inappropriate equipment and discuss what could have been used instead.

Autumn Term

Lesson 3

Introduction   **10 mins**
Review yesterday's work and discuss what would happen if everybody measured in different units. Introduce the standard measure of one metre and show children the metre ruler.

Activities   **25 mins**
Make a metre (individual)
Provide the children with ribbon, string or long strips of paper and metre rulers. They need to make their own metre measure. Ensure they match one end of the ruler to one end of their measuring device.

Find a metre (small groups)
Children use their metre measures to find objects more than, less than and about one metre in length. They make a collection and label each set.

Differentiation
Low Attainers – Make sure they are using their metre measure accurately.
High Attainers – Encourage them to measure objects that are not straight.

Plenary   **5 mins**
Every group shows an item from each set. Give out homework activity.

Lesson 4

Introduction   **10 mins**
Take a metre ruler outside and show the children how to measure a longer distance by marking where the end of the ruler lies to start the next measure. Draw their attention to measurements that are not exact numbers of metres, i.e. '7 and a bit metres'.

Activity   **25 mins**
Metre measuring (pairs)
Provide the children with a list of things to measure including 'How far up the wall can you reach?', 'How far from your desk to the classroom door?', 'How long is your table?', 'How tall is the teacher?', 'How far can you jump from this line?' etc.

Differentiation
Low Attainers – Provide fewer situations for them to measure.
High Attainers – Make initial estimates.

Plenary   **5 mins**
Ask which measurements should be the same for everyone and which will be different.

Lesson 5

Introduction   **10 mins**
Remind the children of the main teaching points of the week then introduce them to a length problem. Read it together and think what it is asking and how it might be solved.

Activity (whole class then individual)   **25 mins**
Model the solution to the word problem, emphasising vocabulary.
Provide each child with a copy of Copymaster 18 and read through together.

Differentiation
Low Attainers – Attempt questions 1–4 only.
High Attainers – Provide more practical problems.

Plenary   **5 mins**
Discuss answers and strategies used in the problem solving activity.

Theme 10 Sorting information

Objectives
- To solve a problem by sorting information using objects or pictures
- To solve simple problems involving time
- To know the days of the week
- To read time to the hour on an analogue clock

Vocabulary
time, clock, o'clock, hour, hands, morning, afternoon, evening, night, day, week, weekday, weekend, Monday … Sunday, now, earlier, later, before, after, set, sort

Resources
Copymasters 19 and 20, large analogue clock, a class set of small analogue clocks, clock stamp, seven large cards on which are written the days of the week, multilink cubes, hoops, trays of stationery items (one tray per table/group with plenty of coloured pens, pencils, crayons, 15 cm and 30 cm rulers, rubbers, pencil sharpeners etc.), a standard pack of 52 playing cards for each group, gummed shapes

Homework Copymaster 10

Mental maths starters 3, 13

Assessment
At the end of this theme is the pupil able to:
- Tell the time to the hour on an analogue clock;
- Solve simple problems about time involving earlier and later;
- Know the days of the week in order;
- Sort objects using different criteria?

Lesson 1

Introduction 10 mins
Stick a large analogue clock on the board. Set the hands at one o'clock. Tell the pupils this time and write it as '1 o'clock' on the board. Explain to the pupils that the time will be moved on by one hour and set the hands at two o'clock. Write down the new time. Describe the positions of the minute and hour hands. Repeat for different 'o'clock' times asking pupils to call out the times.

Activities 25 mins
Calling time (whole class)
Each pupil will need a small clock. Call out a time and ask pupils to set their clocks to that time and show their clocks to the teacher. Check that pupils position both hands correctly.

Clock stamps (individual)
Prepare sheets or workbooks with eight stamped clock faces. Ask pupils to draw in the hands showing eight different o'clock times and write the time underneath each clock.

Differentiation
Low Attainers – Give fewer clock faces to complete and specify times.
High Attainers – Where possible write down an event that happens at each time represented in the completed clock faces.

Plenary 5 mins
Using the large analogue clock ask a pupil to set the hands to show, for example, 9 o'clock. Ask the pupils for an event that happens at this time in the morning, e.g. *school starts*. Continue for other times, remembering to mention whether the time refers to morning or afternoon/evening.

Lesson 2

Introduction 10 mins
Stick a large analogue clock on the board. Set the hands at three o'clock. Ask the pupils this time. Set the time one hour later and ask them to say the time. Now ask the pupils what time it will be one hour later than this, two hours later etc.
Set the hands at ten o'clock. Ask the pupils this time. Explain that you are going to now set the time one hour earlier. Set the hands at nine o'clock and ask them to say the time. Now ask the pupils what time it will be one hour earlier than this, two hours earlier etc.

Activities 25 mins
Earlier or later (individual)
Each pupil needs Copymaster 19. Complete the blank clock faces to show times earlier/later than the times shown. Allow pupils to use small clocks to help work out the times.

Show me the time (whole class)
Each pupil will need a small clock. Call out a time and ask pupils to set their clocks to that time and show their clocks to the teacher. Now ask pupils to set the clock one hour earlier. Now set it two hours later etc. Check that pupils position both hands correctly and ask them to call out the times each time they reset the clock.

Differentiation
Low Attainers – Change Copymaster 19 so that times are just one hour later or earlier.
High Attainers – Include some more difficult times involving four or more hours earlier or later.

Plenary 5 mins
Read out a story 'My School Day' and ask pupils to set their clocks to show the times mentioned in the story, e.g. *At eight o'clock (set time) I got up, got washed and dressed. One hour later (set clock) I arrived at school …*

Autumn Term

Lesson 3

Introduction   **10 mins**

Prepare seven cards on which are written the days of the week. Choose seven pupils and give each a card. Line the children up in no particular order and read out the days each of them is holding. Explain that these are the names given to the seven days of the week but the order shown is not the correct one. Ask the pupils to arrange the seven in order, helping where necessary.
Ask the pupils questions such as 'Which of these days do you go to school', 'Which day comes after/before'. Explain weekdays and weekend.

Activities   **25 mins**

Ordering days of the week (pairs)
Provide each pair with a set of seven cards on which are written the days of the week. Shuffle the cards then set them out in the correct order. Shuffle the cards again then one pupil selects a card and asks the other pupil which day comes before/after the day shown on the selected card.

My week (individual)
Ask the pupils to copy down the days of the week in the correct order and draw a picture of something they do on each of those days where possible.

Differentiation

Low Attainers – Choose two or three days.
High Attainers – Complete pictures for all seven days and write the events in words.

Plenary   **5 mins**

Using the cards used in the introduction select a card and ask questions such as 'Is this a weekday?', 'Which day comes after this?'

Lesson 4

Introduction   **10 mins**

Prepare a tray of multilink cubes as follows: stick two blue cubes together – make several of these; stick two red cubes together – make several of these. Explain that the pairs of blocks are to be sorted by colour. Ask two pupils to sort the blocks and place in adjacent hoops on the floor. Collect in the blocks and add to the pile a few pairs each made from one red and one blue cube. Now ask two pupils to sort the blocks into sets. Ask what should be done about the red/blue blocks. Show and explain how overlapping the hoops creates a space where these blocks can be placed.

Activities   **25 mins**

Sorting objects (group)
Provide each group with a tray of school stationery items (see resources) and two hoops. Ask each group to sort some of the items into two sets using their own criteria, e.g. blue pens/green pens, pens/pencils, short rulers/long rulers.

Sweet sets (individual)
Each pupil needs a copy of Copymaster 20. Cut out the sweets from the bottom of the page. Arrange the sweets into two individual sets and two overlapping sets in as many ways as possible. Ask pupils to complete the activity by selecting one of their methods of sorting and sticking the sweets into the appropriate sets.

Plenary   **5 mins**

Invite pupils to show their completed sets and explain the method used in sorting.

Lesson 5

Introduction   **10 mins**

Use blu-tak to stick a pack of playing cards randomly on the board. Explain that some cards are 'red' and some are 'black', some have pictures on them, some don't, some have different symbols or numbers. Ask a pupil to remove all of the kings to create a set. Ask another pupil to remove all of the twos. Repeat for other sets.

Activities   **25 mins**

Playing card sets (group)
Provide each group with a pack of playing cards. Ask the pupils to discuss amongst themselves different ways of sorting the playing cards into sets.
Pupils should then sort some or all of the cards into sets.

Shape sets (individual)
Provide each pupil with some gummed shapes and a piece of paper. Ask the pupils to sort some of the shapes into sets – this could be by colour (all red, all blue), shape (triangles, squares or shapes with curved edges, shapes with straight edges), shape and size (small squares, large squares). Record their sorting by sticking the shapes on to the paper on which they have drawn circles for the sets

Differentiation

Low Attainers – Sort shapes into two simple sets.
High Attainers – Sort into more than two sets or sets which overlap.

Plenary   **5 mins**

Invite pupils to show the class their sets of shapes and ask the class to guess how each of the pupils has sorted the shapes.

Theme 1 — Two-digit numbers

Objectives
- To read and write numerals from 0 to at least 20
- To know what each digit in a two-digit number represents
- To begin to partition larger two-digit numbers into a multiple of ten and ones
- To say the number that is 1 or 10 more or less than any given number to 20

Vocabulary
number names from zero onwards, digits, two-digit numbers, tens, ones, units, multiple

Resources
Copymasters 21 and 22, number tracks, 100 square, place value cards, tens and units apparatus, 1–100 digit cards

Homework Copymaster 11

Mental maths starters 2, 5

Assessment
At the end of this theme is the pupil able to:
- Read and write two-digit numbers to at least 20;
- Recognise the value of each digit in a two-digit number;
- Partition a two-digit number into tens and ones;
- Show the number 1 or 10 more or less than a given number?

Lesson 1

Introduction — 10 mins
Show the children a large 1–100 square. Start counting together from one as far as they can. Point to each number as it is said. Randomly point to numbers and ask the children to call them out. Ask the children if they can see any patterns in the rows or columns.

Activities — 25 mins
100 line (whole class)
Show a 1–100 line and count as before. Cover some of the numbers and ask if the children can work out which ones are missing.

Missing numbers (individual)
Provide the children with sections of number lines and tracks with numbers missing. They have to fill in the missing numbers, forming their numerals correctly.

Differentiation
Low Attainers – Work with numbers up to 30.
High Attainers – Provide number tracks up to 100 and some showing numbers in reverse order.

Plenary — 5 mins
Show a 100 square or number line and choose a point to start counting backwards from. Draw attention to what happens when changing to a multiple of ten. Show that the first digit in a two-digit number tells how many tens.

Lesson 2

Introduction — 10 mins
Provide the children with a set of tens and units place value cards. Ask the children to show 84, 73, 50, 99, 21 etc.

Activities — 25 mins
Tens and ones (whole class)
Ask a child to pick a card from a set of 1–99 digit cards. Ask what each digit stands for and how many tens and ones it is made up from. Show the number using tens and ones apparatus on the OHP. Clearly partition the tens and the ones. Ensure the children are shown a range of numbers including multiples of tens as tens and no ones. Show how to record the number 56 as 5 tens and 6 ones.

Making numbers (pairs)
Provide each child with some two-digit number cards and tens and ones apparatus. One child picks a number from the pack and the other child has to make the number from tens and ones. This is recorded as shown previously.

Differentiation
Low Attainers – Record as a picture, with a line for a ten and a dot for each one.
High Attainers – Extend notation to 50 + 6 = 56.

Plenary — 5 mins
Use place value cards to show the number made from 7 tens and 9 ones, 3 ones and 6 groups of ten etc. Give out and explain the homework activity.

Spring Term

Lesson 3

Introduction   **10 mins**
Stick some two-digit numbers to the board and ask children which number is the same as six tens and four units, forty and eight units.

Activity   **25 mins**
Numbers pairs (pairs)
Provide each pair with a copy of Copymaster 21, with the last 8 squares filled in with two-digit numbers and their equivalents in tens and ones. The children take 6 cards each and make any pairs. The children take turns to discard one card and pick another off the pile. The winner is the first to make 5 pairs.

Differentiation
Low Attainers – Add more numbers up to 30.
High Attainers – Add some numbers up to 99.

Plenary   **5 mins**
Show some 10p and 1p coins. Say an amount below 20p. One child has to collect that amount in 1p coins. Another child collects the same amount as one 10p and the correct number of 1p coins. Then ask for an amount greater than 20p in 10p and 1p coins.

Lesson 4

Introduction   **10 mins**
Ask children to use place value cards to show a number which has a tens number of 8, 4 ones, 7 group of ten etc. There will be a variety of answers to each question.

Activities   **25 mins**
Tens and ones (whole class)
Show 48 on a number card and ask the children to say how many tens and ones. Four tens are worth 40. Write this as a number sentence: $40 + 8 = 48$. Repeat with several numbers.

What number? (individual)
Provide the children with a selection of number sentences with a missing number in each, e.g. $43 = \Box + 3$, $50 + 2 = \Box$, $37 = 30 + \Box$ etc.

Differentiation
Low Attainers – Work with numbers up to 30 only.
High Attainers – Make up their own for a partner when finished.

Plenary   **5 mins**
Show a large abacus and ask the children to show two-digit numbers on it. Ask how they show a number one more or less or ten more.

Lesson 5

Introduction   **10 mins**
Divide the class into 3 groups – 1 more, 1 less, 10 more. Show a number less than 20 and ask each group to show their new number. Repeat with other numbers and swap the groups around.

Activities   **25 mins**
100 square more or less (whole class)
Point to 17 on the number square and ask 'What is one more than 17?', 'What is one less than 17?', 'What is 10 more than 17?' Draw attention to the direction of movement on the 100 square. Can they work out how to find 10 less? Mark all numbers and ask the children what shape (cross) is formed. Repeat with other numbers less than 20. Ask what happens when finding one more than a multiple of ten or one less than a number ending with a one.

More or less (individual)
Provide each child with a 100 square, a copy of Copymaster 22 and fill in the first number of the sequences as appropriate for each group. Ask the children to continue the sequence by finding the numbers one more or less and ten more or less.

Differentiation
Low Attainers – Work up to 30, for 10 more or less work only with multiples of 10.
High Attainers – Work on numbers up to 100.

Plenary   **5 mins**
Ask the children what step they need to make to turn: 6 into 16, 29 into 30, 35 into 25, 12 into 2 etc. Use the 100 square for reference.

Theme 2 Doubles and near doubles

Objectives
- To understand the operations of addition and subtraction and the related vocabulary
- To identify near doubles using doubles already known

Vocabulary
add, sum, plus, together, total, take away, difference, how many more, subtract, equals, double, near double

Resources
Copymasters 23 and 24, number lines, counters, 1–6 dice, 0–9 dice, +/− dice, playing cards, 0–9 digit cards

Homework Copymaster 12

Mental maths starters 9, 12

Assessment
At the end of this theme is the pupil able to:
- Add two numbers together using some mental recall of addition facts;
- Subtract two numbers using some mental recall of subtraction facts;
- Make own addition and subtraction calculations for a given answer;
- Recall doubles to at least 5 + 5 and use these to identify near doubles?

Lesson 1

Introduction 10 mins
Show 5 + 7 = 12 on the board and ask what the '+' sign means. Revise all vocabulary associated with addition.

Activity 25 mins
Acing addition (pairs)
Provide each pair with one suit of playing cards from Ace (= 1) to 10. Turn the cards face down and each child picks one. Make an addition calculation and record.

Differentiation
Low Attainers – Provide counting apparatus.
High Attainers – Provide two sets to enable higher totals.

Plenary 5 mins
Children share their strategies. Ask if anyone put the largest number first and counted on.

Lesson 2

Introduction 10 mins
Show 9 − 3 = 6 on the board and ask what the '−' sign means. Revise all vocabulary associated with subtraction.

Activity 25 mins
Subtraction suits (pairs)
Provide each pair with one suit of playing cards from Ace to 10. Turn the cards face down and each child picks one. Make a subtraction calculation and record. Remind the children the larger number goes first in subtraction.

Differentiation
Low Attainers – Use a number line for counting back or apparatus for finding the difference.
High Attainers – Make one of the numbers 10 more by using a picture card, then subtract.

Plenary 5 mins
Show subtraction calculations and ask for strategies. Encourage remembering facts.

Spring Term

Lesson 3

Introduction   **10 mins**
Provide each child with a set of 0–9 digit cards. Ask the children to show two cards with a total of 11, 8, 3, 16 etc. Vary the vocabulary used in questioning.

Activity   **25 mins**
Awesome answers (individual)
Show a brainstorm cloud on the board and choose a number. The children think of different addition and subtraction sums with that answer. Provide the children with a different number and challenge them to find as many calculations as possible.

Differentiation
Low Attainers – Provide apparatus when necessary.
High Attainers – Encourage more complex calculations.

Plenary   **5 mins**
Collect some of the calculations the children made. Again emphasise the importance of remembering some of the facts.

Lesson 4

Introduction   **10 mins**
Provide each child with a set of 0–9 digit cards. Ask the children to show two cards with a difference of 5, 2, 8 etc. Vary the vocabulary used in questioning.

Activity   **25 mins**
Five in a row (pairs)
Provide each child with a copy of Copymaster 23, about 15 counters of the same colour, two 1–6 dice and a +/− dice. The children take it in turns to throw the three dice and work out the calculation. They cover the answer on their grid and the first child to get five counters in a row in any direction wins the game.

Differentiation
Low Attainers – Provide a 0–20 number track.
High Attainers – Provide two 0–9 dice and change some of the numbers in the grid to include answers to 18.

Plenary   **5 mins**
Ask some quickfire addition and subtraction questions for children to recall mentally.

Lesson 5

Introduction   **10 mins**
Ask the children for some examples of doubles and write them on the board as, e.g. 4 + 4 = 8.
Show 5 + 4 on the board. Ask the children for the answer and draw attention to the fact that it is very close to 4 + 4. In fact it is one more than 4 + 4 so it is 1 more than 8 which is 9. Ask if it is near to any other double fact (5 + 5). This time it is one less but the same answer is still reached. Show other near double calculations and ask which double can be used to solve it.

Activity   **25 mins**
Domino doubles (pairs)
Provide each child with a copy of Copymaster 24 photocopied onto thin card and 12 coloured counters. Cut out the dominoes at the bottom and turn face down. The children take turns to turn over a domino and calculate the double or near double. They cover the answer on their grid and the first child to cover all 12 totals or whoever has most counters at the end is the winner.

Differentiation
Low Attainers – Provide flash cards with answers to doubles up to 6 + 6.
High Attainers – Remove a counter each time a double or near double is repeated.

Plenary   **5 mins**
Show an answer to a double and ask the children to show what we double to get the answer.

Theme 3 — Money problems

Objectives
- To recognise 1p, 2p, 5p and 10p coins and equivalent values
- To find totals up to 20p
- To choose and use the appropriate number operation and mental strategy to solve problems

Vocabulary
money, coin, penny, pence, value, amount, total, altogether, buy, spend, change, most expensive, costs the most, cheapest, costs the least, exactly

Resources
Copymasters 25, 26 and 46, plenty of plastic 1p, 2p, 5p and 10p coins, blu-tak, trays of priced items (one tray per table/group with at least 20 different items labelled with large price tags/stickers for amounts under 20p)

Homework Copymaster 13

Mental maths starters 17, 19

Assessment
At the end of this theme is the pupil able to:
- Recognise 1p, 2p, 5p and 10p coins;
- Know that different combinations of 1p, 2p, 5p and 10p coins can have the same value;
- Mentally calculate totals up to 20p;
- Record calculations using +, − and = showing totals up to 20p;
- Solve simple problems involving totals, buying two of the same, extra amount needed, cheapest and most expensive?

Lesson 1

Introduction — 10 mins
Place a tray of coins on the table. Show and describe to pupils the 1p, 2p, 5p and 10p coins. Hold up a 5p coin and ask a pupil to exchange the 5p coin for a combination of 1p and/or 2p coins. Repeat for further combinations. Explain that two 5p coins have the same value as a 10p coin. Ask pupils to exchange the 10p coin for combinations of 1p, 2p and 5p.

Activities — 25 mins

Coin rubbings (individual)
Provide each pupil with one of each of the four coins. Make rubbings of a set of coins and ask pupils to record the total value.

Buying up to 20p (whole class)
Each pupil needs a set of money cards (Copymaster 46). Hold up an item with a price of up to 20p. Ask the pupils to lay out cards which make up the total. Continue this reinforcing that there are several ways of making the totals.

Differentiation
Low Attainers — Concentrate on 1p, 2p and 5p coins to start with.
High Attainers — Make rubbings showing different combinations for the same total.

Plenary — 5 mins
Stick a set of coins on the board. Ask pupils to work out the total value of the coins. Remove a coin, or coins, and ask pupils for the new total. Repeat.

Lesson 2

Introduction — 10 mins
Place a tray of coins on the table. Select an item from one of the prepared trays. Ask a pupil to select coins to pay for the item. Explain to the class how the pupil has paid. Ask another pupil to pay using a different combination of coins. Can you pay for the item using only three coins? etc.

Activities — 25 mins

Coin piles (individual)
Ask pupils to select a few coins at random and work out the total value of the pile of coins. Ask pupils to make further piles of coins having the same value but using different combinations. What is the least/greatest number of coins needed to make the total?

Piggy banks (individual/pairs)
Pupils each need a copy of Copymaster 25. Match the piggy banks containing the same total value of coins.

Differentiation
Low Attainers — Create a pile of coins for a given total.
High Attainers — Pupils draw their own piggy bank with coins and ask their partner to draw a piggy bank containing the same total value of coins in a different combination.

Plenary — 5 mins
Write a total, up to 20p, on the board and ask pupils for a combination of coins to make that total. Record the answers on the board until several combinations have been listed.

Spring Term

Lesson 3

Introduction   **10 mins**
Use one of the trays of items from the previous lesson. Ask pupils to identify the item(s) which costs the most/least/more than 15p/less than 4p etc.

Activities   **25 mins**
Most and least (individual)
Each pupil needs a copy of Copymaster 26. Complete the copymaster by totalling and recording the amounts in each child's hand and answering questions about the totals.

How much more? (whole class)
Using a tray of items, hold up an item and ask questions such as: 'I have 10p. How much more do I need to buy this item costing 16p?' Hold up two items and ask 'How much more does the pen cost than the pencil?', 'I want to buy this book and this pen. How much is this altogether?', 'I have 15p. How much more do I need?'

Differentiation
Low Attainers – Use coins to help work out the totals.
High Attainers – Represent the totals in the purses in 'Most and least' using the least number of coins possible.

Plenary   **5 mins**
Tell the pupils that you have two coins in your pocket. Ask pupils what is the smallest total I could have (two 1p's)/highest total (most) I could have (two 10p's). Continue with questions such as: 'I have three silver coins which add up to 20p. What coins do I have?' Continue, ensuring totals do not exceed 20p.

Lesson 4

Introduction   **10 mins**
Hold up an item with a price tag on it, *e.g. a book with a tag for 16p*. Ask a pupil to select the correct coins to pay for the item. Record the combination as a calculation on the board, *e.g. 10p + 5p + 1p = 16p*. Remind them of the use of + and =. Ask another pupil for a different way of paying, *e.g. 5p + 5p + 2p + 2p + 2p = 16p*. Repeat for further objects.

Activities   **25 mins**
Coin calculations (individual)
Using the trays of items, ask pupils to select an item, work out which coins they would use to pay for it and write down the calculation, *e.g.*
     ball   10p + 1p + 1p + 1p = 13p
Repeat for other combinations of coins, *e.g.*
5p + 5p + 2p + 1p = 13p, and other items.

Adding prices (whole class)
Hold up two items and ask pupils for the total cost. Record the calculation on the board, *e.g. 7p + 9p = 16p*. Repeat for other items.

Differentiation
Low Attainers – Record one combination of coins for each item.
High Attainers – Choose more than one item and record the calculation for the total coins needed.

Plenary   **5 mins**
Select two items, *e.g. doll for 10p and a toffee for 2p*, and record the addition calculation on the board, *e.g. 10p + 2p = 12p*. Now record the possible combinations of coins as addition calculations, *e.g. 5p + 5p + 2p, 10p + 1p + 1p etc.*

Lesson 5

Introduction   **10 mins**
Prepare a tray of items with prices of up to 10p. Ask a pupil to select an item from the tray and ask how much it will cost to buy two of them. Write the calculation on the board, *e.g. 6p + 6p = 12p*. Repeat for other items. Then explain that you have 10p and want to buy two items. Choose two items for exactly 10p. Record the calculation on the board, *e.g. 3p + 7p = 10p*.

Activities   **25 mins**
Buying two (individual)
Provide each table/group with a tray of items with prices of up to 10p (remove higher priced items used in previous lessons). Pupils select an item and work out how much it will cost to buy two of that item. They should record their results as follows: 2 books 8p + 8p = 16p.

What can I buy for 10p? (whole class)
Tell the pupils that they have 10p to spend. Ask a pupil to select two items with a total value of exactly 10p. Record results on the board as calculations and repeat. Choose one item and ask pupils 'Which other item could I buy so that I spend exactly 10p?', 'Which items can I not afford?'

Differentiation
Low Attainers – Provide tray of items with prices of 5p or less.
High Attainers – Extend to buying three/four of the same item.

Plenary   **5 mins**
Invite pupils to explain which items they bought two of and show their recorded results.

Theme 4 — Measuring mass

Objectives
- To understand and use the vocabulary related to mass
- To compare two, then more, masses using direct comparisons
- To measure mass using uniform non-standard units

Vocabulary
mass, weigh, weights, heavy, light, balances, scales, heavier than, heaviest, lighter than, lightest

Resources
Copymasters 27 and 28, a wide range of objects of different masses, interlocking cubes, conkers, pebbles, pegs, balances, cards showing 'heavier than', 'lighter than' and arrows

Homework Copymaster 14

Mental maths starters 14, 20

Assessment
At the end of this theme is the pupil able to:
- Use the appropriate vocabulary when talking about measuring mass;
- Directly compare the mass of two, then more than two, objects;
- Measure the mass of an object using non-standard units?

Lesson 1

Introduction   10 mins
Remind children of the previous term's work on measuring length and tell them that this term they are going to do some work on measuring mass. Talk about situations when the mass of objects needs to be known.

Activity   25 mins
Heavier or lighter (whole class then pairs)
Show the children two objects of different masses. Ask them if they can tell which is the heavier. Indicate that they have to feel them to tell rather than look at them. They need to feel both to compare. Show the objects with the labels 'heavier than' and 'lighter than' with the arrow cards pointing in the correct direction. Repeat for several objects then provide a selection of objects and a set of cards for each pair of children.

Differentiation
Low Attainers – Provide pairs of objects that are considerably different in mass.
High Attainers – Record findings in pictures.

Plenary   5 mins
Some pairs show their findings with the labels.

Lesson 2

Introduction   10 mins
Can the children name objects that they think are heavier than an elephant, lighter than a feather?

Activity   25 mins
Comparing masses (small groups)
Remind the children of yesterday's activity comparing the mass of two objects and introduce sets of three objects to be put in order of mass. Provide each group of children with cards 'heaviest' and 'lightest' to put at either end of the set of objects. The children draw the set of three objects and write the correct words underneath.

Differentiation
Low Attainers – Ensure the children are confident comparing two masses first.
High Attainers – Provide sets of objects that have two quite similar in mass.

Plenary   5 mins
Ask one group to bring out their objects and discuss what they did. Write some sentences about the mass of the objects using mathematical vocabulary.

Spring Term

Lesson 3

Introduction   **10 mins**
Discuss with the children that sometimes it is difficult to tell which object is heavier and show them a bucket balance. Put an object in one side and ask the children what they see is happening. Then put a heavier object in the other bucket and ask what they observe.

Activity   **25 mins**
Balancing act (small groups)
Provide each group with a balance and a set of objects. Tell them to pick three of the objects and use the balance to put them in order. The children will have to weigh each object and compare it with the other two to establish the correct order. Record findings by drawing pictures or writing 'the _____ is heaviest, the _____ is lightest and the _____ is in the middle'.

Differentiation
Low Attainers – Children just compare masses and do not order the objects.
High Attainers – Compare the masses of four objects.

Plenary   **5 mins**
Demonstrate how to compare the masses of four objects, encouraging use of vocabulary to describe what is happening.

Lesson 4

Introduction   **10 mins**
Provide each pair with an object and they have to quickly find one object in the classroom heavier than it and one object lighter than it. Check some of the findings using a balance.

Activity   **25 mins**
Heavier and lighter (pairs)
Provide each pair with two copies of Copymaster 27, a balance and an object. The children have to find some objects heavier than and lighter than the object they have been given and record their findings. They then have to write a sentence about their findings.

Differentiation
Low Attainers – Omit the sentence writing activity.
High Attainers – Challenge them to find objects that weigh the same as their given object.

Plenary   **5 mins**
Compare findings and see which pair found the most objects. Give out the homework activity.

Lesson 5

Introduction   **10 mins**
Show the children the bucket balance again with a shoe in one side. Tell them that you want to find something that weighs exactly the same. Ask how they will know when the masses are the same. Introduce the idea of using lots of the same thing to balance the object. Demonstrate with interlocking cubes. Show what happens when there is one cube too much or too few. Tip out the cubes and count them together. Record this as 'the shoe weighs the same as 25 cubes'.

Activity   **25 mins**
How many cubes? (small groups)
Provide each group with a balance, cubes (or conkers, pegs, pebbles etc.), objects to weigh and one copy of Copymaster 28 per child. Weigh each object using one non-standard unit and record the results.

Differentiation
Low Attainers – Provide assistance counting the non-standard units.
High Attainers – Put the objects in order of mass.

Plenary   **5 mins**
Show an object and ask the children to estimate how many pebbles it will weigh the same as. Record estimates then weigh it. Repeat with other objects.

Theme 5 — Shapes and positions

Objectives
- To use everyday language to describe features of familiar 2D and 3D shapes, referring to shapes with faces, number of faces or corners, numbers of sides or edges
- To make and describe models, patterns and pictures using everyday materials
- To use everyday language to describe position and direction
- Talk about things that turn
- Use one or more shapes to make patterns and describe repeating patterns

Vocabulary
As for Autumn Theme 5, also: direction, left, right, forwards, backwards, sideways, across, towards, away from, turn, point, line

Resources
Copymasters 29 and 30, teacher set of coloured cardboard 2D shapes, blu-tak, pupil sets of plastic or cardboard 2D and 3D shapes, everyday 3D objects, e.g. tin of soup, cereal packet, dice, wooden/plastic hollow/solid building blocks, hoops, plasticine or Play-doh, tools for cutting and rolling plasticine, junk materials, packets and containers, everyday objects with repeating patterns, objects that turn, cardboard discs

Homework Copymaster 15

Mental maths starters 8, 15

Assessment
At the end of this theme is the pupil able to:
- Name, sort and describe a variety of 3D shapes using everyday language;
- Use everyday materials to make a 3D model and describe its construction;
- Make and describe a repeating pattern using 2D shapes;
- Use everyday language to describe positions and directions;
- Recognise objects that turn and identify the point or line about which an object turns?

Lesson 1

Introduction — 10 mins
Place a selection of 3D shapes on the table. These should include, for example, solid wooden shapes, hollow plastic shapes and everyday 3D objects. Reinforce the difference between solid and hollow. Place two hoops on the floor and ask pupils to sort the shapes into solid and hollow. Ask pupils if they can think of any other ways in which they could sort the shapes, *e.g. shapes with and without curved faces, cubes and not cubes.*

Activities — 25 mins
Sorting into sets (groups)
Provide each group with three hoops and a wide selection of 3D shapes including plastic and wooden blocks and everyday objects. Encourage pupils to choose a method for sorting their shapes into two or three groups. Ask each group to explain how they have sorted their shapes to the rest of the class. Pick up on any shapes in incorrect sets.

Shape match (whole class)
Ask pupils to choose a shape that they have been working with. Ask pupils to stand up and hold up their shape if it matches the description: Does your shape have all square faces? Is your shape a sphere? Does your shape have a triangular face? Is your shape the same shape as a straw?

Differentiation
Low Attainers — Limit to sorting into two sets with fewer shapes and for a given criterion.
High Attainers — Sort shapes into two sets using the hoops as a Venn diagram.

Plenary — 5 mins
Have ready a selection of packets and containers which have been cut and flattened into nets. Ask the pupils to describe the shapes of the faces. Reassemble the nets to show how the faces fit together to make a 3D shape with corners and edges.

Lesson 2

Introduction — 10 mins
Demonstrate the different ways in which plasticine or Play-doh can be formed, *e.g. rolled into strings, rolled flat like pastry, cut, formed into solid shapes.* Make hollow cylinders from plasticine using different methods — from coiled strings, from a rolled out sheet and by poking a pencil through a solid rolled cylinder.

Activities — 25 mins
Plasticine modelling (individual)
Provide each pupil with lumps of plasticine and tools and ask them to make as many different shapes as possible (these could be either 2D or 3D). Ask pupils to choose their favourite shape and make a display on a table.

Junk modelling (individual)
Ask pupils to construct a robot from junk materials and containers and record their design on paper.

Differentiation
Low Attainers — Assist with choice of materials and construction of robot. Omit recording of design if necessary.
High Attainers — By outcome.

Plenary — 5 mins
Ask pupils to describe and explain the shapes used for their robot models.

Spring Term

Lesson 3

Introduction   **10 mins**

Use stick-on shapes to create a pattern of 2D shapes on the board, e.g.

○ ○ □ □ ○ ○
▽ ○ ▽ ○ ▽ ○ ▽ ○

Ask pupils to describe the patterns, e.g. *'circle, circle, square, square, circle, …'* or *'two circles then two squares then the same again'*. Encourage the children to identify the names of the shapes, the numbers of shapes and the colours used, e.g. *two red circles, two blue squares*. Explain that the pattern is repeated. Ask how many times. Ask pupils to suggest other patterns using the same shapes.

Activities   **25 mins**
Experimenting with patterns (individual)
Ask the pupils to use plastic or card 2D shapes to experiment with repeating patterns.

Making and describing a repeating pattern (individual)
Draw and colour a repeating pattern on paper. Describe the pattern by writing the names and colours of the shapes and write down the number of times it is repeated.

Differentiation
Low Attainers – Use two or three basic shapes and colours.
High Attainers – Use a wider range of shapes of different sizes.

Plenary   **5 mins**
Have some objects with repeating patterns, e.g. *wallpaper, fabric, wrapping paper, crockery*, and ask pupils to describe them in terms of shapes, sizes, colours, how often the pattern repeats.

Lesson 4

Introduction   **10 mins**
Ask the pupils to stand up. Stand at the back of the class facing the same way as the pupils. Explain that they are to follow your directions, e.g.

    'Turn left'
    'Take one step forward'
    'Walk towards the board'

Activities   **25 mins**
In the forest (whole class)
This should be done in the PE Hall. Ask the children to imagine that they are in a forest and explain that they are to follow the instructions you are giving about their positions and directions, e.g.

    'Walk forwards along the path'
    'Stand next to a tree'
    'Climb up the tree'

Repeat for other imaginary situations, e.g. *a busy street*.

Maze (individual)
Each pupil needs Copymaster 29. Draw the route through the maze to its centre. Write down the directions using the words 'left', 'right', 'forwards', 'backwards'.

Differentiation
Low Attainers – They should explain their directions orally.
High Attainers – Draw their own maze and test it on another pupil.

Plenary   **5 mins**
Ask pupils to describe their journey to school using everyday language for positions and directions.

Lesson 5

Introduction   **10 mins**
Have a variety of objects which either turn about a point (clock, scissors, windmill, wheel, spinning top) or a line (book, box with hinged lid, CD case). Demonstrate that part of these objects turn in some way. Explain that some turn about a point, such as the clock, and some turn about a line, such as the pages of a book. Ask the pupils to sort the objects into two groups, allowing pupils to play with the objects to help them decide.

Activities   **25 mins**
Objects that turn (individual)
Each pupil needs Copymaster 30. Identify whether the objects turn about a point or line and mark in colour the points or lines about which the object turns.

Spinners (individual)
Provide each pupil with a cardboard disc. Ask them to colour it in sectors or spiral or circular patterns (demonstrate if required) and stick a pencil through the centre into plasticine. Ask them to test their spinners.

Differentiation
Low Attainers – Provide examples of some of the objects on the sheet to help identify the points or lines about which they turn.
High Attainers – Use hexagons or pentagons to create numbered spinners for a game.

Plenary   **5 mins**
Ask pupils to look around the classroom and find objects that turn. Make a list on the board or flipchart.

Theme 6 — Counting patterns

Objectives
- To count in tens from zero to 100
- To count on in twos from zero, then one and begin to recognise odd and even numbers to ten
- To count in steps of five from zero to 20 or more
- To solve mathematical problems or puzzles
- To suggest extensions 'What if?' and 'What could I try next?'

Vocabulary
number, zero, nought, one, two, … twenty, thirty, … one hundred, count, forwards, backwards, count on, count back, share, pattern, before, after, between, add, plus, equal to, is the same as, odd, even, every other

Resources
Copymasters 31 and 32, set of teacher's number cards from 0 to 20 and a set of 0 to 100 in tens, blu-tak, pegs, clothes line, three small trays, five packets of crisps, multilink cubes, sets of number cards from 0 to 20 – sufficient for half the class, number lines, counters, 100 squares

Homework Copymaster 16

Mental maths starters 6, 13

Assessment
At the end of this theme is the pupil able to:
- Count on and back in tens from zero to 100 and from other multiples of ten;
- Count on and back in twos from zero to twenty and from one to nineteen;
- Start to recognise odd and even numbers;
- Count on and back in fives from zero to twenty;
- Start to complete number sequences involving steps of 1, 2, 5 and 20;
- Investigate number patterns?

Lesson 1

Introduction   10 mins
Write the numbers 1 to 10 on the board and explain that by writing a zero after each one further numbers are made. Point to and read out these numbers – ten, twenty, … one hundred. Point to a number at random and ask pupils to say the number.

Activities   25 mins
Tens pattern (individual)
Each pupil needs a 100 square. Ask the pupils to colour the numbers 10, 20, … 100. Point out the pattern of these numbers in the square.

Washing line tens (whole class)
Peg cards with the numbers zero, 10, 20, … 100 on to the clothes line. Explain that you are going to count up in tens from zero to 100. Recite the numbers forwards and then backwards. Repeat as necessary. Ask questions about the numbers such as 'What number is after 60/ before 30/ between 80 and 100/ …?' Now ask pupils to turn away and then remove one number. Ask which number is missing. Repeat. Go on to remove two numbers and ask which are missing.

Differentiation
By outcome.

Plenary   5 mins
Using the washing line, ask the pupils to start from e.g. 40 and count on/back in tens from that number. Continue and then repeat without the use of the washing line.

Lesson 2

Introduction   10 mins
Draw a number line from 0 to 20 on the board. Point to zero and ask the pupils to count on two and ask 'Which number are we at now?' Write the number above the line. Keep counting on in twos and recording the numbers until the list of numbers 2, 4, … 20 is obtained. Explain that these are called even numbers.

Activities   25 mins
Even squares (individual)
Each pupil needs Copymaster 31. Explain that pupils are to colour in two squares in red, four squares in green, and continue to 20 in different colours.

Washing line evens (whole class)
Each pupil needs a set of number cards from 0 to 20 with the odd numbers removed. Peg cards with the even numbers from 0 to 20 on the line. Firstly count from 0 to 20 in twos and back. Explain that you are now going to remove a card and that they are going to show you the number that is missing by holding up one of their set of cards. Repeat several times.

Differentiation
By outcome.

Plenary   5 mins
Explain that the pupils are going to use their number cards again to show the correct answer to each of your questions. Ask questions such as 'Count on 2 from 12 – which number is this?', 'Count back two from 18 – which number is this?', 'Which is the next even number after 6?', 'Which is the even number before 14?'

38

Spring Term

Lesson 3

Introduction   **10 mins**

Draw a number line from 0 to 20 on the board. Point to one and ask the pupils to count on two and ask 'Which number are we at now?' Write the number above the line. Keep counting on in twos and recording the numbers until the list of numbers 1, 3, … 19 is obtained. Explain that these are called odd numbers.

Activities   **25 mins**

Odd rods (individual)
Provide each pupil with a large pile of multilink cubes. Link cubes to make rods which are 1, 3, 5, … 19 cubes in length. Arrange the rods next to each other in order of length/number of cubes and show how each rod is two cubes longer than the previous rod.

Odds pattern (individual)
Each pupil needs a grid of the numbers from 1 to 20. Ask pupils to use one colour to colour in all of the odd numbers in the grid. Ask them which numbers are not coloured. Do you recognise these numbers? Now colour all of these even numbers in a different colour. When pupils have finished their grid ask questions as to whether a given number is odd or even.

Differentiation
Low Attainers – Focus on numbers 1, 3, 5, 7, 9 only.
High Attainers – Up to 100 grid.

Plenary   **5 mins**
On the board write some even number and odd number sequences with missing numbers. Ask pupils to identify the missing numbers.

Lesson 4

Introduction   **10 mins**

Draw a number line from 0 to 20 on the board. Point to zero and ask a pupil to count on five. Ask 'Which number are we at now?' Write the number above the line. Keep counting on five and recording the numbers until the list of numbers 5, 10, 15, 20 is obtained. Count on five up to 20 then back from 20 to 0. Now count on from 1 in ones and clap each time you reach a multiple of 5. Repeat this counting backwards from 20.

Activities   **25 mins**

Fives pattern (individual/whole class)
Each pupil needs a grid of the numbers from 1 to 20. Ask pupils to use one colour to colour in all of the numbers 5, 10, 15, 20. Ask the pupils which of these are odd? Which are even? Notice that the numbers 10, 20 are coloured. These are the first two numbers in the pattern 10, 20, 30, …

Complete the patterns (individual)
Each pupil needs Copymaster 32. Ask pupils to fill in the missing numbers in the patterns which include tens, evens, odds, fives. Encourage them to use a number line or their coloured grids to help them count on.

Differentiation
Low Attainers – Edit the copymaster to provide easier sequences.
High Attainers – Colour in all multiples of 5 on a 100 grid.

Plenary   **5 mins**
On the board write the number 2. Ask pupils to count on in twos up to 20. Ask pupils what name is given to these numbers. Write 1 on the board and ask pupils to count on in twos. Ask what name is given to these numbers. Write 10 and count on in tens to 100 and five and count on in fives to 20.

Lesson 5

Introduction   **10 mins**

Choose three pupils, write their names on the board and give them each a small tray. Explain that you have five packets of crisps to share amongst the three pupils. Ask the pupils 'If I give Daniel 1 packet and Stevie 2 packets how many are left for Clare?' Repeat and record for other combinations,

e.g.   Daniel   Stevie   Clare
           1   2   2
           3   0   2
Check for any which are the same.

Activity   **25 mins**

Counters in boxes (individual)
Prepare sheets with three squares drawn on them to represent three boxes. Each pupil needs 3 counters of the same colour. Ask the pupils to work out as many ways as possible of sharing out 3 counters into three boxes. Point out that not all boxes have to contain counters. Record work on paper.

Differentiation
Low Attainers – Share between two boxes only.
High Attainers – Use more than three counters.

Plenary   **5 mins**
Ask pupils to show the class some of their results. Discuss that there are many ways to share the counters. Point out that they should always check to see if they have some identical combinations.

Theme 7 — Ordering numbers

Objectives
- To understand the vocabulary of comparing and ordering numbers including ordinal numbers to at least 20
- To compare two familiar numbers and say which is more or less
- To understand the vocabulary of estimation, give a sensible estimate of a number of objects and check by counting

Vocabulary
count, most, least, more than, less than, equal to, the same as, compare, order, first, second, … twentieth, before, after, between, guess, estimate, close to, far away, near, too low, too high

Resources
Copymasters 33 and 34, multilink cubes, two small trays, set 0–20 number cards for each pupil, 0–30 cards if required, cards with the words first, … twentieth, pegs, clothes line, containers holding small items, e.g. jar containing marbles, small dish of buttons, box of multilink cubes, bucket of tennis balls, flipchart, gummed shapes

Homework Copymaster 17

Mental maths starters 7, 8

Assessment
At the end of this theme is the pupil able to:
- Compare two numbers up to 20 using correct vocabulary;
- Order cardinal numbers to at least 20;
- Order ordinal numbers to at least 20;
- Make a sensible estimate of up to 30 objects, comment on closeness of estimate and check by counting?

Lesson 1

Introduction   10 mins
Give two pupils each some multilink cubes (between 10 and 20) on a small tray. Ask the pupils to count how many cubes each has. Ask the question 'Who has the most/least cubes?' Write the answers on the board as 'Ben has more then Sarah, Sarah has less then Ben. Now ask 'How many cubes should I give Sarah so that they have equal amounts/the same?'

Activities   25 mins
More, less, the same (individual)
Each pupil needs Copymaster 33. Compare the prices of items using comparing vocabulary.

Comparing numbers (pairs)
Each pair needs two sets of 0–20 number cards. Turn over one card from each pile and take turns to compare the numbers.

Differentiation
Low Attainers – Use two sets of 0–10 cards.
High Attainers – Use two sets of 0–30 cards.

Plenary   5 mins
Write two numbers on the board and ask pupils to compare the numbers using appropriate vocabulary.

Lesson 2

Introduction   10 mins
Write the following on the board: 13   16 and stick number cards 11, 14, 15, 16, 18 on the board. Ask the pupils which numbers can and can't fit between 13 and 16 and explain their answers.

Activities   25 mins
Which fit? (whole class)
Continue with further examples of the type used in the introduction, e.g. 14   17; 7   13.

Ordering numbers (pairs)
Each pair needs a set of 0–20 number cards. Take turns to select five cards from the pile and place them in the correct order.

Differentiation
Low Attainers – Use a set of 0–10 cards.
High Attainers – Use a set of 0–30 cards.

Plenary   5 mins
Use further examples of finding numbers to fit the blank spaces, reinforcing the correct use of vocabulary to explain answers.

Spring Term

Lesson 3

Introduction   **10 mins**

Stand ten pupils in a line at the front and give them cards with the words 'first', 'second', ... 'tenth' to show their positions. Ask pupils questions such as 'Who is first?', 'Which position is Jay?', 'Who is between third and fifth?' Add ten more pupils to the line and give cards in order for 'eleventh', ... 'twentieth'. Ask further questions. Now place cards in order on the board and ask pupils to recite the words.

Activities   **25 mins**

Ice cream queue (individual)

Each pupils needs Copymaster 34. Answers questions about the positions of people in the queue. Ensure that the word cards used in the introduction are displayed in position in the classroom.

Alphabet (whole class)

Write the first twenty letters of the alphabet on the board. Ask a pupil to come out and work out which is the thirteenth letter by counting along.

Differentiation

Low Attainers – Read Copymaster 34 questions and answers orally.
High Attainers – Work without referring to the displayed word cards.

Plenary   **5 mins**

Peg the word cards in order on a clothes line. Recite them. Now swap the positions of two cards and ask pupils to identify them.

Lesson 4

Introduction   **10 mins**

Hold a handful of multilink cubes and show the class saying that you have less than ten. Ask them to look at the cubes and guess how many you have. Write some names of pupils on the board and record their guesses. Explain that another word for 'guess' is 'estimate' and that estimates can be good or bad depending on how close they are to the real number. Count the cubes and discuss the estimates using appropriate vocabulary. Repeat for a handful of cubes between 10 and 20.

Activities   **25 mins**

Estimating cubes (pairs)

One pupil makes a pile of multilink cubes then the other pupil estimates the number of cubes in the pile. The first pupil counts the cubes and comments on the other's estimate. Repeat, taking turns.

Estimating game (individual/whole class)

Set up several containers holding small items, *e.g. jar containing marbles, small dish of buttons, box of multilink cubes, bucket of tennis balls*. Allow pupils a short time to look, estimate and record (on a pre-prepared sheet) the number of items in each container.

Differentiation

Low Attainers – Choose small numbers of cubes to estimate.
High Attainers – Choose larger numbers of cubes to estimate.

Plenary   **5 mins**

Ask pupils to count the number of items in each container and ask pupils to check their estimates. Ask questions about their estimates.

Lesson 5

Introduction   **10 mins**

On three sheets of a flipchart draw three identical squares. In the first square draw up to 10 dots, in the second up to 20, in the third up to 30. Show the pupils the first square for a short time, tell them that there are less than 10 dots and then ask them to estimate the number of dots. Write down their estimate on a piece of paper. Repeat for the other two squares. Discuss the estimates.

Activity   **25 mins**

Too low, too high (pairs)

A pupil either draws spots or sticks gummed shapes on a piece of paper and then counts them. The pupil then asks their partner to estimate the number of spots/shapes and comments on their estimate, *e.g. 'too low', 'too high', 'very close'*. The other pupil keeps estimating until they say the correct number. Repeat, taking turns.

Differentiation

Low Attainers – Choose smaller numbers of dots/shapes.
High Attainers – Start to estimate quantities in the classroom, *e.g. pencils in the drawer, books on the shelf.*

Plenary   **5 mins**

Place a number of mixed objects (between 20 and 30) on a tray. Ask a pupil to estimate the number and comment on their estimate. Keep asking until the correct number is called.

Theme 8 — Adding and subtracting

Objectives
- To understand the operation of addition
- To understand the operation of subtraction as 'how many more?'
- To partition into 5 and a bit when adding 6, 7, 8, 9
- To bridge through 10 when adding single-digit numbers
- To find totals and give change
- To work out how to pay an amount using smaller coins
- To solve simple mathematical problems and puzzles
- To explain methods orally
- To choose and use the appropriate number operation and mental strategy to solve a problem

Vocabulary
add, sum, together, total, difference, how many more? subtract, equals, change, 1p, 2p, 5p, 10p coin, penny, pence, cost, spend, pay, money, how much?

Resources
Copymasters 35 and 36, counters, hoops, interlocking cubes, coins, classroom shop, number tracks, 0–9 digit cards

Homework Copymaster 18

Mental maths starters 13, 15

Assessment
At the end of this theme is the pupil able to:
- Add and subtract using a wider range of mental strategies, including bridging through 10 and adding 5 and a bit;
- Calculate totals and give change in different coins;
- Solve problems using appropriate number operations and mental strategies, explaining methods orally?

Lesson 1

Introduction — 10 mins
Put a set of 7 counters on the OHP and count them together. Switch off the OHP and remove 4 of the counters. Ask how many counters are there now, how many were taken away and how do they know. Gradually write it as a number sentence, 7 − 4 = 3. Repeat the activity with 9 counters, taking 6 away and use a range of vocabulary in questioning. Show them to work out how many were taken away by saying 'We have three left so how many more are needed to make 9?' Model counting on using the number line. Remind the children not to count the starting number.

Activity — 25 mins
How many more? (pairs)
Provide each pair of children with a set of 0–10 digit cards and access to a number line. Turn the cards face down and each child picks a card. They have to work out how many more the larger number is than the smaller number or how many more needs to be added to the smaller number to make the larger number. They each record this as a subtraction sentence.

Differentiation
Low Attainers – Provide with two 1–6 dice instead of digit cards.
High Attainers – Provide number cards to 15.

Plenary — 5 mins
Children share some of their solutions and strategies. Practise some subtraction calculations using a range of vocabulary in questioning.

Lesson 2

Introduction — 10 mins
Show a 3 on a digit card and ask the children to show the double of this. Write the number sentence on the board. Repeat for all doubles to 6 + 6. Draw attention to 5 + 5 = 10 as an important double to be used later.

Activities — 25 mins
5 and a bit (whole class)
Show how to partition 6, 7, 8, 9 into 5 + 1 = 6, 5 + 2 = 7 etc. Now write 5 + 6 on the board and ask the children what the 6 can be made from, i.e. 5 + 1. So 5 + 6 = 5 + 5 + 1. Show the children to use double 5 and one more, 10 + 1 = 11. Repeat with adding 7, 8 and 9. Then show how to split two numbers into 5 and a bit, e.g.
7 + 8 = 5 + 2 + 5 + 3 = 10 + 2 + 3 = 15

Using facts (individual)
Write some addition calculations on the board involving numbers that can be split into 5 and a bit.

Differentiation
Low Attainers – Provide interlocking cubes that can be split into 5 and a bit.
High Attainers – Provide a challenge of larger numbers, 14 + 10 = 10 + 10 + 4, splitting into 10 and a bit.

Plenary — 5 mins
Discuss some of the answers and how the numbers were partitioned.

Spring Term

Lesson 3

Introduction   **10 mins**
Call out a number less than 10 and ask the children to show the digit card that when added to it makes 10. Display a number line from 0–20. Write 7 + 5 on the board and ask the children to work this out mentally. Discuss the methods they used. Show this calculation using apparatus. Put groups of 7 and 5 counters on the OHP. Count one counter at a time to the pile of 7 until 10 is reached. Count how many are left (2) and add this on to 10 (12). So 7 + 5 = 7 + 3 + 2 = 10 + 2. Demonstrate this on a number line by showing a spearate jumps from 7 to 10 to 12. Repeat this with different calculations when bridging 10 is needed.

Activity   **25 mins**
Crossing the tens bridge (individual)
Provide each child with 5–9 digit cards. Shuffle the cards then turn two over and write an addition sentence. Encourage use of bridging through ten to solve the calculations.

Differentiation
Low Attainers – Provide a 0–20 number line.
High Attainers – How many different calculations can be made with all of the cards?

Plenary   **5 mins**
Show a calculation that requires bridging through 10 and ask a child to show the stages by writing number sentences, e.g. *8 + 6 = 8 + 2 + 4 = 10 + 4 = 14.*

Lesson 4

Introduction   **10 mins**
Revise recognition of coins to 10p. Show large cards and ask for totals e.g. *How much will I have if I have a 2p coin and a 5p coin?* etc.

Activities   **25 mins**
Which coins? (whole class)
Tell the children 'I have 8p in my pocket, what coins might I have?' Write all the possibilities on the board, counting them together. Work with amounts less than 10p. If the children are confident with this try with amounts up to 20p.

All change (pairs)
Provide each pair with a selection of coins up to 20p and Copymaster 35 cut into cards. Tell the children they are taking turns to go shopping with 20p. They choose no more than 3 objects on the cards making sure they do not cost more than 20p altogether. The shopkeeper adds the prices then gives the change. Together they show all the different ways of giving the change using the coins they have. They then record this by drawing the coins or writing their value. Repeat taking turns to be customer and shopkeeper.

Differentiation
Low Attainers – Choose two items to buy.
High Attainers – Increase their spending money to 30p.

Plenary   **5 mins**
Ask some totals and change questions using a range of vocabulary. Encourage showing change in different ways. Give out the homework activity.

Lesson 5

Introduction   **10 mins**
Review the homework activity with the children. Ask some mental addition and subtraction questions that involve using the strategies learnt earlier in the theme.

Activities   **25 mins**
Shopping (whole class)
Use the context of the classroom shop for problem solving. Ask a range of questions where children have to pick the appropriate operation and mental strategy, e.g. *How much more is a bag of crisps than an apple?, What two items can I buy for 12p?, I have 20p: if I buy a carton of milk will I have enough to buy a banana?* etc.

Money problems (individual)
Provide each child with Copymaster 36 and read through some of the questions together. Remind them to think how they are going to solve it and do they know a quick way using a mental strategy.

Differentiation
Low Attainers – Do 1–6 only with support for reading.
High Attainers – Make own money problems for a partner using the cards from Copymaster 35.

Plenary   **5 mins**
Discuss strategies used and answers to the problems.

Theme 9 Measuring

Objectives
- To suggest suitable non-standard and standard units and measuring equipment to estimate then measure mass
- To record estimates and measurements as 'about as heavy as 20 cubes', 'nearly 2 kilograms'
- To know the seasons of the year
- To solve simple problems involving time and mass

Vocabulary
mass, weigh, weights, heavy, light, balances, scales, heavier than, heaviest, lighter than, lightest, kilogram, Spring, Summer, Autumn, Winter, season, after, before, next

Resources
Copymasters 37 and 38, kilogram weights, balances, objects to weigh, non-standard weighing objects, small plastic bags

Homework Copymaster 19

Mental maths starters 4, 6

Assessment
At the end of this theme is the pupil able to:
- Choose suitable non-standard units to weigh objects with;
- Estimate and measure the mass of objects using non-standard units and a kilogram;
- Record measures as 'about as heavy as 20 cubes' etc.?

Lesson 1

Introduction — 10 mins
Remind the children of the work carried out earlier in the term and revise some of the vocabulary. Show how to use a balance to compare the mass of two objects and how to weigh an object using non-standard units.

Activity — 25 mins
My object weighs ... (pairs)
Provide each pair of children with an object to weigh and a range of non-standard units. They have to estimate the mass of the object using each of the different non-standard units then accurately measure and record their findings.

Differentiation
Low Attainers – Provide non-standard units that have a relatively high mass so there are not too many to count.
High Attainers – Provide a wider range of non-standard units.

Plenary — 5 mins
Ask the children which they think was the most suitable unit to measure with. Ask if the balance was always level.

Lesson 2

Introduction — 10 mins
Remind the children of the different units used for measuring in the previous lesson. Indicate that it is better that the heavier the object being weighed, the larger the unit used to measure with. Demonstrate that an object does not always weigh the same as an exact number of non-standard units and that one unit less does not balance and one unit more does not balance. Show how to record this as … and a bit, or nearly …

Activity — 25 mins
Weight a bit (small groups)
Provide each group with a selection of objects to be weighed and non-standard units. The children have to pick the most appropriate unit, estimate and then take turns to weigh the object. They then record this as shown above.

Differentiation
Low Attainers – Provide a limited range of objects to be weighed and non-standard units.
High Attainers – Provide a wider range of non-standard units.

Plenary — 5 mins
Show objects and ask which of the non-standard units are most appropriate. Take some estimates then measure.

Spring Term

Lesson 3

Introduction **10 mins**
Discuss the situation when everybody was weighing using different units. Ask what would happen in shops if you asked for apples weighing the same as 50 cubes etc. Introduce the idea of a standard weight and pass round some kilogram weights for the children to get the feel of.

Activities **25 mins**
Make a kilogram (small groups)
Provide each group of children with a kilogram weight, a balance and a plastic sealable bag. The children have to use some objects to make their own measuring device of a bag weighing exactly one kilogram.

More or less than a kilo? (small groups)
The group use their measuring device and collect together objects weighing more than, less than or about the same as one kilogram. The children label each group.

Differentiation
Low Attainers – Not applicable.
High Attainers – Use some kilogram weights also and find objects that are 'nearly 3 kilograms'.

Plenary **5 mins**
Make a collection from each group of an object less than, more than and about one kilogram. Give out the homework activity.

Lesson 4

Introduction **10 mins**
Ask the children what the weather is like outside. Discuss different types of weather at other times of the year. Show photographs of weather, trees etc. in different seasons. Tell the children that each part of the year is called a season and show them the names of the four seasons, saying them together. Ask the children if they know which season it is now. Identify special events that happen in each season.

Activities **25 mins**
Ordering seasons (whole class)
Attach the seasons cards to the board. Discuss what they know about each season and write or draw this under the name of each one. Show the children the order of the seasons on a circular cycle. Ask questions, e.g. 'Which season is before Winter?', 'What comes after Spring?' etc.

Season pictures (individual)
Provide each child with a copy of Copymaster 37 copied onto thin card. Ask the children to draw a picture of each season. Cut the cards up to make a set and ask the children to put them in order. These cards can be put together and the children can play matching and ordering games with them.

Differentiation
Low Attainers – Provide photographs of seasons to help with their drawings.
High Attainers – Not applicable.

Plenary **5 mins**
Children show their cards and talk about what they have drawn and why.

Lesson 5

Introduction **10 mins**
Read some rhymes and poems about the seasons. Ask the children questions about the seasons and they show their cards to answer, *e.g. what season comes before Autumn, all show Summer card etc.*

Activity **25 mins**
Solving problems (individual)
Provide each child with a copy of Copymaster 38 and read together some of the problems. The children complete as many as possible.

Differentiation
Low Attainers – Work through questions 1–6.
High Attainers – Not applicable.

Plenary **5 mins**
Discuss the strategies and answers to the questions.

Theme 10 — Lists and tables

Objectives
- To solve a problem by sorting, classifying and organising information in a list or simple table

Vocabulary
set, group, sort, list, table, pictogram, block graph, vote

Resources
Copymasters 39 and 40, everyday items for sorting, e.g. toys, food packets/tins, clothes – sufficient for several groups, examples of lists used in everyday life, e.g. shopping lists, TV programme listings, class register, book contents, white card, blu-tak, multilink cubes, empty crisp packets of up to four different flavours, examples of tables used in everyday life, e.g. conversion tables, nutrition tables, timetables

Homework Copymaster 20

Mental maths starters 12, 18

Assessment
At the end of this theme is the pupil able to:
- Make a list of items;
- Make a two-column table;
- Start to use pictograms and block graphs with real objects;
- Sort objects using different criteria;
- Solve problems by sorting?

Lesson 1

Introduction   10 mins
Write the names of the four seasons on the board as headings of lists. Ask pupils to think of things that remind them of each season, e.g. Spring – lambs, daffodils; Summer – holidays, sunshine; Autumn – leaves, Halloween; Winter – snowmen, Christmas. Explain that lists are used to organise words so that they are easy to read. Each of the four lists records information about different things.

Activities   25 mins
Making lists (individual)
Ask pupils to make lists of objects in the classroom which are green/red/white or in the toy cupboard/on the teacher's desk/on the windowsill. Encourage clear setting out of work and use of headings.

Shopping list (individual)
Each pupil needs Copymaster 39. Write a list of all of the items shown on the conveyor belt by writing down the name of the item and its price.

Differentiation
Low Attainers – List items only.
High Attainers – Make their own lists by sorting items on the conveyor belt into categories, e.g. number of tins, number of pieces of fruit, items costing more than 10p.

Plenary   5 mins
Play the listing game. Start by saying 'I went to the shop and bought an apple'. Ask a pupil to repeat this and add an item, e.g. 'I went to the shop and bought an apple and a cake'. Repeat. Other topics could be zoo animals, names.

Lesson 2

Introduction   10 mins
Have a list of eight pupils written on the board. At the start of the lesson ask them to come to the front. Explain that they must organise themselves, with the help of the class, in order of their height. List the pupils' names on the board in height order, smallest to tallest. Ask questions such as 'Who is the tallest pupil?', 'How many are shorter than Chloe?'

Activities   25 mins
Sorting into lists (groups)
Provide each group with a collection of objects (toys, food packets/tins, clothes) and ask them to sort them into sets and record the objects in each set in a list, e.g. Toys – doll, car, teddy, …; Food – beans, soup, crisps, …; Clothes – shoe, sock, tie, …

Favourites (whole class)
Ask each pupil to write their name on a card. Explain that you are going to make lists of pupils whose favourite pet is a cat/dog/rabbit/hamster. Ask pupils in turn to bring their name card and stick on the board in the appropriate list. Repeat for other categories, e.g. favourite colour, number of brothers and sisters.

Differentiation
Low Attainers – Provide titles lists to complete with fewer items.
High Attainers – Encourage own methods of sorting and listing.

Plenary   5 mins
Show pupils and explain some examples of lists used in everyday life, e.g. shopping lists, TV programme listings, class register, book contents.

Spring Term

Lesson 3

Introduction   **10 mins**
Prepare a two-column table with some of the pupils' names listed down the first column. In the second column ask for and record those pupils' birth months. Repeat for other tables using other pupils' names and record eye colour, hair colour. Explain how tables are used to record information.

Activities   **25 mins**
Class tables (whole class)
Use the tables created in the introduction and ask pupils to read information from them, e.g. 'What colour eyes does Kirsty have?', 'Tell me the names of the children who were born in April?', 'How many children have brown hair?'

Colour table (individual)
Provide each pupil with a pile of multilink cubes of different colours.

Prepare and copy a simple table listing colours in the first column. Explain to pupils that they are to count the number of cubes for each colour and list their results in the table provided.

Differentiation
Low Attainers – Limit the number of different colours of cubes.
High Attainers – Create and complete a table for information of their own choice.

Plenary   **5 mins**
Draw a table on the board listing different hair colour. Ask pupils to put up their hands if they have blond hair. Record the total in the table. Repeat for all colours.

Lesson 4

Introduction   **10 mins**
Write down the names of four fruits on the board – apple, pear, banana, peach. Ask each pupil in turn which of the four is their favourite. Give each pupil a pre-prepared card with either a picture or the name of the fruit on it. Ask pupils to sort themselves into four groups based on their selection. Count the number in each group and record the results in a simple table on the board.

Activities   **25 mins**
Fruit pictogram (whole class)
Draw an empty pictogram on the board and ask pupils to stick, using blu-tak, their fruit cards in the relevant row. Explain that each picture represents one pupil's choice. Ask them to add up the number for each fruit. Ask questions about the results, e.g. 'Which is the most popular fruit?', 'How many like apples best – how do we know this?', 'How many more people like apples than pears?'

Ladybirds (individual)
Each pupil needs Copymaster 40. Cut out each ladybird and complete the empty grid by sticking the ladybirds with one, two, three or four spots into the correct row.

Differentiation
Low Attainers – Target simpler questions such as 'How many people like apples best?'
High Attainers – Target harder questions such as 'How many more people like apples than pears?'

Plenary   **5 mins**
Use a large prepared pictogram, created by sticking pictures or shapes, in labelled columns or rows and use it to ask questions about the data represented in it.

Lesson 5

Introduction   **10 mins**
Prepare an empty two-column table on the board. Ask pupils to suggest popular crisp flavours. Complete the first column using their suggestions. Ask pupils to vote for their favourite flavour. Record the totals in the second column.

Activities   **25 mins**
Favourite crisps (whole class)
Prior to the lesson collect empty crisp packets for up to four different flavours. Either prepare a grid on the board or on the floor to make a real block graph. Give each pupil a packet and ask them to place it in the correct column. When the graph is complete question the pupils by asking 'Which flavour has the most packets?', 'How many salt and vinegar packets are there?'

Cube graph (individual)
Provide each pupil with a pile of multilink cubes of four different colours. Explain to pupils that they are to sort the cubes into piles of each colour and connect the cubes into rods. Prepare and copy a simple empty block graph on which the pupils should place the linked cubes. Encourage pupils to discuss their results with each other in terms of totals of each colour, colour with most/least cubes, total number of cubes used altogether.

Differentiation
Low Attainers – Limit the number of different colours of cubes.
High Attainers – Increase the number of cubes.

Plenary   **5 mins**
Show pupils and explain some examples of tables used in everyday life, e.g. conversion tables, nutrition tables, timetables.

Theme 1 — Comparing & ordering numbers

Objectives
- To say the number that is one or ten more or less than a given number to 30
- To compare two familiar numbers, say which is more or less and give a number that lies between them
- To order numbers to at least 20 and position them on a number track

Vocabulary
more than, less than, between, smaller, larger, smallest, largest, order, before, after, more, less, most, least

Resources
Copymasters 41 and 42, washing line, 0–30 digit cards, 100 square, blank dice

Homework Copymaster 21

Mental maths starters 3, 10, 20

Assessment
At the end of this theme is the pupil able to:
- Say one or ten more or less than any number;
- Compare the size of two different numbers, saying which is larger or smaller and saying a number that lies between them;
- Order numbers and position them on a number line?

Lesson 1

Introduction — 10 mins
Show a number line and count from 0 to 30 altogether. Point to a number and ask the children to show the number one more than it. Repeat and ask them to show a number which is one less than a given number.

Activities — 25 mins
Where on the square? (whole class)
Show a 100 square and point to 17 and ask 'What is one more than 17?', 'What is one less than 17?', 'What is 10 more than 17?' Draw attention to the direction of movement on the 100 square. Can they work out how to find 10 less? Mark all numbers and ask the children what shape (cross) is formed. Repeat with other numbers less than 30. Ask what happens when finding one more than a multiple of ten or one less than a number ending with a one. Model how to record the numbers.

More or less (individual)
Provide each child with the first 3 rows of a 100 square. They choose a number in the middle row and find the numbers one more or less and ten more or less. Record this as demonstrated earlier.

Differentiation
Low Attainers — Provide a framework for recording answers.
High Attainers — Provide a whole 100 square and encourage them to also find 20 and 30 more or less than a chosen number.

Plenary — 5 mins
Show an OHT of a 100 square. Blank out the numbers one and ten more or less than a chosen number. Ask the children what the missing numbers are. Repeat for a few numbers. Encourage the children to use the language of comparing.

Lesson 2

Introduction — 10 mins
Show a card with a number less than 30. Ask for the number one more and less and ten more and less. Show on the 100 square how to find 20 more or less by moving down or up two rows. Repeat for 30 more or less.

Activity — 25 mins
The more or less dice game (pairs)
Provide each pair of children with a 100 square, a dice marked 'more' x 3 and 'less' x 3 and a dice marked 1, 1, 1, 10, 10, 10. One child chooses a number on the 100 square. The other child rolls both dice and has to find one or ten more or less than the given number and write the appropriate calculation. The other person checks it. A point is scored for each correct answer. The person with the most points when time runs out is the winner.

Differentiation
Low Attainers — Only use the first 3 rows of the 100 square.
High Attainers — Provide a dice marked 1, 1, 10, 10, 20, 30.

Plenary — 5 mins
Ask a child to open a book randomly at a page and say the page number. Ask the children what page was 10 before, 10 after etc. Repeat with other page numbers.

Summer Term

Lesson 3

Introduction   **10 mins**
Show a washing line with 0 and 30 positioned at either end. Shuffle a pack of 1–29 number cards and ask a child to pick two of them. Show the children the cards and ask which is the smaller number, how do they know? Ask them to position the cards on the washing line. If the cards have a difference greater than one ask for suggestions as to what number could go between them, where would it be? Repeat until all the cards are used.

Activity   **25 mins**
Numbers in order (individual)
Provide each child with a copy of Copymaster 41 and red and blue coloured pencils. Complete Copymaster 41 with numbers appropriate to each group. They have to colour the larger number blue and the smaller number red then put a number which lies between the two numbers in the box.

Differentiation
Low Attainers – Work with numbers up to 30 and make the difference between the two numbers 2.
High Attainers – Work with numbers up to 99.

Plenary   **5 mins**
Show two numbers and ask for all the possibilities that lie in between using a number line to help. Give out the homework activity.

Lesson 4

Introduction   **10 mins**
Give two different amounts of money on cards or in purses to two children. Ask who has the most/least amount of money. Use values up to 30p

Activity   **25 mins**
Highest wins (pairs)
Provide each pair with a selection of cards from a pack of 0–100 number cards and some counters. Shuffle them and place in a pile. The children take turns to turn over a card. They compare the size of them and whoever has the highest card wins a counter. The first child with ten counters wins the game.

Differentiation
Low Attainers – Provide cards with numbers less than 30.
High Attainers – The winner of the counter can get a bonus counter if they can say a number which lies between the two.

Plenary   **5 mins**
Ask questions in various contexts comparing the size of two numbers, e.g. *Rob is 23 and Ellie is 19, who is the younger?*

Lesson 5

Introduction   **10 mins**
Show a washing line from 0–30 but with some cards missing. Point to the gap and ask the children to show the missing number on their digit cards.

Activity   **25 mins**
Ordering numbers (individual)
Provide each child with a copy of Copymaster 42 filled in appropriate to each group with sets of numbers up to 50 to be ordered.

Differentiation
Low Attainers – Use a number line to check the order.
High Attainers – Work with higher numbers then provide random sets of cards to be ordered.

Plenary   **5 mins**
Play What's My Number? Tell the children you are thinking of a number between 13 and 20. They ask questions to find out what it is. Repeat with higher numbers when they are more confident.

Theme 2 Adding and taking away

Objectives
- To use +, − and = signs to record mental calculations in a number sentence
- To recognise and use □ and △ to stand for an unknown number
- To use number facts to add/subtract a pair of numbers in the range 0 to 20

Vocabulary
add, sum, together, total, difference, how many more? subtract, equals

Resources
Copymasters 43 and 44, blank dice, 1–6 dice, counters, number lines, 0–9 digit cards

Homework Copymaster 22

Mental maths starters 9, 11

Assessment
At the end of this theme is the pupil able to:
- Write addition and subtraction sentences using the correct signs;
- Recognise that missing numbers can be represented in different ways and solve the missing numbers in number sentences;
- Use number facts already known to mentally calculate addition and subtraction facts up to 20?

Lesson 1

Introduction   10 mins
Revise the vocabulary of addition through questioning and children's responses to questions.

Activities   25 mins
Addition sentences (whole class)
Roll two large dice and record the two numbers, e.g. 4 and 2. Ask the children to add them and show the total on a digit card. Show them how to write this calculation as a number sentence 4 + 2 = 6 and also as 2 + 4 = 6. Throw the dice again and repeat, emphasising that the order of numbers when adding does not matter.

Counter calculations (pairs)
Provide the children with some counters. Each child takes a handful of counters and then counts them. The pair of children have to find how many counters they have altogether and record this as two numbers sentences.

Differentiation
Low Attainers – Allow no more than 10 counters each.
High Attainers – Allow the children to work with higher numbers of counters.

Plenary   5 mins
Show some calculations, without answers, for numbers less than 10. The children have to pair up the calculations, e.g. 7 + 2 = □ and 2 + 7 = □ then find the total. Emphasise that the total for both calculations will be the same.

Lesson 2

Introduction   10 mins
Revise the vocabulary subtraction through questioning and the children's response to questions.

Activities   25 mins
Subtraction sentences (whole class)
Shuffle a pack of 0–9 digit cards and ask a child to pick two. Tell the children they are going to subtract one number from the other. Remind them that the smaller number is taken away from the larger number. Show the numbers then as a number sentence, e.g. 8 − 3 = 5.

Subtraction sign (pairs)
Provide each pair with a 1–6 dice and a 7–12 dice. Throw a dice each and record the two numbers. Put these into a number sentence and find the difference. Take turns for throwing the different dice.

Differentiation
Low Attainers – Use 2 1–6 dice.
High Attainers – Use a 7–12 dice and a 15–20 dice.

Plenary   5 mins
Invite children to share some of their subtraction sentences, checking answers.

Summer Term

Lesson 3

Introduction   **10 mins**
Provide children with 0–9 digit cards. Ask questions such as 'What needs to be added to 8 to make 12?', 'How many more than 5 is 9?'

Activities   **25 mins**
Number bonds (whole class)
Ask the children for number bonds to 9 and record them all on the board. Choose one sentence and rub out one of the numbers, replacing it with a box. Discuss how to work out what the missing number is asking the children for suggestions. Then show a number sentence with both numbers missing and give the answer. Ask for all possibilities for the two missing numbers.

Missing numbers (individual)
Provide each child with a copy of Copymaster 43, filled in appropriately for each group with addition signs in all of the circles and one or two of the other numbers missing.

Differentiation
Low Attainers – Limit totals to numbers up to 10.
High Attainers – Work with numbers up to 20.

Plenary   **5 mins**
Show an addition sentence with just the total. Ask the children to use their digit cards to show what the two numbers could be.

Lesson 4

Introduction   **10 mins**
Provide each child with a set of 0–9 digit cards to show answers. Ask questions such as 'What needs to be taken away from 7 to leave 4?', 'How many less is 7 than 12?'

Activities   **25 mins**
Subtraction facts (whole class)
Ask the children for subtraction facts for 9 and record them all on the board. Choose one sentence and rub out the number being subtracted, replacing it with a box. Discuss how to work out what the missing number is asking the children for suggestions. Then show a number sentence with the subtracted number and the answer missing and suggest missing numbers. Ask for all possibilities they can think of for the two missing numbers.

Missing numbers (individual)
Provide each child with a copy of Copymaster 43 filled in appropriately for each group with subtraction signs in all of the circles and one or two of the other numbers missing.

Differentiation
Low Attainers – Work on subtraction facts up to 10.
High Attainers – Miss out the number being taken away from in some of the sentences.

Plenary   **5 mins**
Show a subtraction sentence with missing numbers. Discuss possibilities for which numbers are missing and share strategies.

Lesson 5

Introduction   **10 mins**
Show a large 0–9 digit card and ask 'What number is one less than this?', 'Give two numbers which add together to give this number', 'What number is 10 more than this?' Then show the teens numbers on the board. Ask the children what they all have in common, partition them.

Activities   **25 mins**
Adding teens (whole class)
Show an addition sentence which has an answer less than 10, e.g. $5 + 3 = 8$. Now show a corresponding sentence with a teens number in it, i.e. $15 + 3 =$. Discuss strategies for calculating. Draw attention to using $5 + 3 = 8$, so $15 + 3 = 18$. Write the sentences underneath each other. Repeat with another pair of sentences then with subtraction facts.

Using facts (individual)
Provide each child with Copymaster 44. Remind the children to look at the calculations to see if they can use any facts they already know.

Differentiation
Low Attainers – Provide a number line for checking.
High Attainers – Provide some extra calculations with larger numbers where a tens boundary has to be crossed.

Plenary   **5 mins**
Write 0–9 on one side of the board and 11–19 on the other. Point to two numbers that can be added without crossing a tens boundary, e.g. $13 + 6$. Ask the children to say what number fact they knew that could help them.

Theme 3 — Money problems

Objectives
- To recognise coins of different values up to 20p
- To find totals, give change from up to 20p
- To work out how to pay using smaller coins
- To choose and use the appropriate number operation and mental strategy to solve problems

Vocabulary
money, coin, penny, pence, value, amount, total, altogether, enough, buy, spend, change, most expensive, costs the most, cheapest, costs the least, exactly

Resources
Copymaster 45, full set of real coins from 1p to £2 for each group, feely bag, purse, sets of cards on which are written amounts from 1p up to 20p – enough for half the class, plenty of plastic 1p, 2p, 5p, 10p and 20p coins, blu-tak, trays of priced items (one tray per table/group with at least 20 different items labelled with large price tags/stickers for amounts up to 20p), cash box or till for each group.

Homework Copymaster 23

Mental maths starters 2, 12

Assessment
At the end of this theme is the pupil able to:
- Recognise all coins from 1p up to £2;
- Know that amounts up to 20p can be made up of different combinations of 1p, 2p, 5p and 10p coins;
- Mentally calculate totals up to 20p;
- Record calculations using +, − and = showing totals up to 20p;
- Work out how to pay using smaller coins;
- Work out how to give change from larger coins;
- Solve simple problems involving totals and change?

Lesson 1

Introduction — 10 mins
Show the pupils a full set of real coins from 1p up to £2. Ask the pupils to identify the coins from 1p to 10p. Describe the 20p, 50p, £1 and £2 coins, explaining that these are worth more. Place the coins on the table and ask pupils to come out and pick up a coin and tell the class what it is and describe what it looks like.

Activities — 25 mins
Coin rubbings (individual)
Provide each group with at least one full set of coins. Ask the pupils to make a rubbing of each coin and write its value next to it.

Coin quiz (whole class)
Each pupil needs a 1p, 2p, 5p, 10p, 20p, 50p, £1 and £2 card from their set of money cards. Place a full set of coins on the table. Hold up a coin and ask the pupils to match the coin to one of their cards. Repeat for all coins. Ask pupils to match a card to a given description of a coin, e.g. *it is a circle and is only gold; small, silver and has straight sides.*

Differentiation
By outcome.

Plenary — 5 mins
Ask a pupil to describe a coin hidden from the rest of the class. Pupils need to guess the coin from the description. Put a coin in a feely bag and ask a pupil to describe it to the class and ask them to guess the coin.

Lesson 2

Introduction — 10 mins
Show pupils and describe again the appearance of the 20p coin and explain that other coins can be used to make up the same value. Ask pupils which two coins have the same value as the 20p coin. Ask pupils which four coins of the same type make 20p. Ask which three coins can be used to make 20p. Stick the combinations of coins on the board.

Activities — 25 mins
Sets worth 20p (groups)
Provide each group with plenty of coins. Set a time limit of 10 minutes and ask the groups to make as many sets of coins worth 20p as possible. Tell pupils to keep checking that each set is different.

Rubbing coins (individual)
Using the sets of coins from the group activity, ask pupils to choose up to five different combinations of coins totalling 20p and make rubbings. Tell the pupils that they must arrange the coins in order from the highest value to the lowest, e.g. 10p, 5p, 5p; 10p, 5p, 2p, 2p, 1p.

Differentiation
Low Attainers – Make rubbings of only two different sets of coins.
High Attainers – Investigate a more concise method of recording the coin combinations, e.g. instead of 5p, 5p, 5p, 5p rub 5p coin once and write 4 next to it.

Plenary — 5 mins
Record as many of the combinations as possible on the board in the form of addition calculations.

Summer Term

Lesson 3

Introduction   **10 mins**

Stick the following coins on to the board – 10p, 5p, 2p, 2p, 1p. Ask the pupils how much these coins make altogether. Explain that these five can be used to make any amount from 1p up to 20p, e.g. make 6p using 5p and 1p, make 13p using 10p, 2p and 1p.

Hold up an item priced up to 20p. Give a pupil the 5 coins and ask him/her to come and pay for the item. Tell the class which coins were used, ask the pupil to show which coins remain and explain that this is his/her 'change'. Repeat for other items.

Activities   **25 mins**

Working out change (individual)
Each pupil needs Copymaster 45. For each object colour in the coins needed to pay for it. Complete the box by writing down the change from 20p.

Paying up to 20p (pairs)
Each pupil needs the set of 5 coins totalling 20p. Prepare a set of cards on which are written amounts up to 20p. One pupil turns a card from the pile and gives the other pupil the correct amount of money and states the amount of change.

Differentiation

Low Attainers – Give pupils 4 coins totalling 10p and limit prices to up to 10p.
High Attainers – Use more than 5 coins totalling 20p.

Plenary   **5 mins**

Place some coins in a purse, e.g. 5p, 5p, 2p, 2p, 1p totalling 15p. Tell a pupil to buy an item costing 8p and ask them to give you the money and total up the change. Repeat for other amounts in the purse and prices of items to buy.

Lesson 4

Introduction   **10 mins**

Give a pupil a 10p coin. Hold up an item with a price tag of 6p. Ask the pupil how they are going to pay for the item with the one coin. Explain to the pupils that they can pay with a coin that is worth more than the item they are buying and the shopkeeper will give them change. How much change will the pupil get from 10p when he/she buys the item costing 6p? Record the calculation on the board: 10p – 6p = 4p. You give the pupil the item and the change, e.g. 2p, 2p. Repeat.

Activities   **25 mins**

Change/no change (whole class)
Give each pupil a 10p, 5p and 2p coin. Hold up an item worth up to 20p. Ask pupils to select the coins they will use to buy the item. Ask if they will need any change, e.g. item costing 8p – need to give 10p and get 2p change; item costing 12p – need to give 10p and 2p and no change; item costing 20p – can't buy it.

Giving change (pairs)
Give each pair of pupils a set of cards on which are written amounts up to 20p. One pupil has one 10p coin and two 5p coins, the other has a selection of coins from 1p to 10p. The first pupil turns a card from the pile and 'pays' for the card with his/her coins. The second pupil must give the other the correct change.

Differentiation

Low Attainers – Use amounts to 10p.
High Attainers – Use amounts to 30p.

Plenary   **5 mins**

Give a pupil a 10p coin. Hold up an item with a price tag of 7p. Ask the pupil to pay with a 10p coin and give them the wrong change. Ask the pupil to check their change and work out what it should be and by how much it is wrong. Repeat for other items.

Lesson 5

Introduction   **10 mins**

I have a 10p piece and want to buy a bar of chocolate costing 8p. How much change will I get? What coins could I have in my change? I have a 10p and a 5p and want to buy a book costing 12p. Question as before. Go on to include paying with a 20p coin.

Activity   **25 mins**

Shop (groups)
Provide each group with a variety of items priced up to 20p, a till or cash box and each pupil with some coins. Ask one pupil to act as the shopkeeper and others to act as customers, making sure that each pupil has a turn as shopkeeper. Encourage pupils to talk about what they wish to buy, how much it will cost altogether, which coins they will use to pay with and how much change they should receive.

Differentiation

Low Attainers – Give a few coins to enable items to be bought without change.
High Attainers – Give a larger amount of money and encourage to them to make a shopping list.

Plenary   **5 mins**

Ask pupils to discuss their shop experiences. What did you buy? How much did it cost altogether? Did you ever get the wrong change? Did you ever not have enough money to buy what you wanted? What was the most expensive thing you bought?

Theme 4) Capacity

Objectives
- To understand and use the vocabulary related to capacity
- To compare two, then more, capacities using direct comparisons
- To measure capacity using uniform non-standard units or standard units (litres)

Vocabulary
guess, roughly, nearly, close to, about the same as, too much, too little, enough, not enough, full, half full, empty, partly full, litre, capacity, container, estimate

Resources
Copymasters 47 and 48, variety of containers, litre bottles/containers, sand, water, rice, cards showing 'holds more than' and 'holds less than', hoops, funnels, labels showing: 'about one litre', 'more than one litre' and 'less than one litre'.

Homework Copymaster 24
Mental maths starters 5, 19

Assessment
At the end of this theme is the pupil able to:
- Use and understand vocabulary related to capacity;
- Compare two or more containers saying which has a greater capacity;
- Measure the capacity of containers using non-standard measures or litres?

Lesson 1

Introduction   10 mins
Provide each group of children with a set of various containers, about half of them full and the rest empty. Use sand or rice instead of water to fill the containers. Ask the children to sort the containers into groups of full and empty.

Activities   25 mins
Which holds more? (whole class)
Take one container from each set and ask which of the two they think has the greatest capacity (holds the most). Demonstrate how to find out by pouring the contents of one container to another.

More or less? (pairs)
Provide each pair with a selection of bottles. They choose two and have to say which they think holds more than the other. They test this by pouring the contents of one to the other as demonstrated. They then place a card between the two showing either 'holds more than' or 'holds less than'. Ensure the order of the containers is correct.

Differentiation
Low Attainers – Provide containers that have very different capacities.
High Attainers – Provide them with bottles that have quite similar capacities.

Plenary   5 mins
Each pair show two containers and the appropriate label.

Lesson 2

Introduction   10 mins
Show a selection of 3 different size containers. Ask the children which they think has the largest capacity and the smallest capacity and which container goes in the middle. Check this by pouring sand from the largest to the smallest.

Activity   25 mins
Putting them in order (pairs)
Provide each pair with 3 different containers and ask them to put them in order from smallest to largest capacity. Label the containers with stickers marked 1, 2, 3.

Differentiation
Low Attainers – Consolidate direct comparison of two containers.
High Attainers – Provide each pair with 4 containers.

Plenary   5 mins
Children demonstrate how they checked the order of the capacities of the containers.
Give out the homework activity.

Summer Term

Lesson 3

Introduction — **10 mins**
Show a collection of small containers, *e.g. egg cup, yogurt pot, teaspoon, screw cap etc.*, and some larger containers, *e.g. tea cup, jug, small pop bottle etc.* Ask the children to estimate, *e.g. how many egg cupfuls would fill a tea cup*. Demonstrate how to do it.

Activity — **25 mins**
Fill it up 1! (pairs)
Provide each pair with one small and one larger container and the labels from the top half of Copymaster 47. They fill the larger container with a certain number of the smaller container and record their findings on a label. They then change to a new pair of containers.

Differentiation
Not applicable.

Plenary — **5 mins**
Refer back to the estimates made at the beginning of the lesson and check how close they were.

Lesson 4

Introduction — **10 mins**
Discuss the homework activity and ask how they found who had the biggest cup at home.

Activity — **25 mins**
Fill it up 2! (pairs)
Provide each pair with one small and one large container, preferably different containers from the previous lesson, and the bottom half of Copymaster 47 cut into labels. This time the children have to find out how many of the small container the large one fills. They then record their findings for each pair of containers on the labels.

Differentiation
Low Attainers – Provide one small container only, *e.g. an egg cup.*
High Attainers – Provide a wider selection of small containers and encourage estimation beforehand.

Plenary — **5 mins**
Ask the children to discuss what systems they used to count and draw attention to how to measure carefully.

Lesson 5

Introduction — **10 mins**
Discuss some of the measuring from this unit and some of the vocabulary used. Ask the children what would happen if things were sold in different size containers and why a standard measure is needed. They may know the names of some measures, particularly a pint of milk or beer! Introduce the litre and show a selection of containers that have a one litre capacity.

Activity — **25 mins**
Lots of litres (small groups)
Provide each group with three hoops, a selection of containers, three labels marked: 'about one litre', 'more than one litre', 'less than one litre' and a copy each of Copymaster 48. The children have to sort the containers into groups using a given litre container as a standard. They can work by estimation or actual measuring by direct comparison as carried out in Lesson 1 of this unit. On this occasion the comparison is always with a litre measure. The children then write the name of or draw the container in the correct circle.

Differentiation
Low Attainers – Provide containers that are considerably more or less than a litre.
High Attainers – Provide some containers that are very close to one litre in capacity.

Plenary — **5 mins**
Each group shows one container from each set and discuss how they found out.

Theme 5 — Shapes and positions

Objectives
- To make symmetrical patterns by folding shapes in half
- To begin to relate solid shapes to pictures of them
- To use one or more shapes to make, describe and continue repeating patterns
- To make whole turns and half turns
- To use everyday language to describe direction and movement
- To investigate general statements about shapes

Vocabulary
As for Spring Theme 5, also: whole turn, half turn, straight, slide, roll, symmetrical

Resources
Copymasters 49 and 50, teacher set of coloured cardboard 2D shapes, blu-tak, pupil sets of plastic or cardboard 2D and 3D shapes, everyday 3D objects, wooden/plastic hollow/solid building blocks, hoops, plasticine or Play-doh, tools for cutting and rolling plasticine, junk materials, packets and containers, everyday objects with repeating patterns, objects that turn, cardboard discs

Homework Copymaster 25

Mental maths starters 6, 18

Assessment
At the end of this theme is the pupil able to:
- Make a 3D model from a given picture;
- Make, describe and continue a repeating pattern using 2D shapes;
- Use everyday language to describe movement, including straight and turning movements, sliding and rolling;
- Recognise whole turns and half turns;
- Name, sort and describe a variety of 3D shapes in terms of the way they move;
- Make a picture or pattern having one line of symmetry?

Lesson 1

Introduction   10 mins
Place a selection of simple hand drawn pictures of familiar objects, *e.g. the school building, a car, a bridge, a church*, on the board. Ask pupils to identify any 3D shapes they can see in the pictures.

Activities   25 mins
Models from pictures (small groups)
Provide each group with Copymasters 49 and 50 and a set of wooden 3D shapes. Ask pupils to build the models shown on the copymaster. Encourage pupils to discuss the shapes and methods they are using.

Shape walk (whole class)
Take the class on a walk around the school and its grounds and ask questions about 3D shapes, for example, 'Can you see anything in the playground which is a cylinder?' (rubbish bin, netball post), 'What shape is the TV set?'

Differentiation
Low Attainers – Provide them with only the pieces required for each model.
High Attainers – After building models depicted in the copymaster ask them to build a model and then attempt to make a sketch of it.

Plenary   5 mins
Ask pupils to describe the models made earlier to the class. Explain the shapes used and the method used to build it, *e.g. from bottom up, in sections*.

Lesson 2

Introduction   10 mins
Use coloured stick-on shapes, or draw, the following pattern on the board ▽ ○ ▽ ○ and ask the pupils to suggest how the pattern should be continued.
Repeat with other patterns, gradually increasing the complexity of the pattern to include several repeating shapes, for example:

○ ○ ○ ○
▽ ▽ ▽ ▽

Activities   25 mins
Paired patterns (pairs)
Provide each pupil with a long strip of plain paper (15 cm wide), a selection of 2D plastic or cardboard shapes and coloured pencils. Ask pupils to create a repeating pattern and then swap with another pupil and continue each other's repeating pattern.

Pupil patterns (whole class)
Provide each pupil with a sheet of paper/card on which is drawn a shape, *e.g. square, star, circle, etc.* Ensure that there are sufficient identical shapes distributed around the class so that various repeating patterns are possible. Call out two pupils' names at random and ask them to stand at the front holding up their shapes. Ask volunteers to come with their shapes to continue the pattern. Repeat.

Differentiation
Low Attainers – Pair pupils of similar ability, stick to simple patterns and focus discussion on prediction.
High Attainers – Use a wider variety of shapes and encourage more complex patterns.

Plenary   5 mins
Start to orally describe a pattern, *e.g. 'circle, square'*. Ask a pupil to continue the pattern orally by adding the next shape – 'Circle'. The next pupil then continues by saying 'Square'. Gradually increase the complexity of the pattern.

Summer Term

Lesson 3

Introduction   **10 mins**
Teach the lesson in the PE hall. Explain to the pupils that you are going to give them a series of commands which will be used later in the lesson. As part of the warm-up ask the pupils to perform a series of movements, *e.g. walk in a straight line, turn a whole turn on the spot, turn a half turn on the spot, turn through two whole turns, keep turning on the spot, turn one arm through a whole turn, turn left, turn right.*

Activities   **25 mins**
Taking turns (whole class)
Start by linking the actions covered in the introduction to make sequences of straight and turning movements. Organise yourself and pupils into a circle. Call out instructions, *e.g. 'turn to your left'*, walk through a half turn of the circle, *'turn three times on the spot'*.

Clock turns (whole class)
Invite pupils to demonstrate, using a large clock, a whole turn, a half turn, two whole turns. Set the clock at a time, *e.g. two o'clock*, and ask questions such as 'What time will the clock show after one whole turn, two whole turns, etc?', 'How many turns will it take to change the time from three o'clock to four o'clock?'

Differentiation
Low Attainers – Demonstrate actions.
High Attainers – Make up their own sequences.

Plenary   **5 mins**
Invite pupils to demonstrate whole and half turns using a variety of objects which turn about a point, *e.g. clock, windmill, tap, wheel.*

Lesson 4

Introduction   **10 mins**
Teach the lesson in the PE hall equipped with mats, benches, balls, hoops, bean bags.
Ask pupils to roll on the mat, slide along the bench, roll the ball along the floor, slide the bean bag across the floor, roll the hoop then slide the hoop. Explain that some objects can move by rolling, some by sliding and some can do both.

Activities   **25 mins**
Moving around (whole class)
Ask the pupils to follow instructions which incorporate both movement and direction, for example, *'roll the ball towards the windows'*, *'turn left and walk in a straight line'*, *'slide your bean bag to the person on your right'*.

Slides and rolls (whole class)
Ask pupils to each select one or two objects from around the classroom. Ask pupils to test whether their objects slide or roll when moved. Can any of their objects do both?
Sort the collection of objects into three groups. Ask if they can explain why an object slides and/or rolls (has flat and/or curved surfaces).

Differentiation
Low Attainers – Demonstrate actions; help in choice of suitable objects.
High Attainers – Look specifically at an object which either slides, rolls or both.

Plenary   **5 mins**
Hold up different objects and ask pupils to state whether it will only slide (bar of chocolate, cereal packet, book), only roll (apple, potato, tennis ball, egg), or both roll and slide (plastic cup, cone, roll of sticky tape). Test pupils' predictions.

Lesson 5

Introduction   **10 mins**
Draw or pin up a simple picture of a symmetrical house. Show how a line drawn through its centre splits the house into two halves. Fold a number of simple 2D shapes in half to show that folding splits the shape into two halves.

Activities   **25 mins**
Cutting shapes (individual)
Provide each pupil with a piece of paper and ask them to fold in half. Cut a shape from the folded sheet, ensuring that pupils include the fold in the shape. Open out the paper to reveal a symmetrical shape and paint in the line made by the fold.

Butterflies (individual)
Provide each pupil with a folded sheet with a half butterfly outline drawn on it. Paint the half shape and fold the paper back in half to create a symmetrical butterfly pattern.

Differentiation
Low Attainers – Will need help with cutting and folding.
High Attainers – Experiment with their own ideas, *e.g. flowers, ladybird, tree.*

Plenary   **5 mins**
Stick a variety of 2D shapes having one line of symmetry on the board and invite pupils to draw on the line of symmetry.

Theme 6 — Counting patterns

Objectives
- To begin to count on in steps of three from zero
- To recognise and extend number sequences with differences of 1, 2 or 3
- To investigate a general statement about familiar numbers by finding examples that satisfy it
- To explain method and reasoning orally

Vocabulary
number, zero, nought, one, two, … twenty, thirty, … one hundred, count, forwards, backwards, count on, count back, share, pattern, before, after, between, add, plus, equal to, is the same as, odd, even, every other, digit

Resources
Copymasters 51 and 52, 100 squares, one enlarged 100 square, sets of number cards with 3, 6, … 27 – sufficient for half the class, percussion instruments, number lines (up to at least 30), 30 A4 cards each with one number from 1 to 30, large number grids with numbers 1 to 30, multilink blocks, counters, gummed paper shapes, straws, beads, small toys

Homework Copymaster 26

Mental maths starters 1, 8, 16

Assessment
At the end of this theme is the pupil able to:
- count on and back in threes first from zero to thirty, then from any number;
- count on and back in twos from any given number less than 30;
- start to recognise odd and even numbers;
- count on and back in tens from any number using a 100 square;
- describe and start to continue simple number sequences;
- represent a simple number sequence by objects, pictures and patterns?

Lesson 1

Introduction   10 mins
Write 0 on the board. Ask pupils to count on three from zero – 1, 2, 3. Write the number 3 on the board. Count on a further three – 4, 5, 6. Write number 6 on the board. Continue to 30. Recite the sequence forwards and backwards.

Activities   25 mins
Grid threes (individual)
Each pupil needs a 100 square. Ask pupils to colour in the number sequence 3, 6, … 30. What do they notice about the pattern of coloured squares? Can they extend the sequence?

Number cards (pairs)
Each pair of pupils needs a set of number cards on which are written the numbers 3, 6, … 27. Pupils take turns to draw a card and state the number three less than and the number three more than the number on the card.

Differentiation
Low Attainers – Give smaller numbers only on the number cards.
High Attainers – Encourage them to complete all multiples of 3 on the 100 square.

Plenary   5 mins
Provide each pupil with a percussion instrument and ask them to count from 0 to 30 in ones. Each time they count on three they must say the number and hit their instrument. Repeat several times both counting on and back.

Lesson 2

Introduction   10 mins
Each pupil needs a number line from 0 to 30. Ask pupils to use their number lines to help them to count on and back in twos from 0, then from 1, then count on in threes from 0. Now ask them to count on and back in twos from different numbers.

Activities   25 mins
Odds and evens (whole class)
Prepare a set of 30 A4 cards with the numbers 1 to 30 written on them. Give each child a card. Explain that you are going to count from 1 to 30 in ones and when their number is called they come and line up on the left side of the classroom if their number is odd and on the right if it's even. Two sequences are formed. Ask the 'odds' to read out the numbers opposite them and vice versa. Ask pupils to swap cards with the pupil opposite and read out the sequences again. Point out that all even numbers end in 0, 2, 4, 6, 8 and all odd numbers end in 1, 3, 5, 7, 9.

Counting in threes (individual)
Each pupil needs a large grid with the numbers 1 to 30 and some counters. Give pupils a number and ask them to place a counter on that number in the grid. Count on in threes from that number covering each number with a counter. Ask pupils to record the list of numbers. Repeat from other numbers both counting on and back in threes.

Differentiation
By outcome.

Plenary   5 mins
Shuffle the set of 30 A4 cards and place them face down. Select a card and stick it on the board. Ask the pupils whether the number is odd or even and ask them to explain why. Now ask them to count on in threes, back in twos, …

Summer Term

Lesson 3

Introduction — 10 mins
Stick an enlarged 100 square on the board. Start at 10 and ask pupils to count on in tens and then back in tens. Repeat by starting at other multiples of ten. Now colour a number, *e.g. 23*, and write this number on the board. Explain that you are going to count on in tens from 23. Point to the numbers in the square as you count aloud up to 33. Colour the square and write 33 underneath 23 on the board. Continue up to 93. Ask pupils what they notice – numbers in a line on 100 square, digits in the sequence 23, 33, 43, …

Activities — 25 mins
Counting on in tens (individual)
Each pupil needs a 100 square and some counters. Give pupils numbers to count on in tens from. Ask pupils to use the counters to cover the numbers and then write down the sequence.

Ten more, ten less (individual)
Each pupil needs Copymaster 51, a 100 square and counters. Complete the boxes either side with numbers which are ten less and ten more than the given number.

Differentiation
Low Attainers – Provide several copies of 100 square and allow them to colour the squares rather than record the sequences.
High Attainers – By outcome.

Plenary — 5 mins
Call out a number and ask pupils to count on and back in tens using their 100 squares.

Lesson 4

Introduction — 10 mins
Write the numbers 5, 6, 7, 8, 9 on the board. Ask pupils to describe this sequence of numbers, i.e. they go up in ones, start at 5 and count on one each time, count in ones from 5 to 9. Repeat for other sequences, *e.g. 5, 10, 15, 20; 8, 6, 4, 2, 0*.

Activity — 25 mins
Creating sequences (individual)
Each pupil needs Copymaster 52 and a 100 square. Pupils study each sequence of numbers and use the number square to describe the sequence. They then go on to create their own sequences according to the given instructions.

Differentiation
Low Attainers – Describe the sequences orally only.
High Attainers – Make up and describe their own number sequences.

Plenary — 5 mins
Write the number sequence 1, 3, 5, 7, 9 on the board. Ask pupils to describe the sequence and continue it for three more numbers. Repeat for other sequences in a similar way.

Lesson 5

Introduction — 10 mins
Write the sequence 2, 4, 6, 8, 10 on the board and explain that these numbers can be shown with objects, pictures or patterns, *e.g. wooden blocks can be arranged as shown below*:

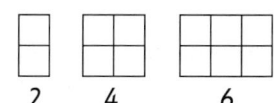

```
 □   □□   □□□
     □□   □□□
 2   4    6
```

Also represent the sequence in pictures, *e.g. as petals on a flower, spots on a ladybird, etc.*

Activities — 25 mins
Object sequences (individual/groups)
Set out table with resources for making patterns, *e.g. multilink blocks, counters, gummed paper shapes, straws, beads, small toys*. Ask pupils to use the resources to create sequences.

Picture sequences (individual)
Ask pupils to represent a sequence of numbers on paper using patterns or pictures.

Differentiation
Low Attainers – Write a sequence on paper and ask them to use objects/draw pictures to represent it.
High Attainers – Use objects to create sequences and record their results.

Plenary — 5 mins
Ask pupils to describe their sequences – objects used, numbers going up in ones/twos, etc.

Theme 7 Addition

Objectives
- To add more than two numbers
- To use number facts to add/subtract a pair of numbers within the range 0–20
- To add 9 to a single-digit number by adding 10 then subtracting 1
- To bridge through 20 when adding a single-digit number

Vocabulary
add, sum, together, total, difference, how many more? subtract, equals, bridge, answer

Resources
Copymasters 53 and 54, 100 squares, 0–20 and 0–30 number lines, digit cards, 1–6 dice, blank dice, counting apparatus, hoops

Homework Copymaster 27

Mental maths starters 10, 13

Assessment
At the end of this theme is the pupil able to:
- Add three or more numbers using a range of strategies;
- Use known number facts to add and subtract pairs of numbers up to 20;
- Add 9 by adding 10 and subtracting 1;
- Bridge through 20 when adding a single-digit number?

Lesson 1

Introduction — 10 mins
Put out three hoops with 4, 5 and 2 objects in them. Count the number of objects in each hoop and record, gradually adding the numbers, as $4 + 5 = 9$, $9 + 2 = 11$ so $4 + 5 + 2 = 11$.
Repeat several times with different numbers of objects and record the number sentence each time. Discuss different strategies used.

Activity — 25 mins
Adding three numbers (pairs)
Provide each child with Copymaster 53 and three 1–6 dice for each pair. One child rolls the three dice and records the numbers on Copymaster 53. The other child records the same numbers in a different order and they both calculate the total.

Differentiation
Low Attainers — Provide a number line to count in jumps.
High Attainers — Provide 0–9 dice.

Plenary — 5 mins
Share strategies used and emphasise that the order of adding does not matter by doing a few examples. Give out the homework activity

---

Lesson 2

Introduction — 10 mins
Go over the homework activity and see what the highest totals were from the number plates. Recap on the previous lesson of adding three numbers.

Activities — 25 mins
Missing numbers (whole class)
Show a number sentence with a missing number, e.g. $6 + 2 + \square = 14$. Discuss how to solve it by adding 6 and 2 then asking what needs to be added on to 8 to make 14 and modeling on the number line.

What's the missing number? (individual)
Provide each child with a copy of Copymaster 53 filled in appropriately for each group. Leave one of the numbers to be added blank and fill in the rest of each sentence.

Differentiation
Low Attainers — Work with totals less than 10.
High Attainers — Work with higher totals and leave two numbers blank.

Plenary — 5 mins
Pick examples that the children have done and ask individuals to share the strategy they used.

Summer Term

Lesson 3

Introduction   **10 mins**
Provide each child with a set of 0–9 digit cards. Ask them to show a pair of numbers that total 10. Show a digit card and ask them to show the number that can be added to it to total 10.

Activities   **25 mins**
Using facts (whole class)
Show the calculation 7 + 8 = . Ask the children for ideas how to solve it. Show that 8 = 3 + 5 so 7 + 8 = 7 + 3 + 5 = 10 + 5 = 15. Tell the children to look for ways to make 10 first. Also show that 8 + 7 = 8 + 2 + 5 = 15, where the larger number has been put first.
Repeat with other pairs of numbers that total more than 10 and less than 20. Model on a number line as two steps if necessary.

Number sentences (pairs)
Provide each pair with a dice numbered 4–9. The children take turns to roll the dice twice and record the numbers in a number sentence. Encourage them to look for facts to 10 to solve the calculation.

Differentiation
Low Attainers – Provide flash cards with number bonds to 10.
High Attainers – Set a time limit to do a certain number of calculations.

Plenary   **5 mins**
Show a subtraction calculation *e.g.* 7 – 3 = ☐ and ask the children to solve it. Then show 17 – 3 = ☐ and ask for it to be solved. Ask what they notice about the numbers. Repeat with other numbers, subtracting a single-digit number from a teens number without crossing the tens boundary.

Lesson 4

Introduction   **10 mins**
Show a two-digit number and ask the children to use digit cards to show the number that is 10 more or less. Repeat with several numbers, drawing attention to the tens digit changing by one.

Activities   **25 mins**
Add 9 (whole class)
Show 7 + 9 = ☐ and ask children to solve it then share strategies. Tell the children that 9 is very close to ten which is an easier number to work with. Show on a number line 7 + 10 = 17 and the units digit remains the same, then subtract 1 which makes the unit digit now one less. Show that 7 + 10 – 1 = ☐ gives the same answer as they had worked out previously. Illustrate this with other examples.

Add 10, take 1 (individual)
Write some calculations that involve adding 9. Put the 9 first in the sentence for some examples. Encourage quick calculation by adding 10 and subtracting 1.

Differentiation
Low Attainers – Provide a 0–20 number line.
High Attainers – Provide calculations where they have to add 9 to two-digit numbers up to 50.

Plenary   **5 mins**
Show that this strategy can be applied to subtracting 9 by subtracting 10 then adding 1. Demonstrate with examples on a number line.

Lesson 5

Introduction   **10 mins**
Revise bridging through 10. Show 7 counters and 6 counters on the OHP. Ask how many counters need to be added to 7 to make 10. Move 3 from the 6 to make a group of 10. Ask how many are left (3) then add this to the 10 and record as 7 + 6 = 7 + 3 + 3 = 10 + 3 = 13.

Activities   **25 mins**
Bridge through 20 (whole class)
Repeat the above activity this time using 8 and 15 counters. Add 2 counters to the 8 to make 10, leaving 13. Then add 13 and 10 to make 23. Repeat this calculation, modeling it on a number line. Then show that they can make 20 by adding 5 to 15 then adding 3 again showing this on a number line.

Crossing the 20 bridge (pairs)
Provide each child with a copy of Copymaster 54, 12 counters and two sets of digit cards 3–8 and 13–18 to be kept in separate piles. The children take it in turns to take a card from each pile and find the total. When they make the total, they cover it with a counter on their grid. The first to make a row of 4 counters is the winner. Finish by completing the calculation at the bottom.

Differentiation
Low Attainers – Provide a 0–30 number line.
High Attainers – The first to cover all the numbers is the winner.

Plenary   **5 mins**
Children show answers to calculations using digit cards. Make the 0–30 number line visible.

Theme 8) Solving problems

Objectives
- To choose and use the appropriate number operation and mental strategies to solve simple money problems or 'real life' problems using counting, addition or subtraction, halving or doubling

Vocabulary
double, halve, half, near double, add, subtract, take away, total, altogether, money, spend, change, sell, buy, cost, cheaper, most, least, more, less, number story, number sentence, symbol, puzzle, problem

Resources
Copymasters 55 and 56, set of 1–20 number cards for each pupil, set of money cards for each pupil, coins, counters, multilink cubes, number lines

Homework Copymaster 28

Mental maths starters 14, 17

Assessment
At the end of this theme is the pupil able to:
- Solve problems involving doubles and halves;
- Choose an appropriate number operation and mental strategy to solve problems and puzzles involving real life situations and money?

Lesson 1

Introduction   10 mins
Make a vertical list of the numbers 1 to 10. Remind pupils how to double numbers, *e.g. double 1 means two ones added together, 1 + 1 = 2*. Ask pupils to double the numbers 1 to 10 and next to each number write the addition.
Remind pupils how to halve a number, explaining that it is the number you would need to double to get the number. Ask them to halve the numbers 2 to 20.

Activities   25 mins
Double and half problems (whole class)
Start by asking the pupils simple number questions such as 'What is double 3, half of 10?' Move on to ask pupils problems involving doubles and halves, *e.g. 'I have 14 sweets and give half to my friend. How many sweets do we each have now?', 'Ben scored 5 in his last spelling test. In the next test he doubled his score. How many did he get this time?'*

Near doubles (whole class)
Each pupil needs a set of 1–20 number cards. Remind pupils how numbers which are close together can be worked out by doubling, *e.g. 3 + 4 is close to 3 + 3, so it can be worked out as double 3 add 1.* Write and call out some near doubles and ask pupils to hold up their cards to show their answers. Ask pupils to explain the methods they used to work out the answers.

Differentiation
Low Attainers – Concentrate on doubles up to double 5.
High Attainers – Include some more difficult problems.

Plenary   5 mins
Call out a number, *e.g. 4*, ask pupils to double it to get 8. Now ask pupils to halve the number. Ask what they get. Repeat for other numbers. Ask pupils if they think that doubling then halving always takes you back to the first number.

Lesson 2

Introduction   10 mins
Write a number on the board, *e.g. 5*, and ask pupils which number must be added to it to make 12, 15, 9 … Write a number of the board, *e.g. 11*, and ask which number must be subtracted to make 3, 8, 6 … Repeat for other numbers.

Activities   25 mins
Addition pairs (pairs)
Each pair of pupils needs a set of 1–20 number cards. Pupils take turns to draw a card and think of two numbers which add to give that number.

Number problems (whole class)
Each pupil needs a set of 1–20 number cards. Ask pupils problems such as 'I am thinking of two numbers which add together to give ten. Which numbers could they be?', 'Karen rolled two dice and scored 9. What numbers could she have rolled?', 'Which number would I have to take away from 12 to get 9?', 'Harry has three more marbles than Tom. Tom has 7 marbles. How many does Harry have? How many do Tom and Harry have altogether?' Pupils should hold up the card(s) showing their answers. Allow pupils access to number lines, counters, etc. and encourage them to use them as necessary. Ask pupils to explain how they worked out the answer.

Differentiation
Low Attainers – Use 1–10 cards in card game.
High Attainers – Pupils draw a card from the pile and take turns to say two numbers which add to give the number until they can't think of any more. They should keep a record of their answers.

Plenary   5 mins
Look back at some of the number problems and write down number sentences for them. Record some of the strategies used.

Summer Term

Lesson 3

Introduction   **10 mins**
Explain to the pupils that they are going to solve some money problems. Tell them that where possible they should try to solve the problem mentally but if they can't then they should use coins, counters or a number line to help them. Demonstrate with an example.

Activities   **25 mins**
Coins (whole class)
Each pupil needs a set of money cards. Ask pupils questions such as 'Which three coins could make 12p?', 'Can you make 18p with 3 coins?', 'Paul buys a stamp and gets 6p change. Which coins could he have got in his change?'
Pupils use their money cards to show combinations of coins to answer the problems.

Buying and selling (whole class)
Each pupil needs a set on 1–20 number cards. Ask pupils questions such as 'How much altogether is 8p, 3p and 1p?', 'Bob spent 7p. How much change did he get from 10p?', 'Jane bought a can of pop for 10p and a bar of chocolate for 7p. How much did she spend in total?', 'Toffees cost 3p each. What will it cost for three?' Pupils hold up a number card to show the correct answer. Allow pupils access to number lines, counters, coins. Ask pupils to explain the methods they used.

Differentiation
Low Attainers – Encourage use of counting equipment and assist with the vocabulary.
High Attainers – Encourage use of mental strategies.

Plenary   **5 mins**
Look back at some of the money problems and write down number sentences for them. Record some of the strategies used.

Lesson 4

Introduction   **10 mins**
Write on the board and read out the number story 'I have 2 apples and I buy 5 more. I now have 7 apples altogether'. Show how this can be written as a number sentence, 2 + 5 = 7. Use further examples, including subtractions. Now include some with unknown numbers, e.g. 'Ben has 6 sweets and gives some away. He now has only three left'. Write this as 6 – ☐ = 3. Solve the problem to find out how many sweets he gave away.

Activities   **25 mins**
Complete the missing numbers (individual)
Each pupil needs Copymaster 55. Complete the number sentences by finding the missing numbers.

Number stories (pairs)
Ask pupils to use the completed number sentences from the copymaster and make up number stories for them.

Differentiation
Low Attainers – Use objects to show the number sentences.
High Attainers – Create number stories for their own number sentences.

Plenary   **5 mins**
Ask pupils to read out some of their number stories and write the number sentences on the board.

Lesson 5

Introduction   **10 mins**
Explain to pupils that they are going to use their number skills to solve various puzzles and problems. Work through a puzzle with the class, *e.g. stick cards on the board with the numbers and symbols 1, 3, 6, +, –, =*. Ask pupils to come out and arrange some of the cards to make different number sentences and then work them out, *e.g. 6 + 3 = 9, 13 – 6 = 5*.

Activity   **25 mins**
Number puzzles (individual)
Each pupil needs Copymaster 56. Solve the problems on the copymaster. Record answers on paper or in exercise book where necessary.

Differentiation
Low Attainers – Encourage use of counting equipment and explain puzzles orally.
High Attainers – Encourage them to extend the puzzles in their own way.

Plenary   **5 mins**
Ask pupils to show some of their answers and explain the methods used.

Theme 9 Measuring capacity

Objectives
- To suggest suitable non-uniform standard and then standard units and measuring equipment to estimate, then measure capacity recording estimates and measurements as 'about 3 beakers full' or 'just under 5 litres'
- Solve simple problems involving capacity

Vocabulary
guess, roughly, nearly, close to, about the same as, too much, too little, enough, not enough, full, half full, empty, partly full, litre, capacity, container, estimate

Resources
Copymasters 57 and 58, variety of containers, litre bottles/containers, sand, water, rice, cards showing 'about a litre', 'more than a litre' and 'less than a litre', hoops, funnels

Homework Copymaster 29

Mental maths starters 4, 15

Assessment
At the end of this theme is the pupil able to:
- Estimate and measure capacities about the same as, more than and less than one litre;
- Estimate how many non-standard units fill a container;
- Estimate how many litres fill a container;
- Solve simple problems involving capacity?

Lesson 1

Introduction   10 mins
Show some of the containers from work covered in Theme 4 Summer Term. Ask the children to estimate which containers hold about the same as, more than or less than one litre. Label them.

Activity   25 mins
Estimate a litre (pairs)
Provide each pair of children with a full litre container, about 5 other containers of various sizes, some labels showing 'about one litre', 'more than one litre' and 'less than one litre'. The children pour the contents of the litre container into the other empty containers to find out whether the containers hold about, more or less than a litre. They label them appropriately.

Differentiation
Low Attainers – Provide fewer containers.
High Attainers – Provide a range of containers close to a litre.

Plenary   5 mins
Each pair of children shows one of their collection of containers and make three groups of containers from the whole class. Query any that do not seem right.

Lesson 2

Introduction   10 mins
Revise the vocabulary of capacity. Show a selection of 'real life' measuring equipment, *e.g. a watering can, a teaspoon, measuring jug etc.* Ask the children what would be measured out by each piece of equipment. Ask which equipment holds more than, less than or about a litre.

Activity   25 mins
Estimating litres (small groups)
Provide each group with Copymaster 57, a litre container and some containers that hold several litres. Ask the children to estimate how many litres each container holds. Encourage them to record as 'just over 3 litres', 'nearly 2 litres' etc.

Differentiation
Low Attainers – Work as a large group together with an adult recording estimates on an A3 version of Copymaster 57.
High Attainers – Provide a half litre container.

Plenary   5 mins
Give out and explain the homework activity.

Summer Term

Lesson 3

Introduction   **10 mins**
Show four identical containers: full, empty, partly full, half full. Ask the children to choose two or more of the containers and describe what they see in different ways using appropriate vocabulary.

Activity   **25 mins**
Measuring litres (small groups)
Work in the same small groups as in the previous lesson and measure the capacities of the containers in litres and compare with estimates.
Provide sufficient water, sand etc. so the containers can be filled. Record measures in the same way as the estimates.

Differentiation
Low Attainers – Work as a large group together with an adult recording the measures.
High Attainers – Find the difference between their estimates and measures.

Plenary   **5 mins**
Show containers that have the same capacities. Comment on the range of shapes and sizes of the same capacity containers.

Lesson 4

Introduction   **10 mins**
Show the children a collection of containers that have capacities less than one litre. Remind them of the previous lesson's activity when the capacities of various containers were measured in litres. Now show them a range of small measuring devices. Ask what would be appropriate to fill a milk bottle, a teaspoon or a plastic cup?

Activity   **25 mins**
Non-standard measuring (small groups)
Provide each group with a collection of very small containers (teaspoon, thimble, egg cup, yogurt pot, toy tea cup, screw cap bottle top) and some larger containers (plant pot, milk carton, mug, drinking beaker, small pop bottle). Ask the children to choose a suitable small container to use to fill a larger one and count how many fill it. Record the measurement as 'the milk carton is nearly 4 yogurt pots full' etc.

Differentiation
Low Attainers – Pair together a suitable small and large container.
High Attainers – Choose one small container and use it to fill a variety of larger ones to compare the sizes.

Plenary   **5 mins**
Briefly discuss any issues arising from the activity and explain the homework task.

Lesson 5

Introduction   **10 mins**
Ask the children what they can remember about estimating and measuring capacities.
Discuss the vocabulary in context using a range of containers including those the children have brought in from home.

Activities   **25 mins**
Capacity problems (individual)
Show a capacity problem on the board and discuss it with the children. Work on the solution together and model how to record it.
Provide each child with a copy of Copymaster 58 and read through some of the problems together and discuss possible strategies.

Differentiation
Low Attainers – Work through questions 1–4 only.
High Attainers – Provide some practical problems.

Plenary   **5 mins**
Discuss the answers and solutions to some of the problems. Sort out any misconceptions that have occurred during the lesson.

Theme 10 Sorting information

Objectives
- To read time to half an hour on an analogue clock
- To solve a problem by organising information in a list or a table
- To discuss and explain results

Vocabulary
time, clock, o'clock, hour, hands, half hour, half past, timer, how long? quick, more quickly, less quickly, fast, faster, slow, slower, more slowly, morning, afternoon, evening, night, day, now, earlier, later, before, after, estimate, sort, list, table

Resources
Copymasters 59 and 60, two large analogue clocks, a class set of small analogue clocks, clock stamp, multilink cubes, one minute sand timers – one for each group, a set of cards showing times in words, clock faces between 1 and 12 o'clock including half hours

Homework Copymaster 30

Mental maths starters 2, 20

Assessment
At the end of this theme is the pupil able to:
- Tell the time to the hour and half hour on an analogue clock;
- Solve simple problems about time involving earlier and later and times between events or times;
- Estimate and time activities using a timer;
- Order a list of events based on time;
- Start to discuss and reason about time?

Lesson 1

Introduction 10 mins
Stick a large analogue clock on the board. Start by reinforcing reading times to one hour by firstly setting the hands at three o'clock, writing it as '3 o'clock' on the board. Explain to the pupils that the time will be moved on by one hour and set the hands at four o'clock and write down the new time. Repeat for different 'o'clock' times asking pupils to call out the times.

Activities 25 mins
Half past (whole class)
Set the clock at three o'clock. Move the minute hand to the half past position and explain that the time has moved on by half an hour – this time is called 'half past three'. Repeat for other times, asking the pupils to call out the times.

Calling time (whole class)
Each pupil will need a small clock. Call out a time – mainly 'half past …' times but also include some 'o'clock' times – and ask pupils to set their clocks to that time and show their clocks to the teacher. Check that pupils position both hands correctly.

Differentiation
By outcome.

Plenary 5 mins
Using the large analogue clock ask a pupil to set the hands to show, for example, 'half past ten'. Ask the pupils for an event that happens at this time in the morning, *e.g. break time.* Continue for other times, remembering to mention whether the time refers to morning or afternoon/evening.

Lesson 2

Introduction 10 mins
Stick a large analogue clock on the board. Set the hands at half past three. Ask the pupils this time. Explain that you are going to now set the time one hour later. Ask the time and then set the hands of the clock to show this. Repeat for other times, both 'o'clocks and half pasts, asking for new times one, two … hours earlier/later.

Activities 25 mins
Clock stamps (individual)
Prepare sheets or workbooks with eight stamped clock faces. Ask pupils to draw in the hands showing eight different times to the half hour and write the time underneath each clock.

Half past (whole class)
Each pupil will need a small clock. Call out a 'half past' time and ask pupils to set their clocks to that time and show their clocks to the teacher. Now ask pupils to set the clock one hour earlier. Now set it two hours later etc. Check that pupils position both hands correctly and ask them to call out the times each time they reset the clock.

Differentiation
Low Attainers – Give fewer times to complete.
High Attainers – Provide further stamped clock faces for pupils to draw the hands showing times which are one, two, … hours earlier/later than a given time.

Plenary 5 mins
Read out the following story 'Saturday Morning' and ask pupils to set their clocks to show the times mentioned in the story – I had a lie in until half past eight (set time) on Saturday. I was ready and dressed in one hour (set clock). At ten o'clock we went to the supermarket and spent a whole hour buying food (set clock). We got back home from the supermarket at half past eleven (set time). I played in the garden for an hour until my lunch was ready (set clock).

Summer Term

Lesson 3

Introduction 10 mins
Stick a large analogue clock on the board. Set the hands at two o'clock. Ask the pupils what time it will be in half an hour. Set the clock to half past two. Set the clock at half past seven and ask, then show, what time it will be half an hour later. Repeat, asking for times half an hour earlier.

Activities 25 mins
Earlier or later (individual)
Each pupil needs Copymaster 59. Complete the blank clock faces to show times half an hour earlier/later than the times shown. Allow pupils to use small clocks to help work out the times.

Time problems (whole class)
Stick two large analogue clocks side by side on the board. Set one clock at one o'clock and the other at two o'clock. Ask pupils how many hours there are between the two times. Set one clock at half past seven and the other at eight o'clock. Ask how long between the times. Set one clock at three o'clock and ask a pupil to come out and set the the time on the other clock at half an hour earlier/later.

Differentiation
Low Attainers – Target questions involving whole hours.
High Attainers – Include some more difficult questions involving half and/or whole hours.

Plenary 5 mins
Set a large clock to a time. Ask pupils to come out and set the new time according to your instructions, *e.g.* 'Set the clock to half past five, one hour earlier, to ten o'clock, half an hour later, …'

Lesson 4

Introduction 10 mins
Show the pupils a sand timer and explain that it takes a certain amount of time for the sand to run from one end to the other. This can be used to time things. Ask the pupils to estimate how many times they could clap their hands in the time that it takes for the sand to run out. Carry out the activity, counting with them. Discuss their estimates.

Activities 25 mins
Name game (groups/individual)
Provide each group/table with a timer. Ask pupils to take turns as the timer for their group. Ask the pupils to write their name on a piece of paper as many times as possible until the sand runs out. How many could they manage?

Multilink challenge (groups/individual)
Provide each pupil with a pile of multilink cubes. Ask the pupils to first estimate how many cubes they think they will be able to link together before the sand in the timer runs out, then time this activity. Repeat this several times and ask pupils to record their results in a table, *e.g.*
    1   20
    2   22
    3   25

Differentiation
Low Attainers – Will need help with timing the activity.
High Attainers – Try sorting multilink cubes into coloured sets during the time allowed.

Plenary 5 mins
Discuss the results from the activities. Who linked the most/fewest cubes? Who wrote their name most times? Discuss how pupils with shorter names may have written more – why?

Lesson 5

Introduction 10 mins
Prepare a set of cards showing times, in words and clock faces, between 1 and 12 o'clock, including half hours and stick them on the board at random. Ask pupils 'Which is the earliest time?' Place this at the top of the board. 'Which is the latest time?' Place this at the bottom of the board. Help the pupils to sort the remaining times in order.

Activity 25 mins
The school day (pairs)
Each pupil needs Copymaster 60. Ask pupils to cut out the pictures and put them into the correct order then complete the list of events in order.

Differentiation
Low Attainers – Encourage pupils to say the times as they arrange them in order. Provide adult support.
High Attainers – Write the times in words next to the events.

Plenary 5 mins
Arrange the cards used in the introduction randomly on the board. Remove one and ask the pupils for an earlier time, the time one hour after this time, … Repeat for other times.

Copymaster 1

One more or less

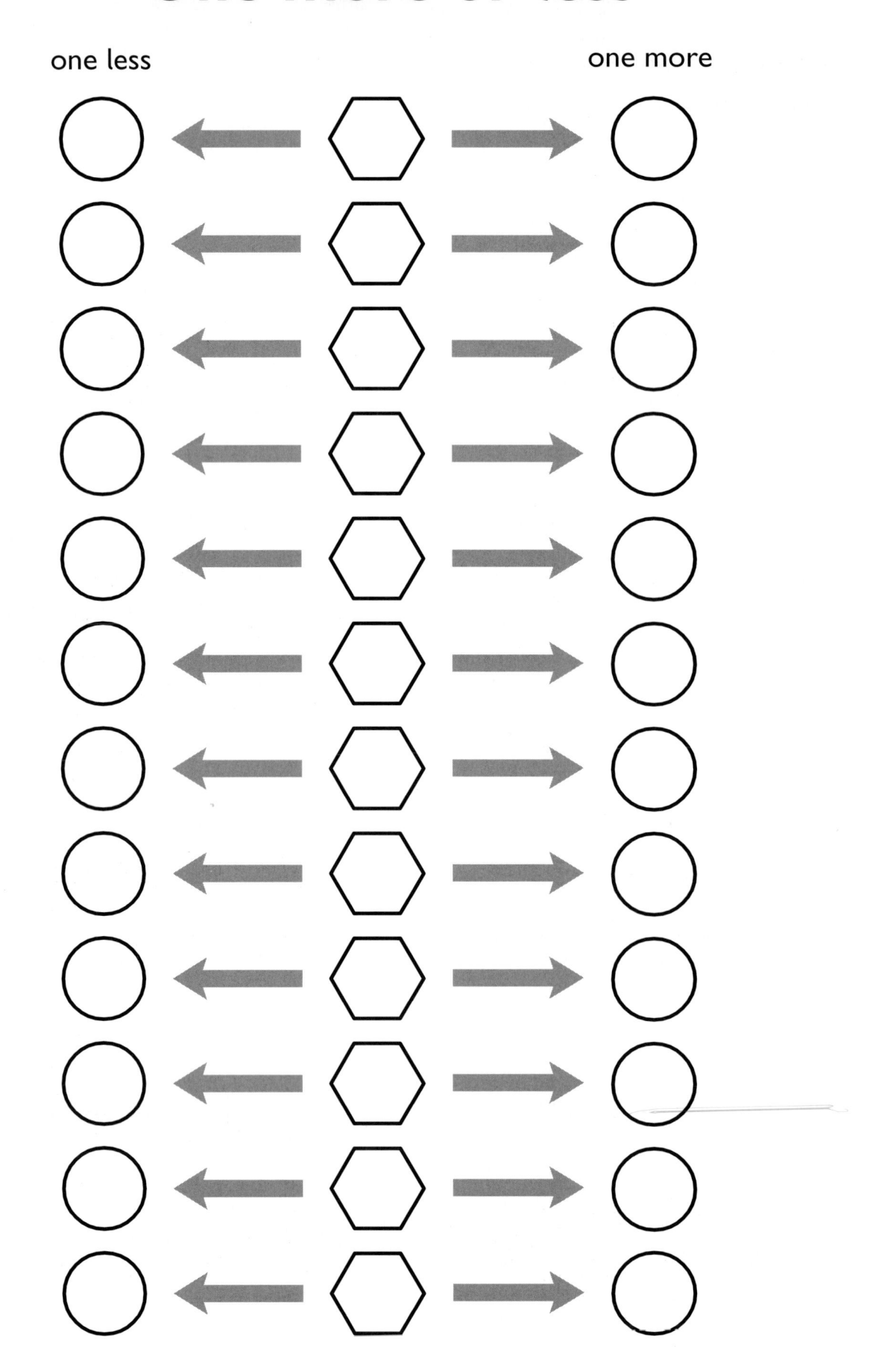

one less   one more

68

Copymaster 2

Tens and ones

- Group the objects into a group of ten and ones.
- Write the number below.

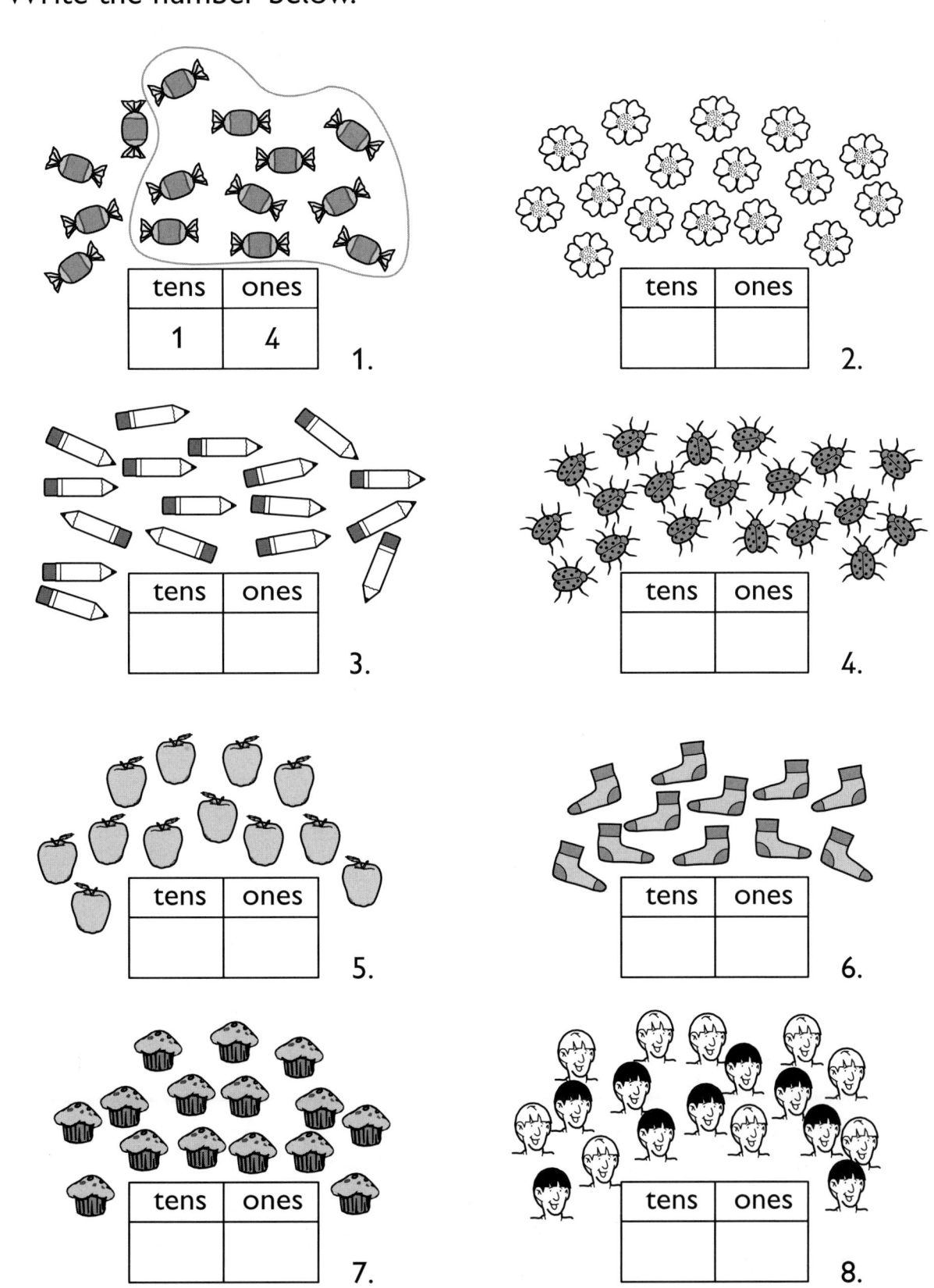

tens	ones
1	4

1.

tens	ones

2.

tens	ones

3.

tens	ones

4.

tens	ones

5.

tens	ones

6.

tens	ones

7.

tens	ones

8.

Copymaster 3

Counting on

1.

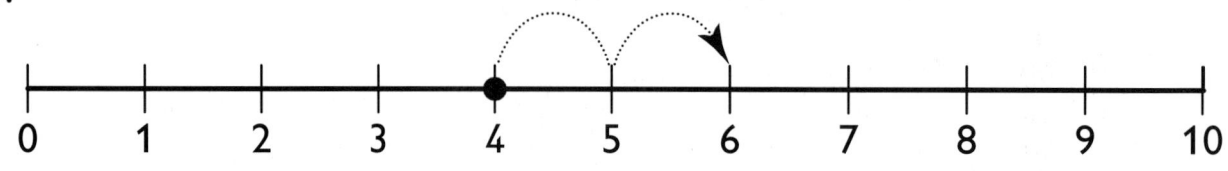

4 + 2 = ☐

2.

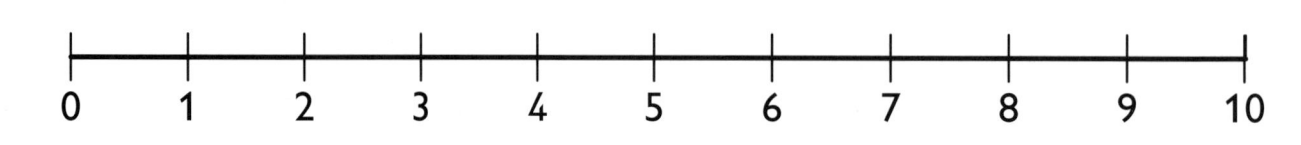

3 + 6 = ☐

3.

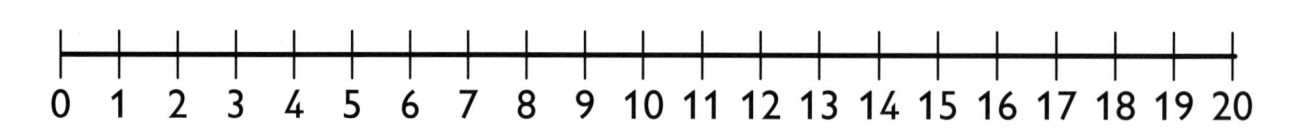

7 + 6 = ☐

4.

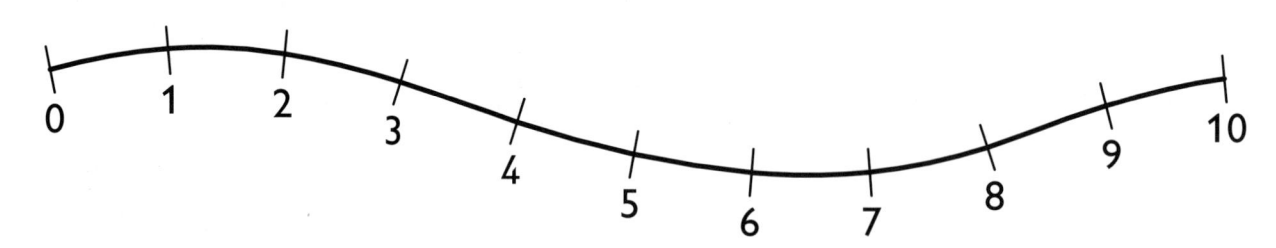

2 + 8 = ☐

5.

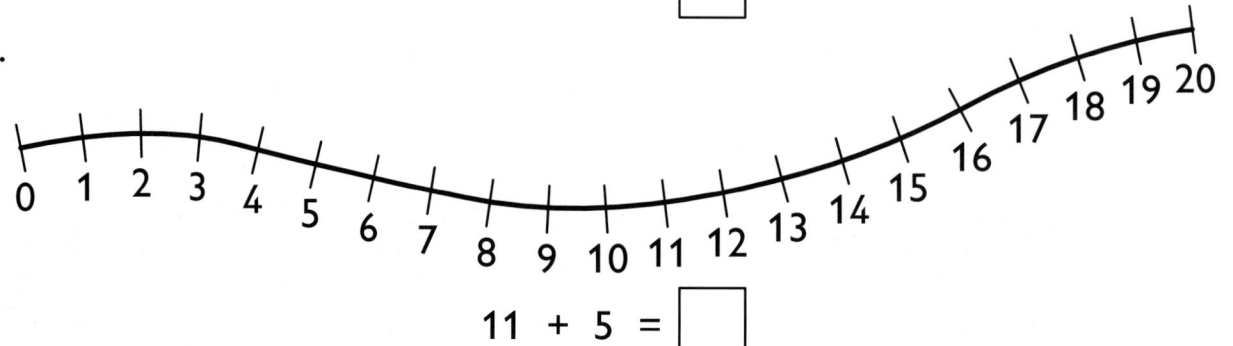

11 + 5 = ☐

Add and subtract game
Dinosaur's Den

FINISH 40 39 38 37 36 35 34 33 32 31 30 29 28 27 26 25 24 23 22 21 20 19 18 17 16 15 14 13 12 11 10 9 8 7 6 5 4 3 2 1 START

- Add the number on your dice
- Take away 3
- Add 3
- Take away the number on your dice
- Take away your age
- Add one more than the number on your dice
- Add 4
- Add the number on your dice
- Take away one
- Take away 5
- Subtract the number on your dice
- Subtract 1

Copymaster 4

Purses

Write the total in each purse.

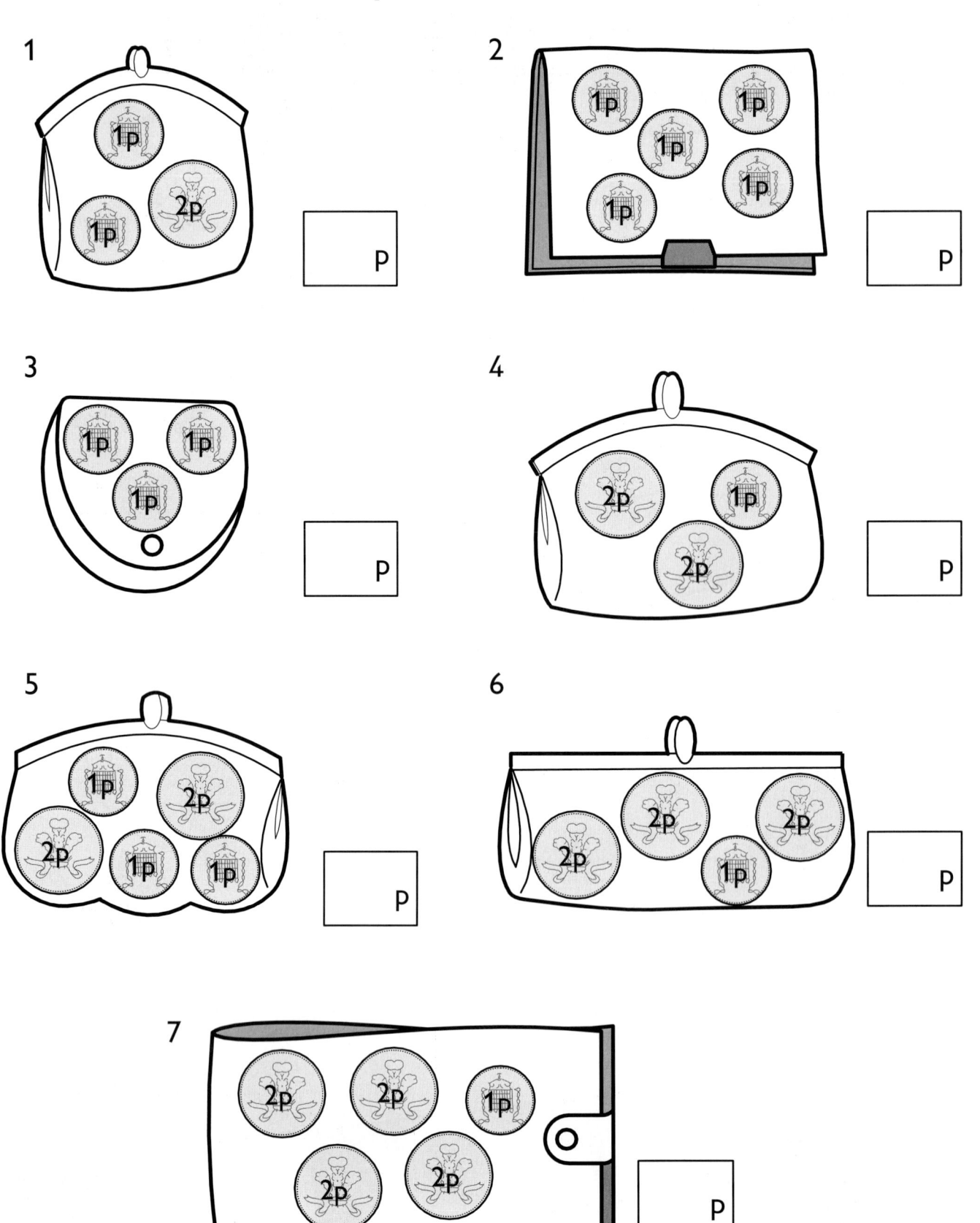

1. 1p, 1p, 2p → ☐ p

2. 1p, 1p, 1p, 1p, 1p → ☐ p

3. 1p, 1p, 1p → ☐ p

4. 2p, 1p, 2p → ☐ p

5. 1p, 2p, 2p, 1p, 1p → ☐ p

6. 2p, 2p, 2p, 1p → ☐ p

7. 2p, 2p, 1p, 2p, 2p → ☐ p

Copymaster 6

Buying things

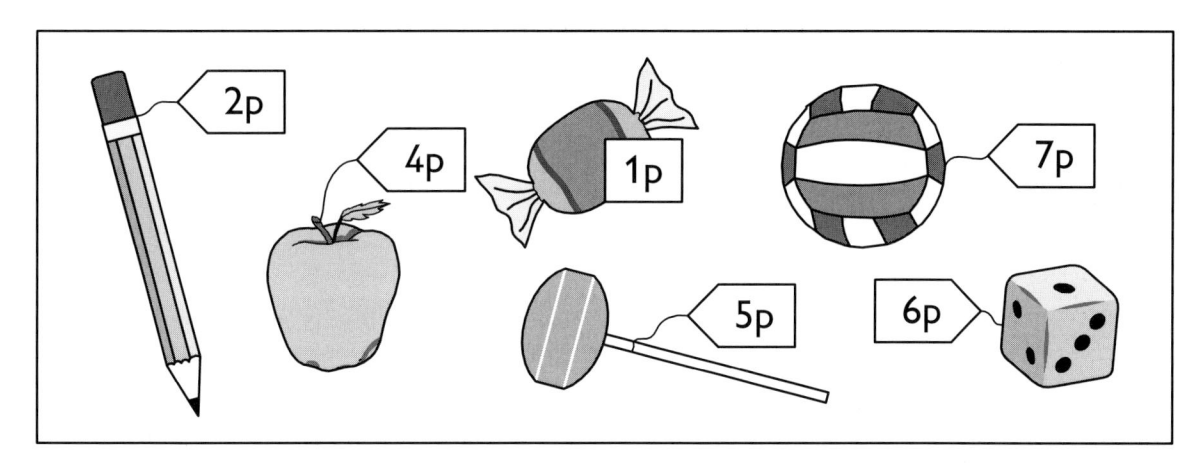

Prices: pencil 2p, apple 4p, sweet 1p, ball 7p, lollipop 5p, dice 6p

Work out the total cost of the items shown.

1.  apple + sweet
   ___ + ___ = ___

2. 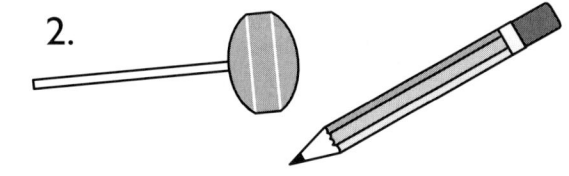 lollipop + pencil
   ___ + ___ = ___

3.  dice + sweet
   ___ + ___ = ___

4.  ball + pencil
   ___ + ___ = ___

5. dice + apple
   ___ + ___ = ___

6. 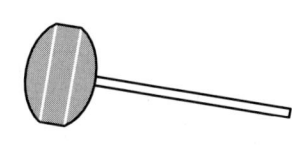 apple + lollipop
   ___ + ___ = ___

73

Copymaster 7

Which order?

74

Non-standard measuring

I am measuring with _____

Object	Object
This is ☐ _____ long.	This is ☐ _____ long.

Object	Object
This is ☐ _____ long.	This is ☐ _____ long.

Object	Object
This is ☐ _____ long.	This is ☐ _____ long.

3D shape quiz

Complete the sentences about each shape.

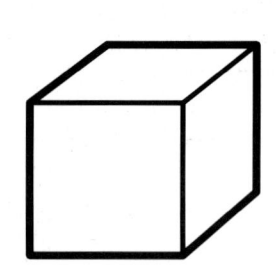

This is a _____.

It has _____ faces.

All faces are _____.

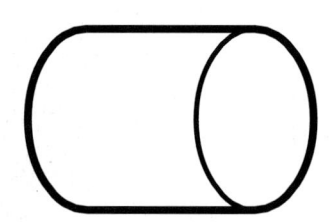

This is a _____.

It has _____ curved face and _____ flat faces. The flat faces are _____.

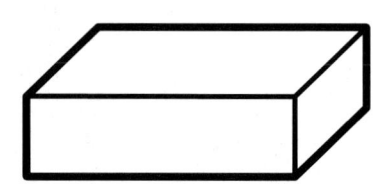

This is a _____.

It has _____ faces.

All faces are _____.

It has _____ corners.

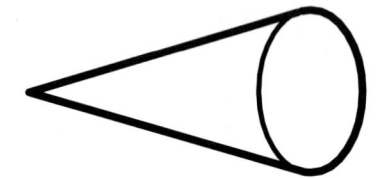

This is a _____.

It has _____ curved edge.

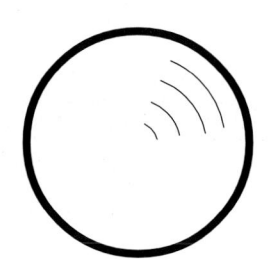

This is a _____.

It has _____ flat faces.

It has _____ corners.

Copymaster 10

Copymaster 11

Join dots

Join the dots in order from 1 to 20.

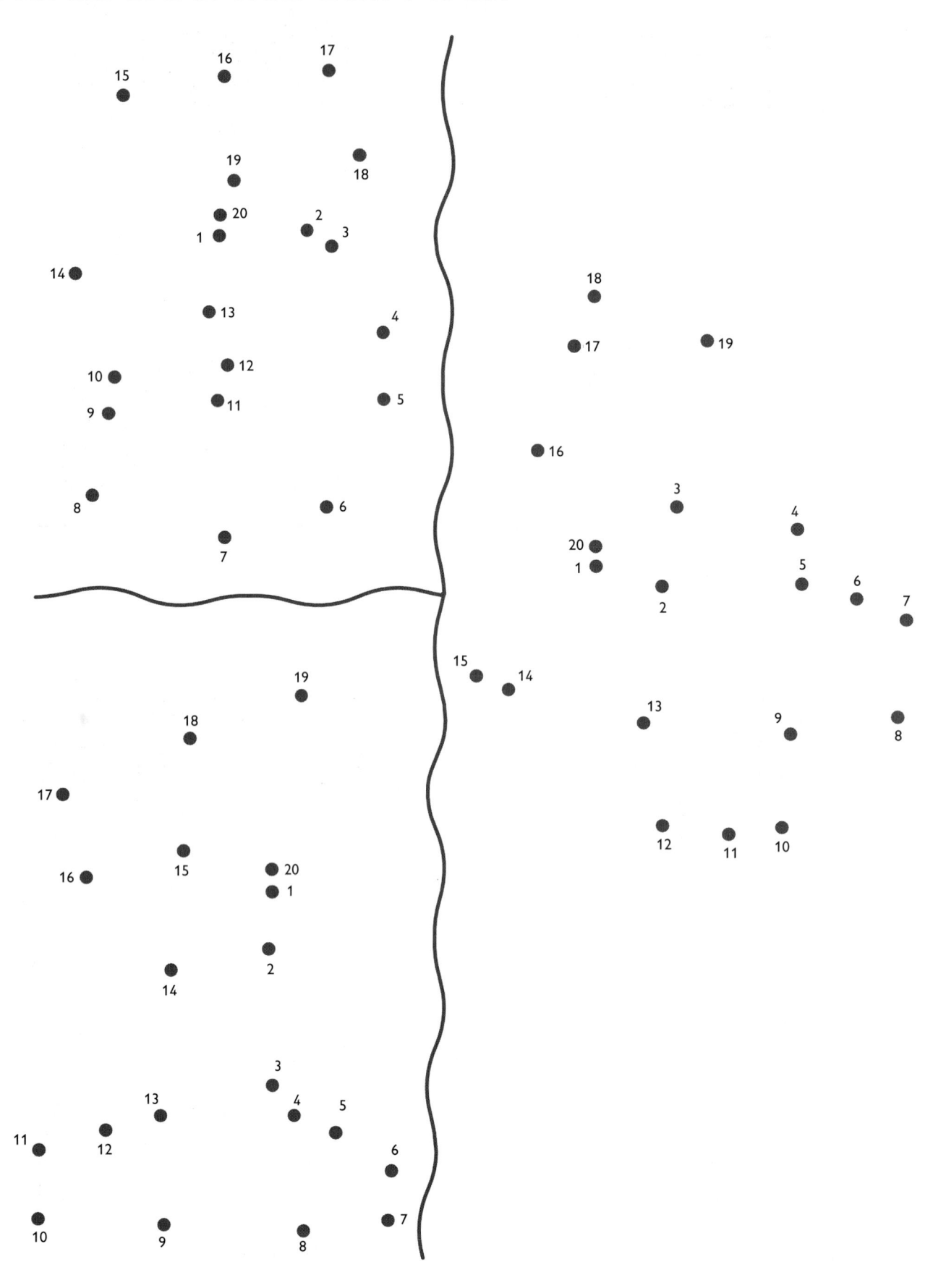

Copymaster 12

Fruit boxes

Fill in the answers.

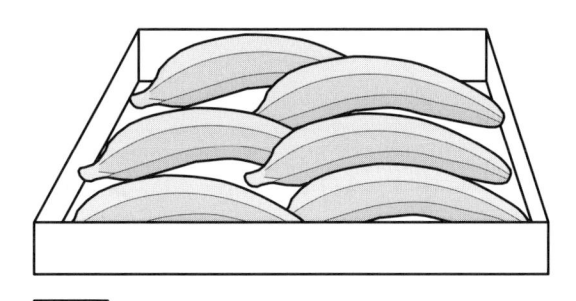

☐ bananas

☐ apples

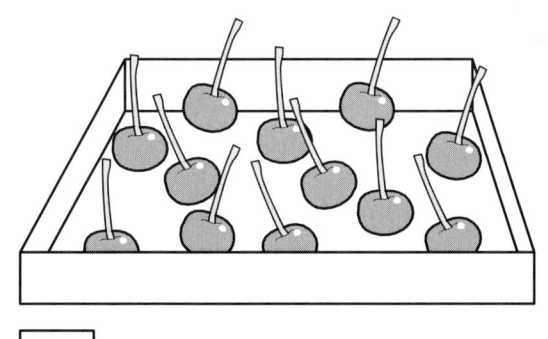

☐ cherries

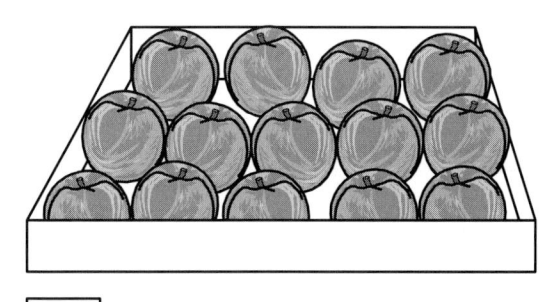

☐ plums

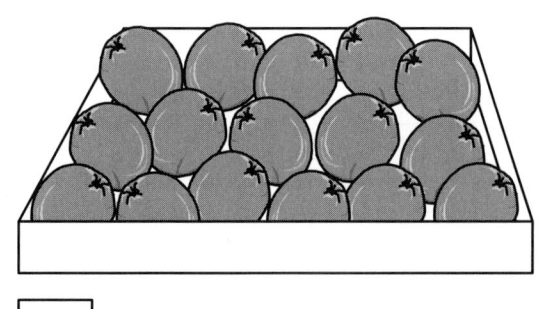

☐ oranges

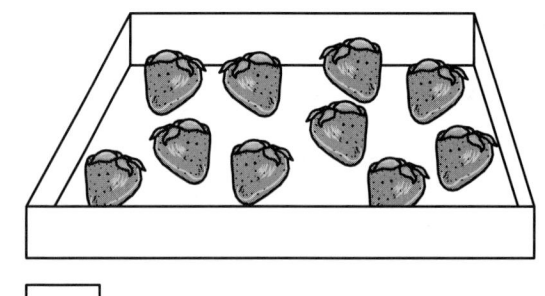

☐ strawberries

Draw the fruit.

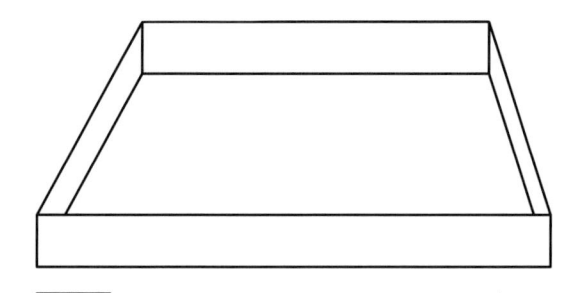

| 11 | apples

| 15 | bananas

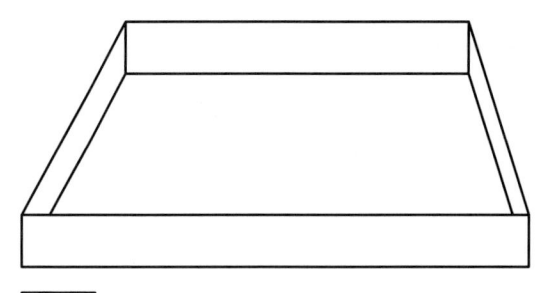

Ten more

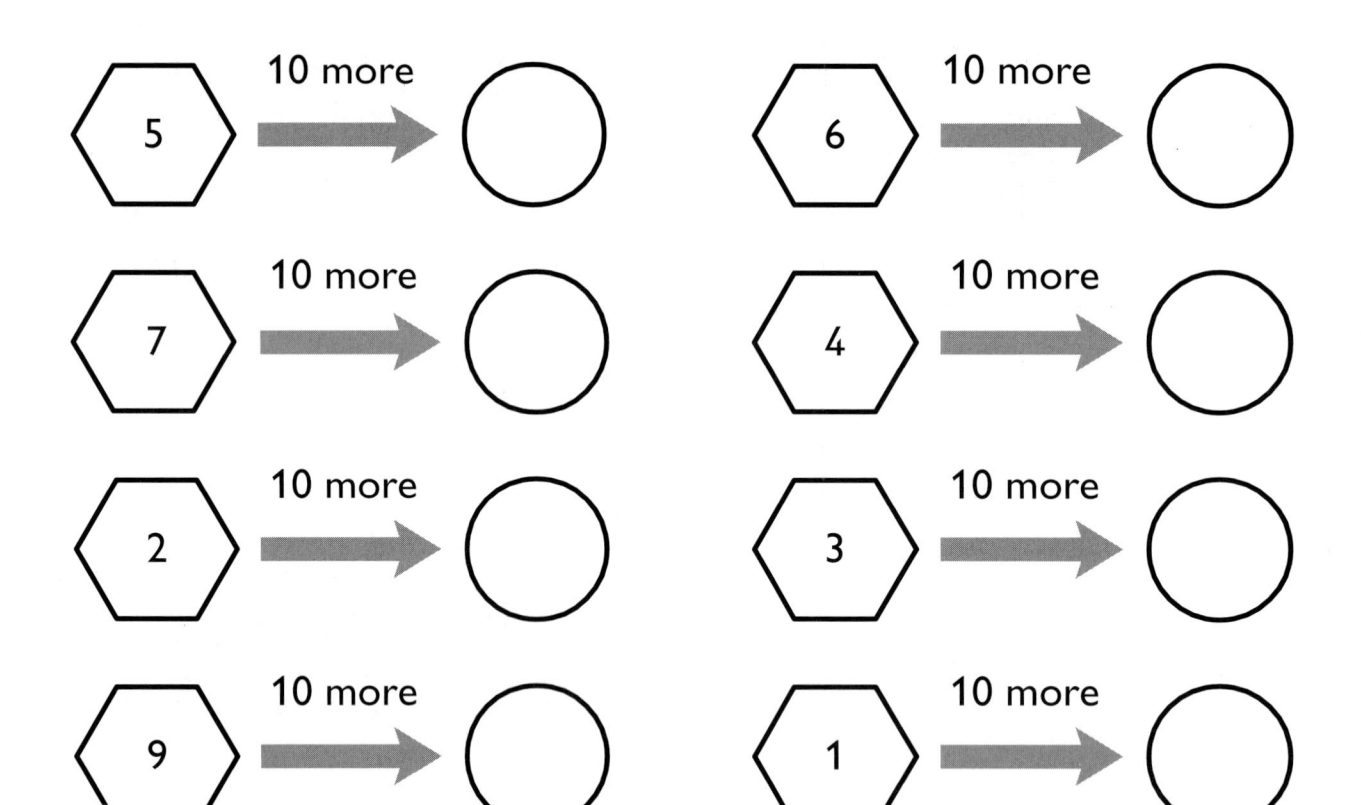

5 →10 more→ ◯   6 →10 more→ ◯

7 →10 more→ ◯   4 →10 more→ ◯

2 →10 more→ ◯   3 →10 more→ ◯

9 →10 more→ ◯   1 →10 more→ ◯

Complete:

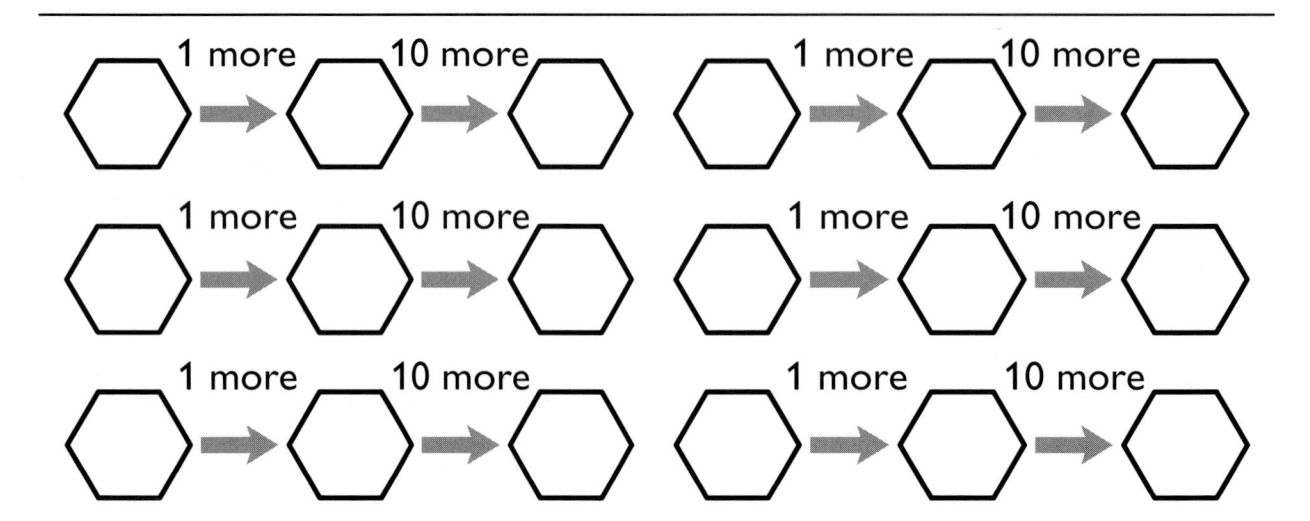

7 + 10 = ☐   8 + 10 = ☐   10 + 5 = ☐

5 + 10 = ☐   10 + 3 = ☐   10 more than 3 = ☐

2 + 10 = ☐   10 + 6 = ☐   9 and ten more = ☐

◯ →1 more→ ◯ →10 more→ ◯   ◯ →1 more→ ◯ →10 more→ ◯

◯ →1 more→ ◯ →10 more→ ◯   ◯ →1 more→ ◯ →10 more→ ◯

◯ →1 more→ ◯ →10 more→ ◯   ◯ →1 more→ ◯ →10 more→ ◯

What a handful!

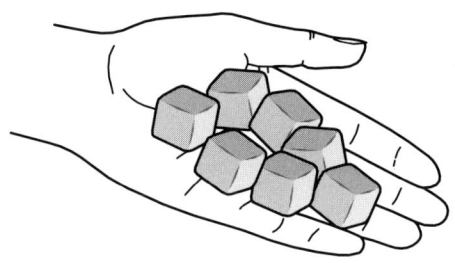

- Grab a handful of objects.
- Write down your estimate.
- Count the objects.

name of objects	estimate	count

Copymaster 15

Difference clowns

Throw the dice and find the difference.

0 – face, 1 – hat, 2 – eyes, 3 – nose, 4 – mouth, 5 – bow tie

82

Calculating clocks

What to do

- Throw the dice.

- If the dice lands on +, add the two numbers.
- If the dice lands on −, find the difference.
- If the answer is zero have an extra turn.

Which measure?

Object being measured	What I am using to measure with	Measure

Length problems

Romana   Hajit   Paul   Lucy   Zoë

1. Who is the tallest? _____

2. Who is the shortest? _____

3. Who is taller than Hajit? _____, _____ and _____

4. Who is shorter than Lucy? _____, _____ and _____

5. Hajit is the same height as 15 straws. Romana is 3 straws taller. How tall is Romana? _____ straws

6. Lucy is 2 straws shorter than Paul. Paul is 22 straws high. How tall is Lucy? _____ straws

7.

   Draw a pencil longer than this.

   Draw a pencil shorter than this.

Copymaster 19

Earlier or later

Draw the times earlier and later.

1.
one hour earlier — one hour later

2. 
one hour earlier — one hour later

3. 
one hour earlier — one hour later

4. 
two hours earlier — one hour later

5. 
one hour earlier — two hours later

6. 
two hours earlier — two hours later

Copymaster 20

Sweets sets

Cut out the sweets from the bottom of the page. Sort some of them into sets using the circles below.

Number pairs

one ten and four ones	two tens and six units	**14**	**30**
12	two tens only	2 tens and 4 ones	**26**
24	one ten and eight ones	1 ten and 2 ones	1 ten and 7 units
18	**17**	3 tens and 0 units	**20**

Copymaster 22

Number sequences

Complete the sequences.

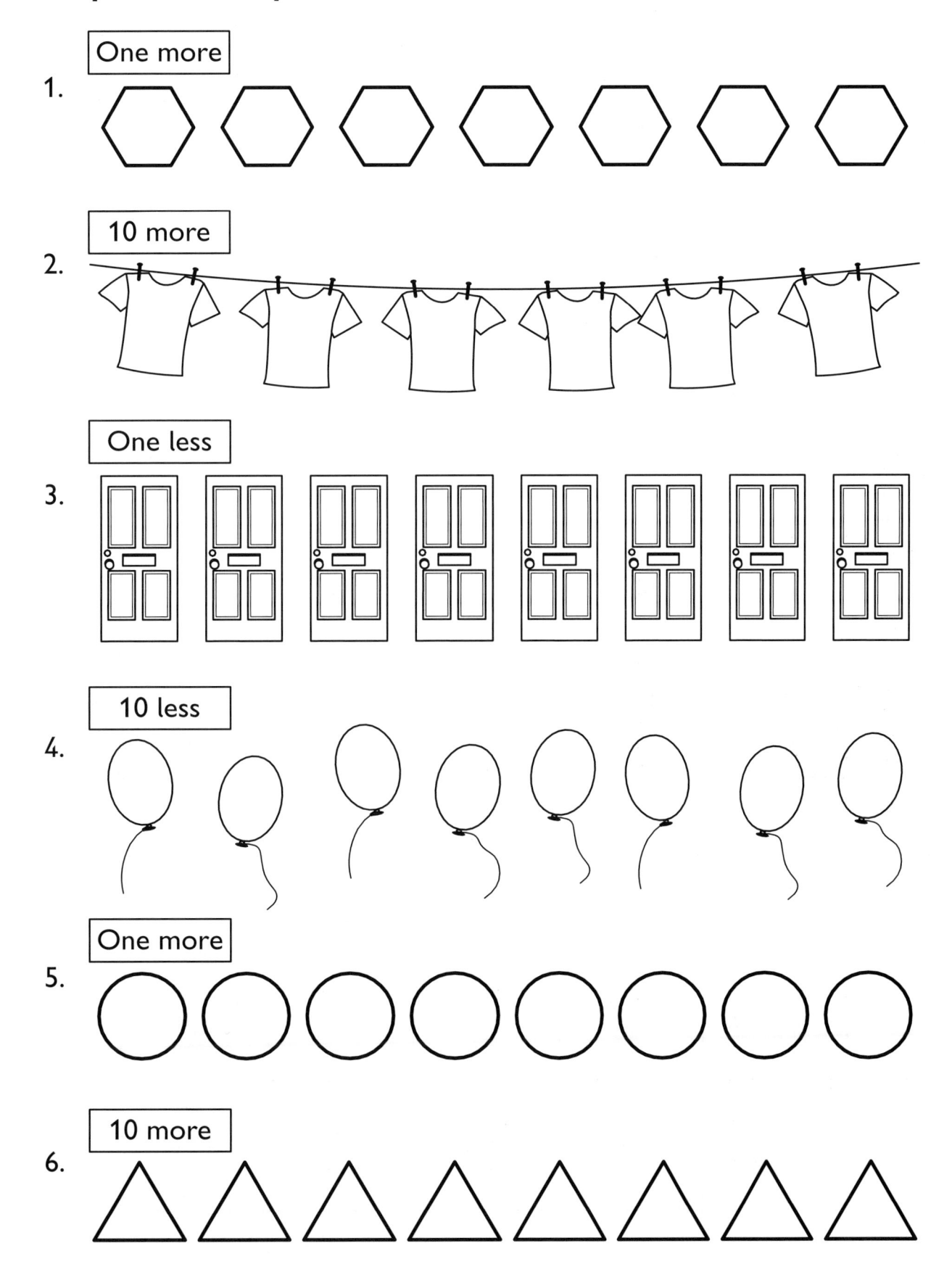

1. One more

2. 10 more

3. One less

4. 10 less

5. One more

6. 10 more

Copymaster 23

Five in a row

- Throw all 3 dice.

- Work out the answer and cover it with a counter.

- The first to get 5 in a row wins.

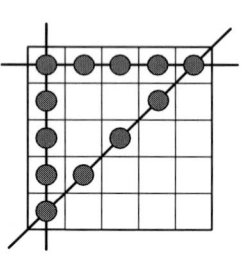

2	6	3	0	7
5	2	12	8	3
7	11	10	1	9
10	6	8	4	5
0	4	9	5	6

Domino doubles

13	6	5
9	2	11
4	12	8
10	7	3

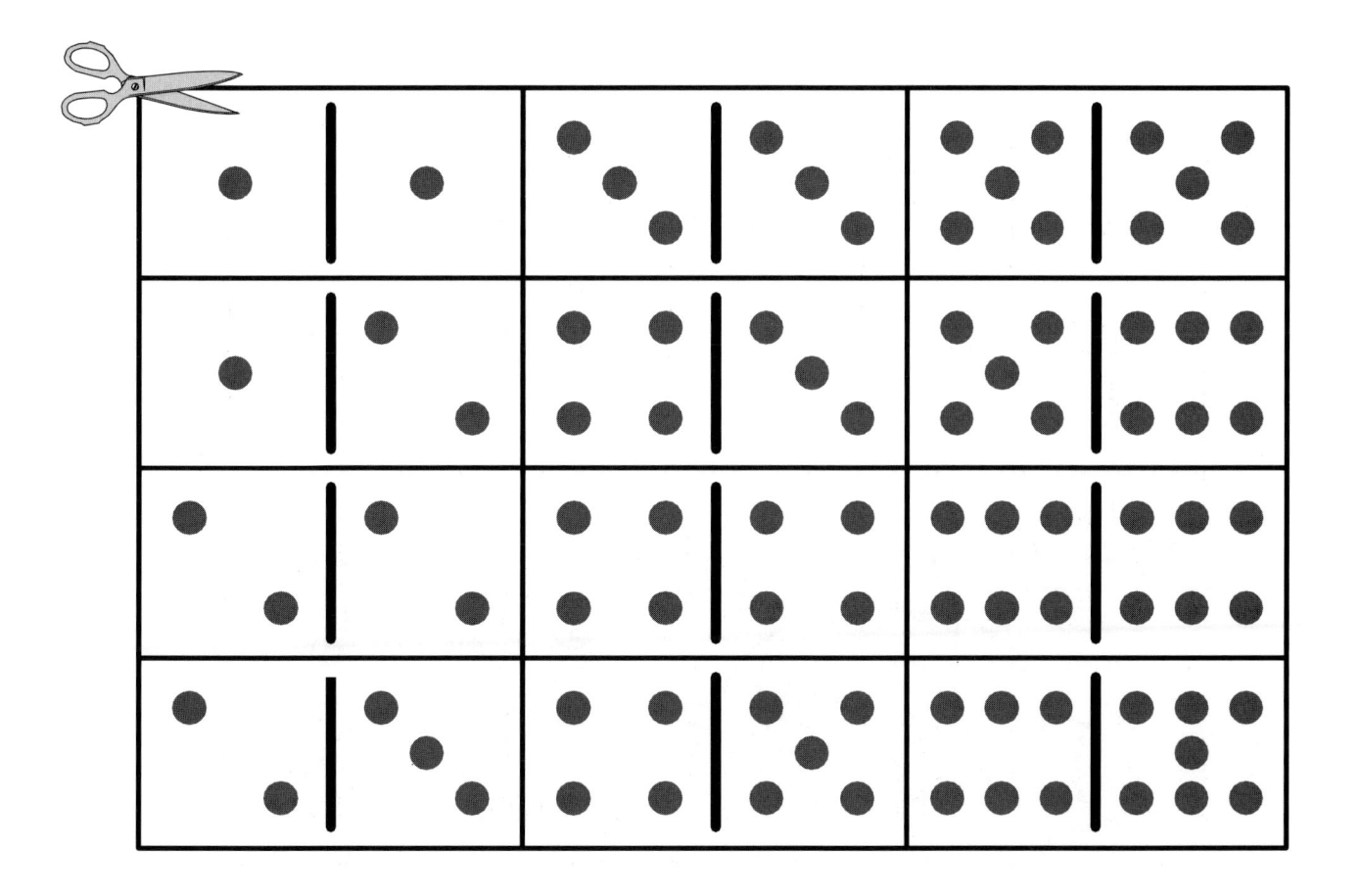

Copymaster 25

Piggy banks

Draw lines to join the piggy banks with the same totals.

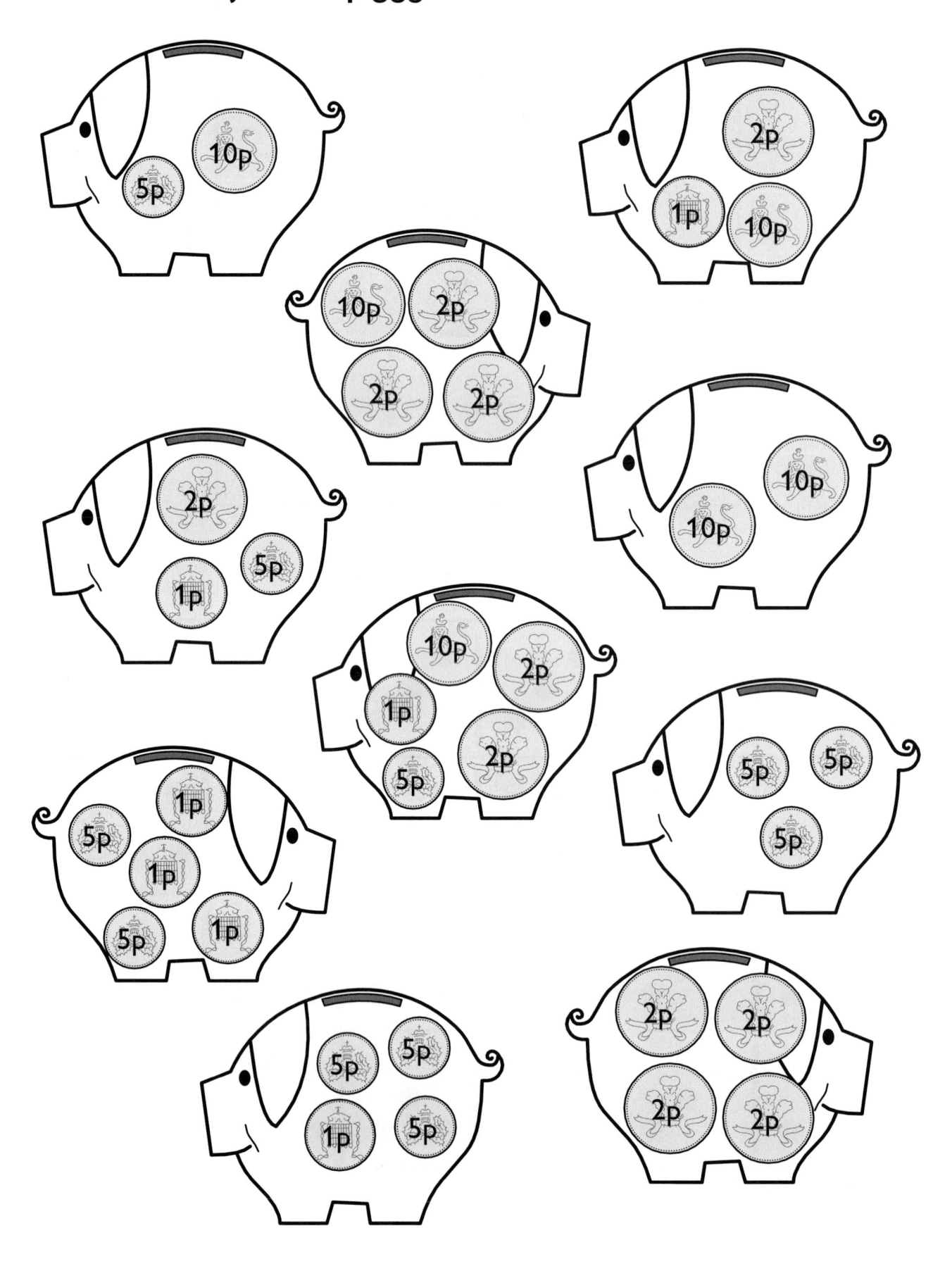

Most and least

Five children hold out the coins in their pockets.

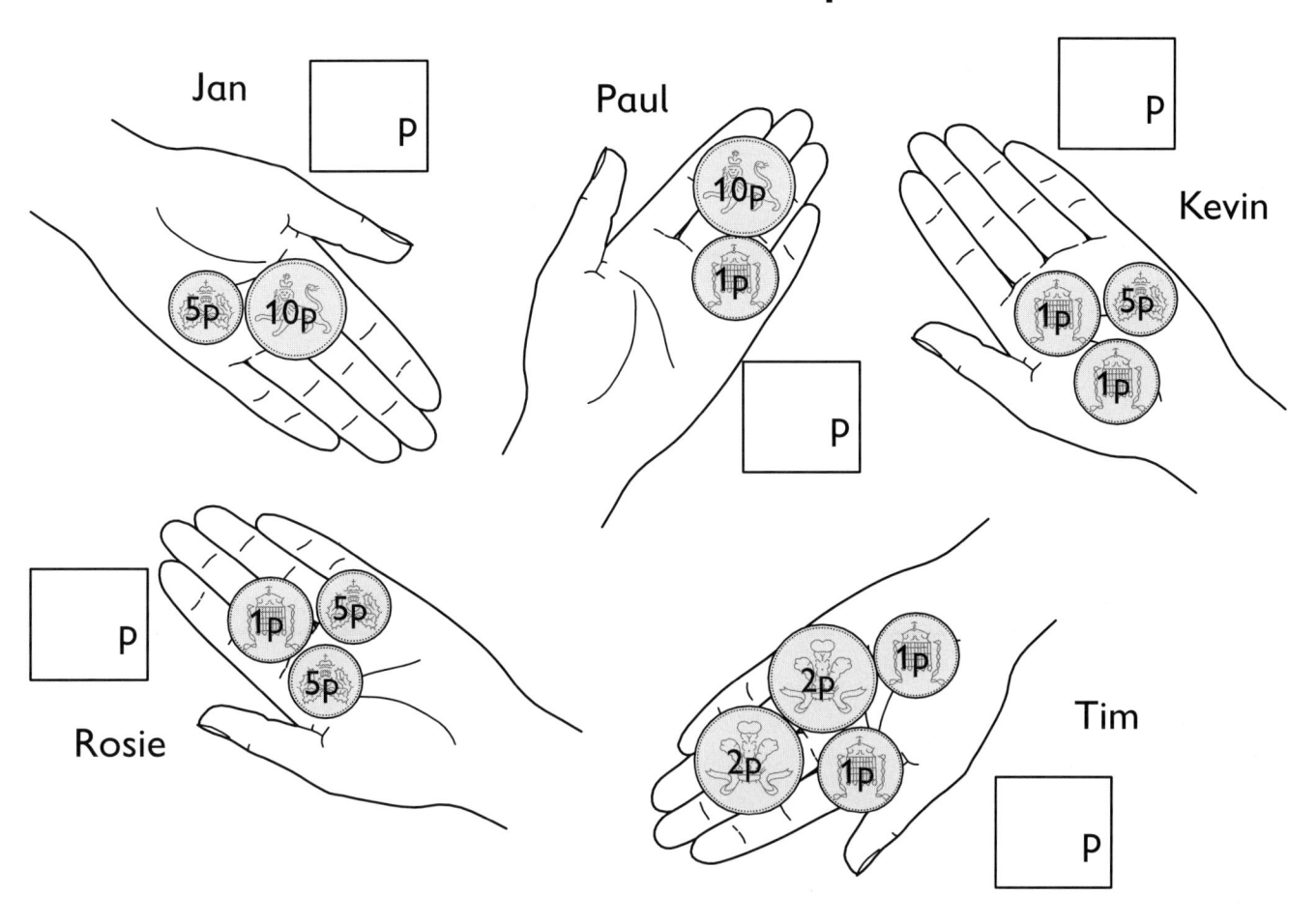

Jan ☐ p

Paul ☐ p

Kevin ☐ p

Rosie ☐ p

Tim ☐ p

Work out each child's total.

Answer these questions about each child's money.

1 How much does Paul have? _____

2 How much does Jan have? _____

3 Who has the most? _____

4 Who has the least? _____

5 Who has more than Paul? _____

6 Who has less than Rosie? _____ and _____ .

7 Who have the same? _____ and _____ .

Copymaster 27

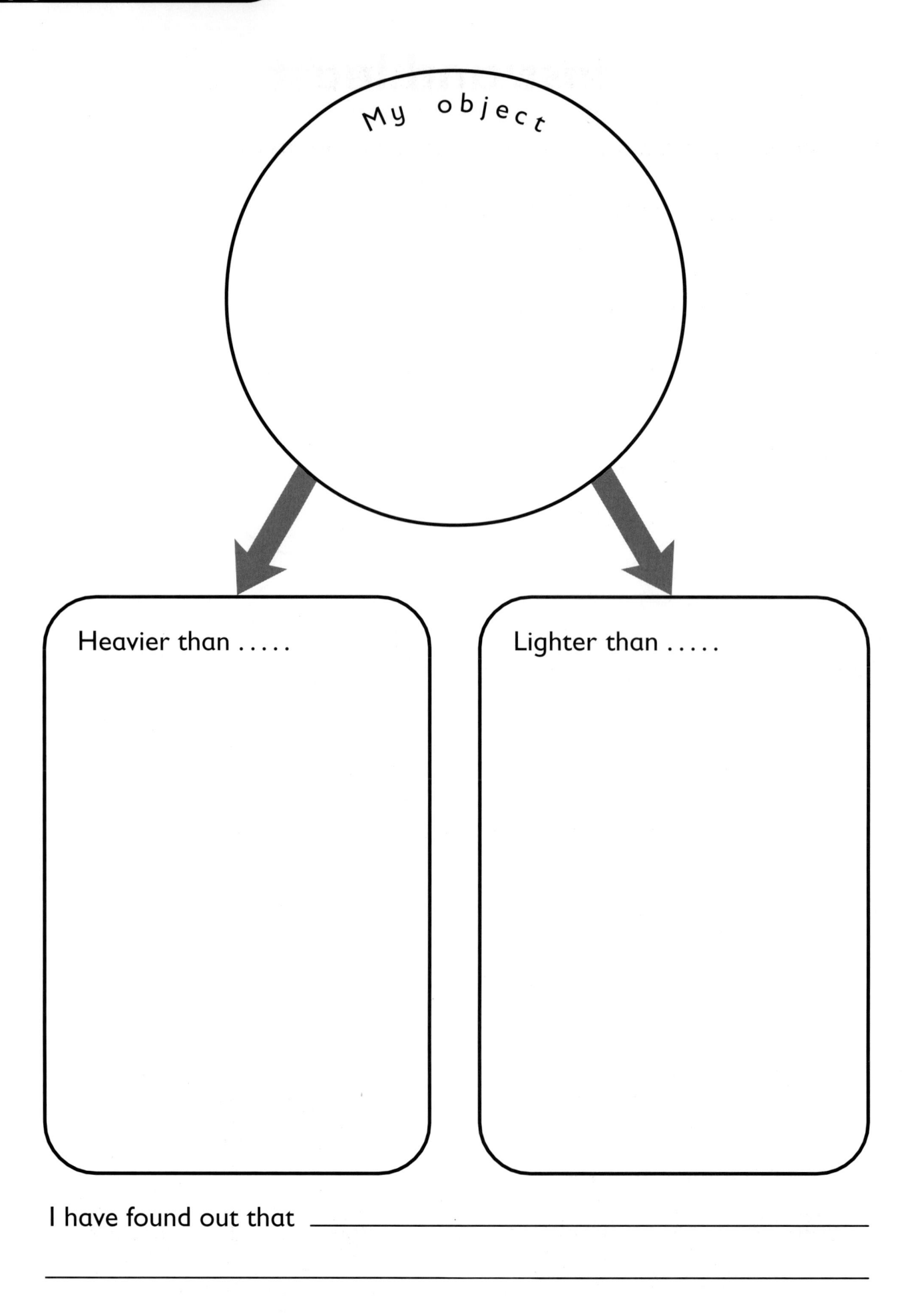

My object

Heavier than . . . . .

Lighter than . . . . .

I have found out that _____
_____

Copymaster 28

How many?

My measuring unit is _____ .

The _____ weighs the same as ☐ _____ .

My measuring unit is _____ .

The _____ weighs the same as ☐ _____ .

My measuring unit is _____ .

The _____ weighs the same as ☐ _____ .

My measuring unit is _____ .

The _____ weighs the same as ☐ _____ .

My measuring unit is _____ .

The _____ weighs the same as ☐ _____ .

My measuring unit is _____ .

The _____ weighs the same as ☐ _____ .

Copymaster 29

Maze

Draw the route through the maze to the middle ✹

Write down the instructions to get from ↑ to ✹ using the words

left   right   forwards   backwards

Copymaster 30

Objects that turn

Mark the point about which each object turns.

Mark the line about which each object turns.

Copymaster 31

Even squares

Colour in the number of squares shown.

Each time use a different colour.

▭▭▭▭▭▭▭▭▭▭▭▭▭▭▭▭▭▭▭▭	2
▭▭▭▭▭▭▭▭▭▭▭▭▭▭▭▭▭▭▭▭	4
▭▭▭▭▭▭▭▭▭▭▭▭▭▭▭▭▭▭▭▭	6
▭▭▭▭▭▭▭▭▭▭▭▭▭▭▭▭▭▭▭▭	8
▭▭▭▭▭▭▭▭▭▭▭▭▭▭▭▭▭▭▭▭	10
▭▭▭▭▭▭▭▭▭▭▭▭▭▭▭▭▭▭▭▭	12
▭▭▭▭▭▭▭▭▭▭▭▭▭▭▭▭▭▭▭▭	14
▭▭▭▭▭▭▭▭▭▭▭▭▭▭▭▭▭▭▭▭	16
▭▭▭▭▭▭▭▭▭▭▭▭▭▭▭▭▭▭▭▭	18
▭▭▭▭▭▭▭▭▭▭▭▭▭▭▭▭▭▭▭▭	20

Patterns

Fill in the missing numbers.

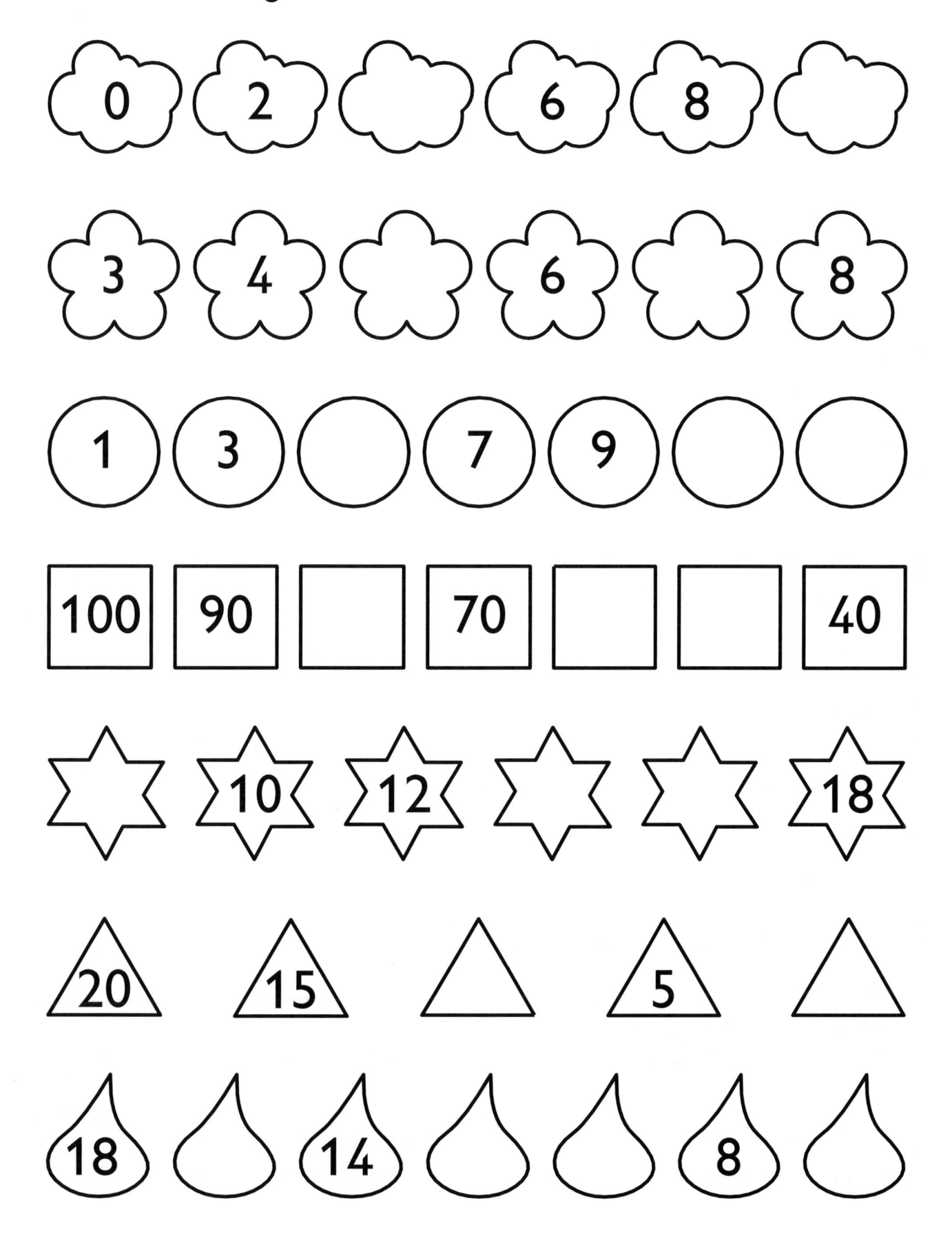

0, 2, __, 6, 8, __

3, 4, __, 6, __, 8

1, 3, __, 7, 9, __, __

100, 90, __, 70, __, __, 40

__, 10, 12, __, __, 18

20, 15, __, 5, __

18, __, 14, __, __, 8, __

Copymaster 33

More/less/the same

Use the words

| more than | less than | the same as |

to compare the prices of the items.

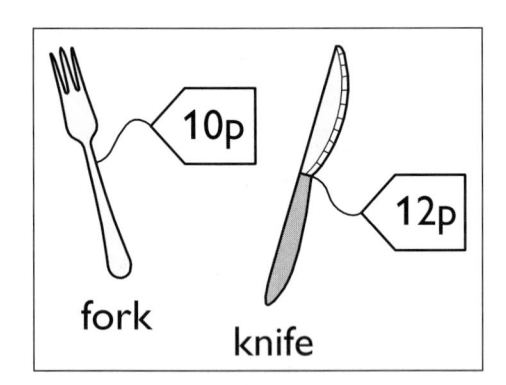

The fork costs _____ the knife.

The knife costs _____ the fork.

The bucket costs _____ the spade.

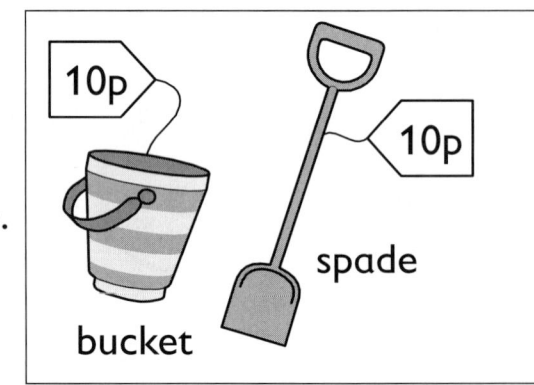

The banana costs _____ the apple.

The apple costs _____ the banana.

The bat costs _____ the ball.

The ball costs _____ the bat.

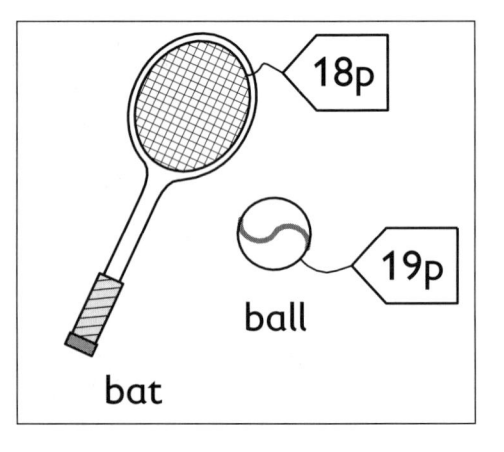

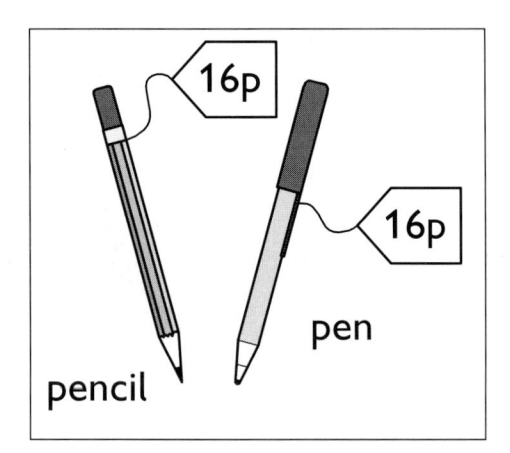

The pen costs _____ the pencil.

100

Ice cream queue

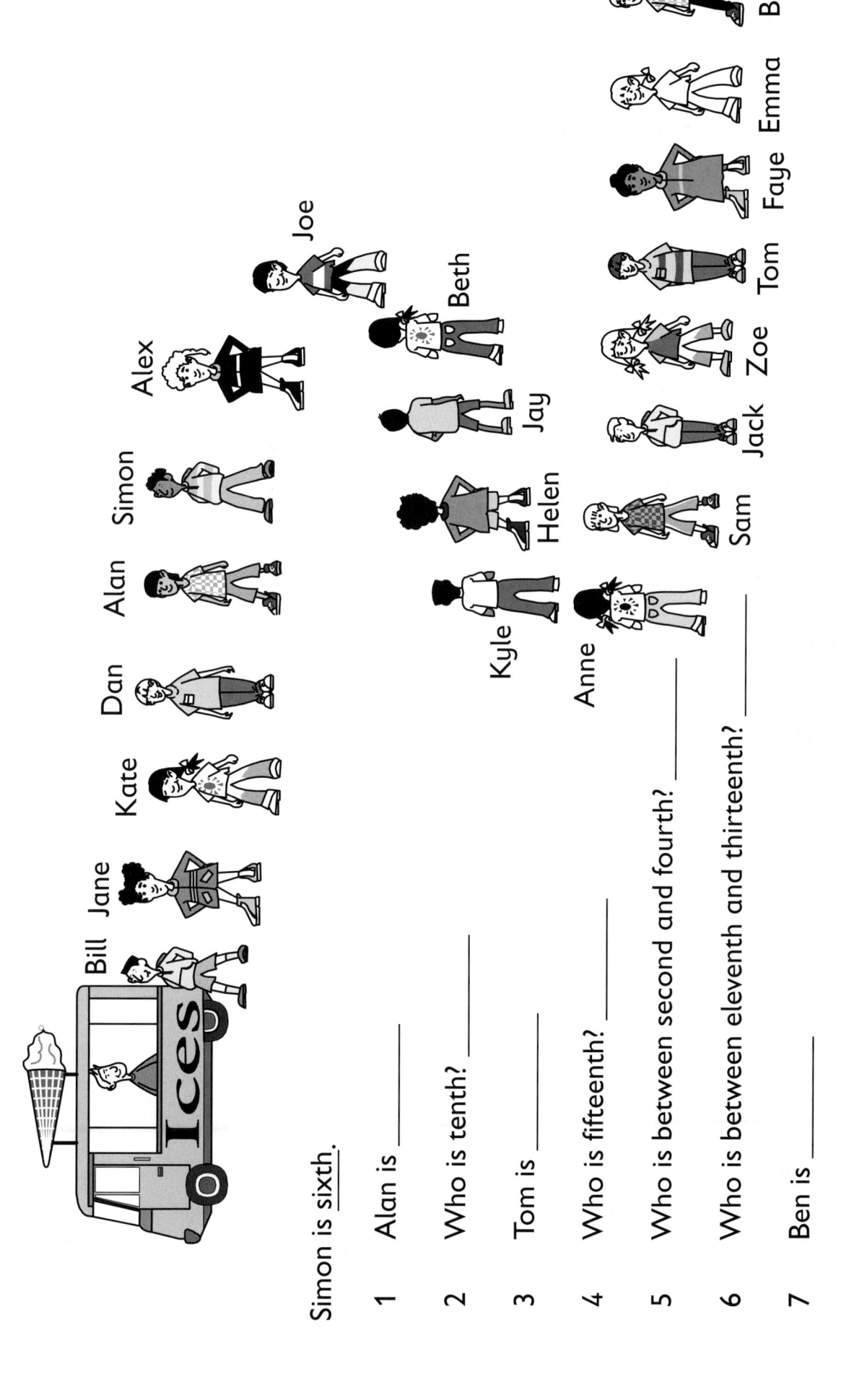

Simon is sixth.

1 Alan is _____

2 Who is tenth? _____

3 Tom is _____

4 Who is fifteenth? _____

5 Who is between second and fourth? _____

6 Who is between eleventh and thirteenth? _____

7 Ben is _____

Copymaster 34

101

Copymaster 35

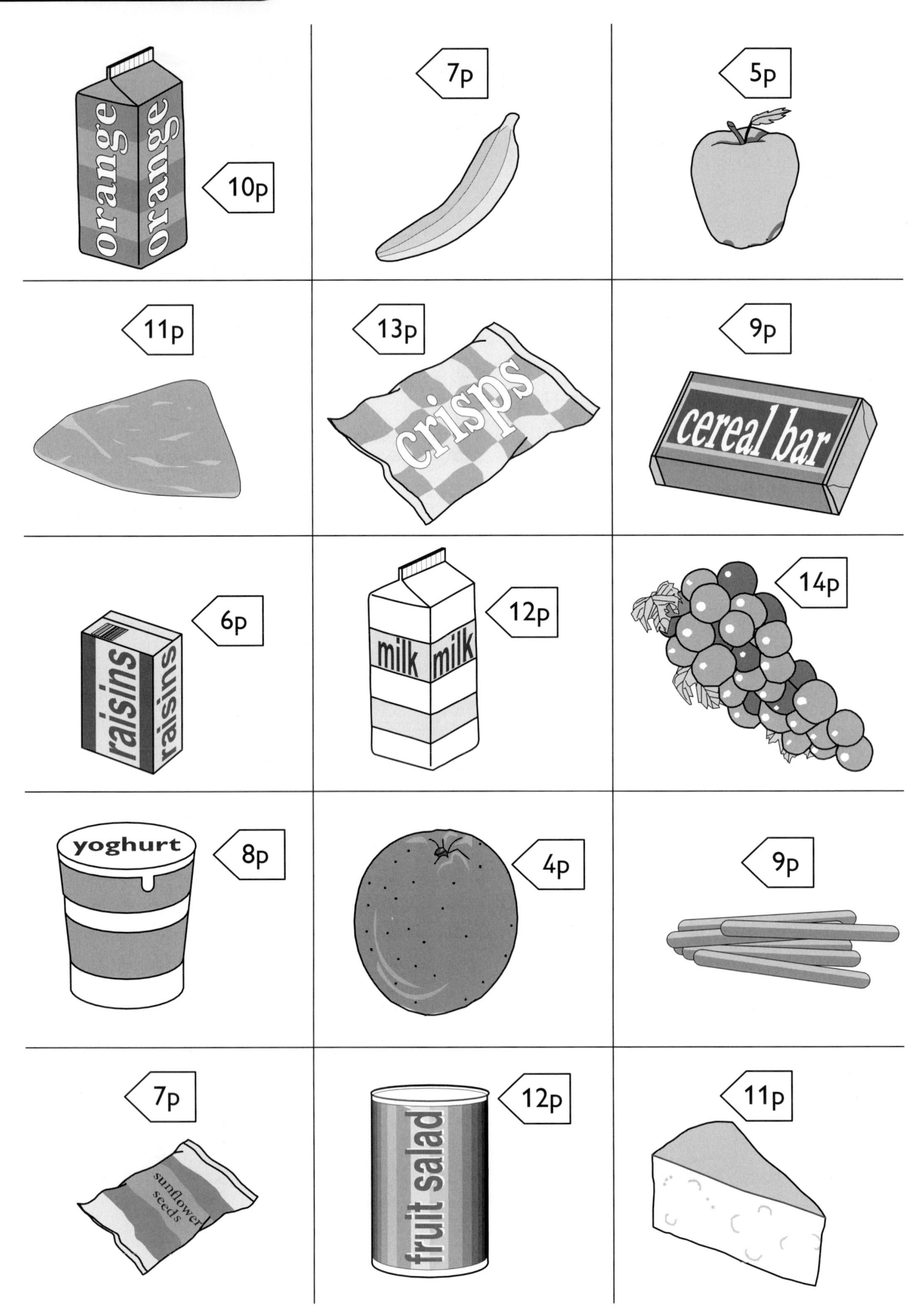

orange squash 10p	banana 7p	apple 5p
11p	crisps 13p	cereal bar 9p
raisins 6p	milk 12p	grapes 14p
yoghurt 8p	4p	9p
sunflower seeds 7p	fruit salad 12p	11p

Money problems

1. Maya spent 4p on a bouncy ball. What was her change from 10p?

2. Strawberry chews cost 3p each. How much do 2 chews cost?

3. A banana costs 7p and an apple costs 8p. How much do they cost altogether?

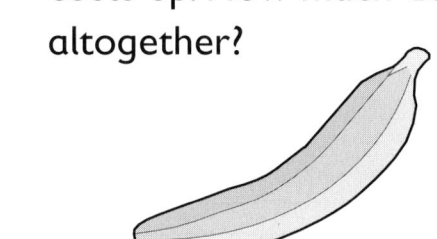

4. Parvin bought a bag of crisps with a 20p coin. He got 6p change. How much were his crisps?

5. A fizzer costs 4p. A whopper costs 3p more than a fizzer. How much does a whopper cost?

6. Sally had 20p. This is her change. How much did she spend?

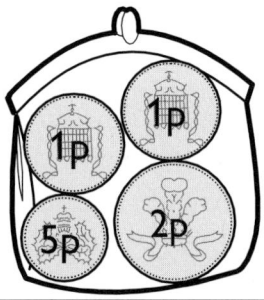

7. Anne bought a pencil for 6p and a notebook for 9p. How much change did she get from 20p?

8. Salam spent 12p. He paid with a 20p coin. What coins could he get in his change?

Copymaster 37

Seasons

- Draw a picture to show what happens in each season.
- Copy the name of the season on each card.

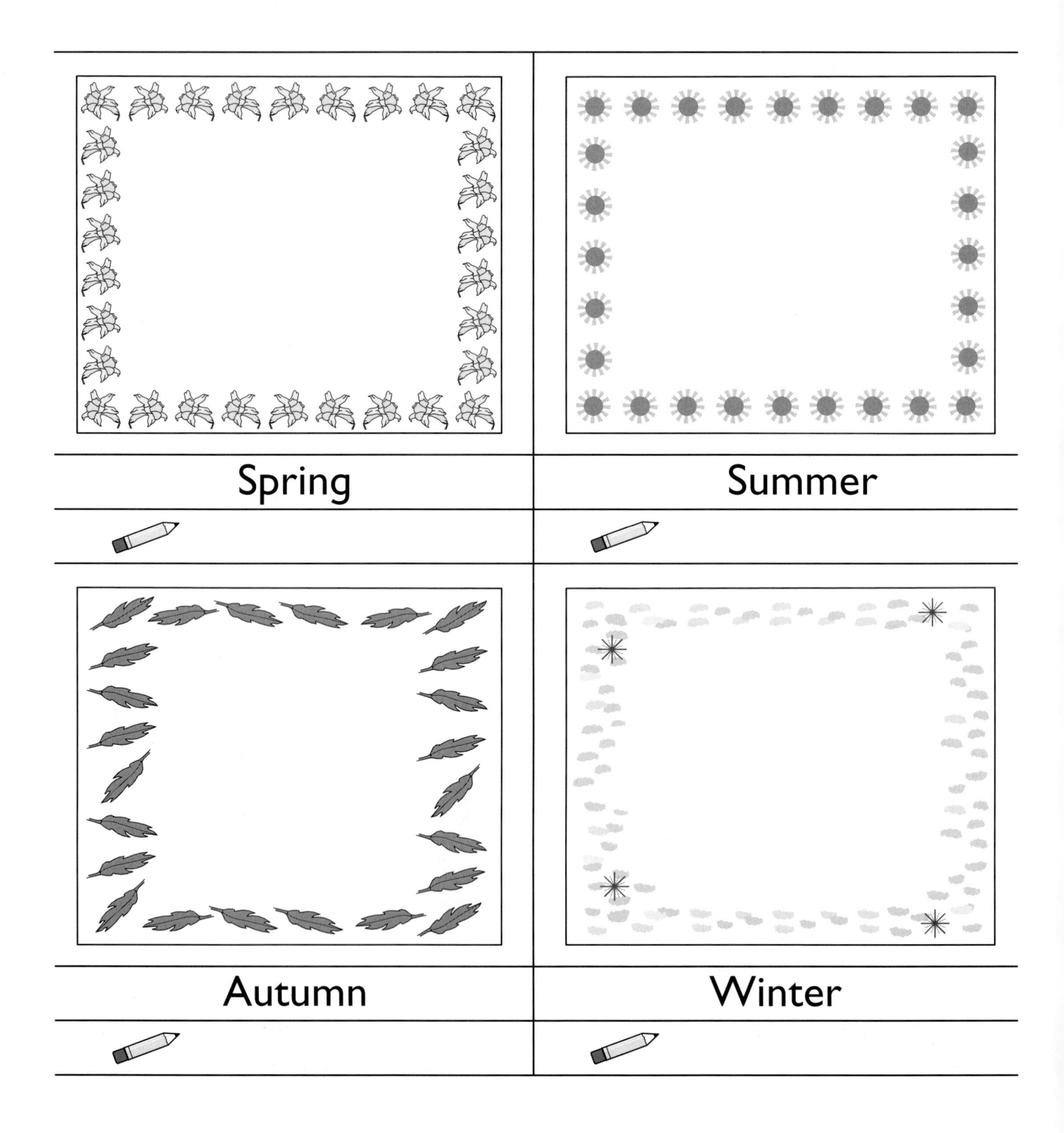

Spring

Summer

Autumn

Winter

Copymaster 38

Solving problems

1. A ball weighs the same as 10 cubes. How many cubes do 2 balls weigh the same as?

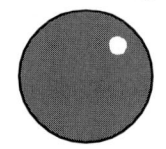

2. Which is heavier, the doll or the train?

3. 15 pebbles balance a book. If there are 12 pebbles in the balance, how many more are needed to weigh the same as the book?

4. A pair of scissors weighs the same as 6 conkers. A pen weighs the same as 4 conkers. Which object is heavier and what is the difference?

5. Wendy estimated that her maths book weighed 25 cubes. She estimated 6 cubes too many. What was the mass of her maths book?

6. Which season is the one before Winter?

7. Which season is two before Autumn?

8. 12 pegs balance a potato. 8 pegs balance a carrot. How many pegs are needed to balance a potato and a carrot together?

9. 4 cubes balance a strawberry. 2 cubes balance a cherry. How many cubes balance 2 strawberries and 2 cherries together?

10. A toy car weighs 7 conkers. A toy lorry weighs 9 conkers more than a toy car. How much does the toy lorry weigh?

Copymaster 39

Shopping list

Complete the shopping list for the items shown.

Shopping List

bananas   9p

Copymaster 40

Ladybirds

Cut out the ladybirds at the bottom of the page.

Count the spots and stick them in the correct row.

1 spot ●	
2 spots ● ●	
3 spots ● ● ●	
4 spots ● ● ● ●	

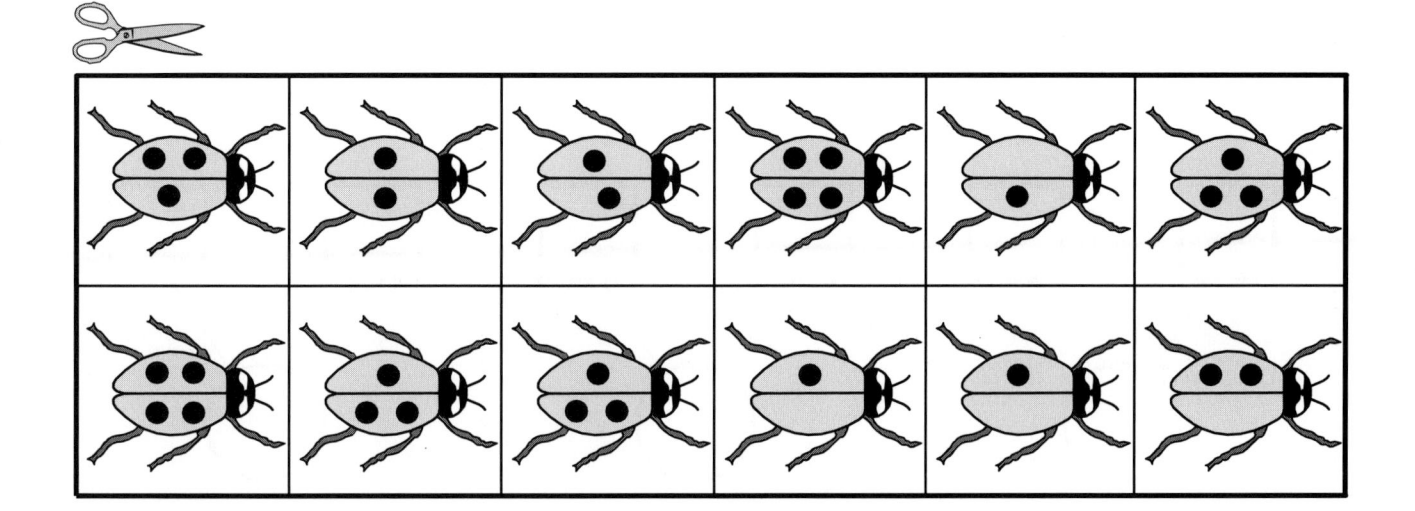

Copymaster 41

Numbers in order

- Colour the higher number blue.
- Colour the lower number red.
- Put a number that lies in between in the circle.

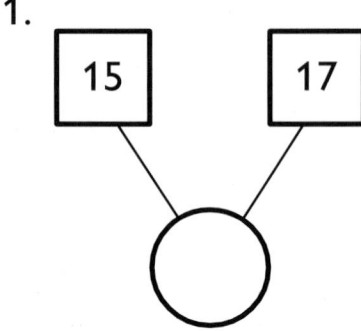

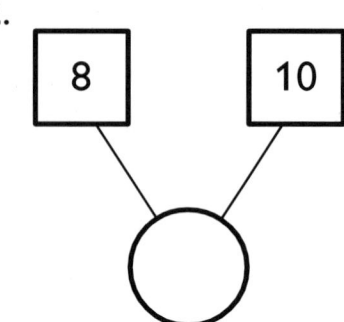

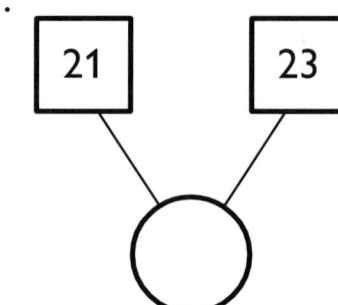

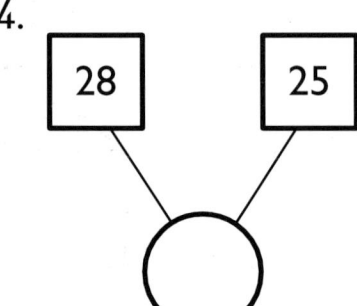

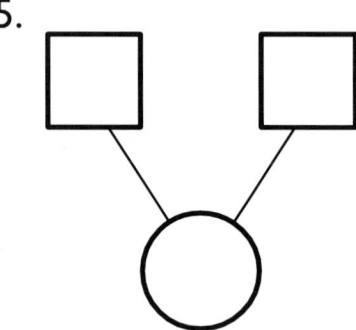

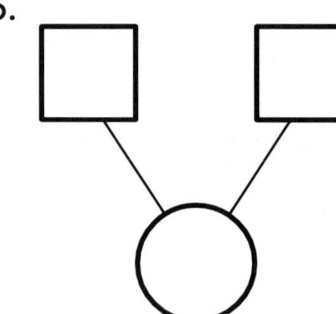

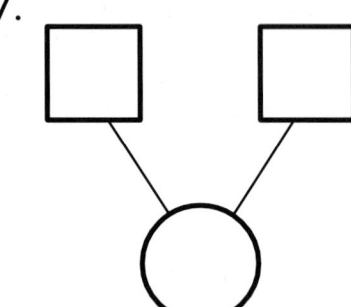

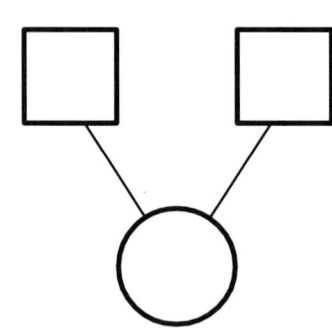

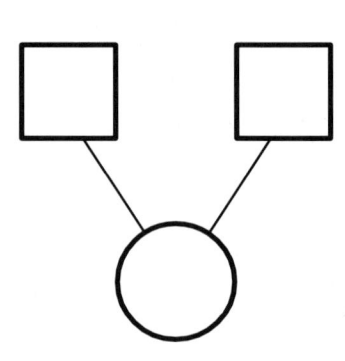

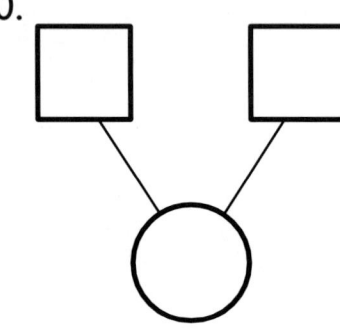

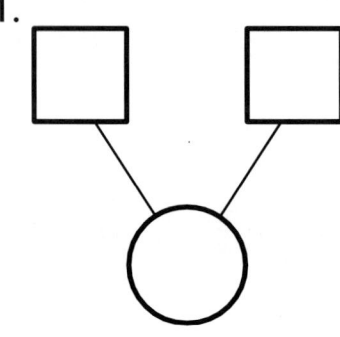

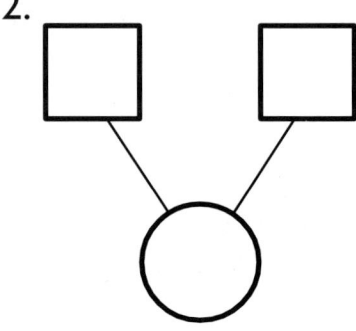

1. [15] [17] ◯

2. [8] [10] ◯

3. [21] [23] ◯

4. [28] [25] ◯

5. [ ] [ ] ◯

6. [ ] [ ] ◯

7. [ ] [ ] ◯

8. [ ] [ ] ◯

9. [ ] [ ] ◯

10. [ ] [ ] ◯

11. [ ] [ ] ◯

12. [ ] [ ] ◯

Copymaster 42

Ordering numbers

Copy out the numbers in the correct order.

1. 7 2 3 9 4 6

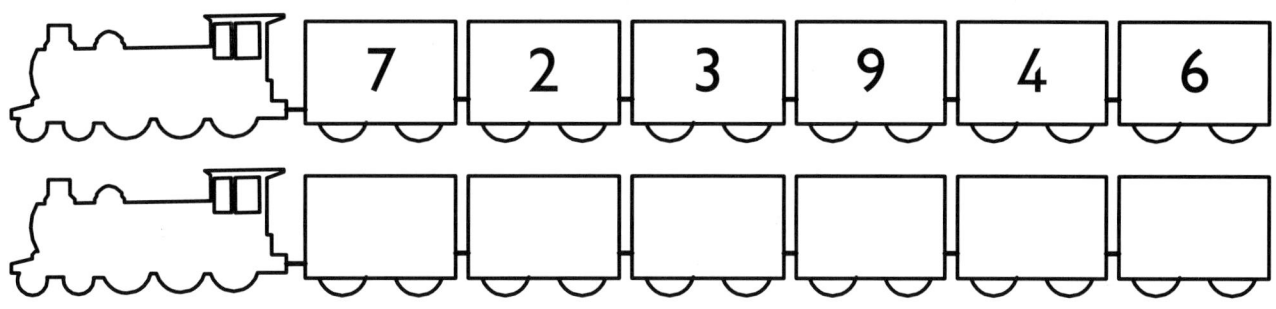

2. 17 6 15 7 12 22

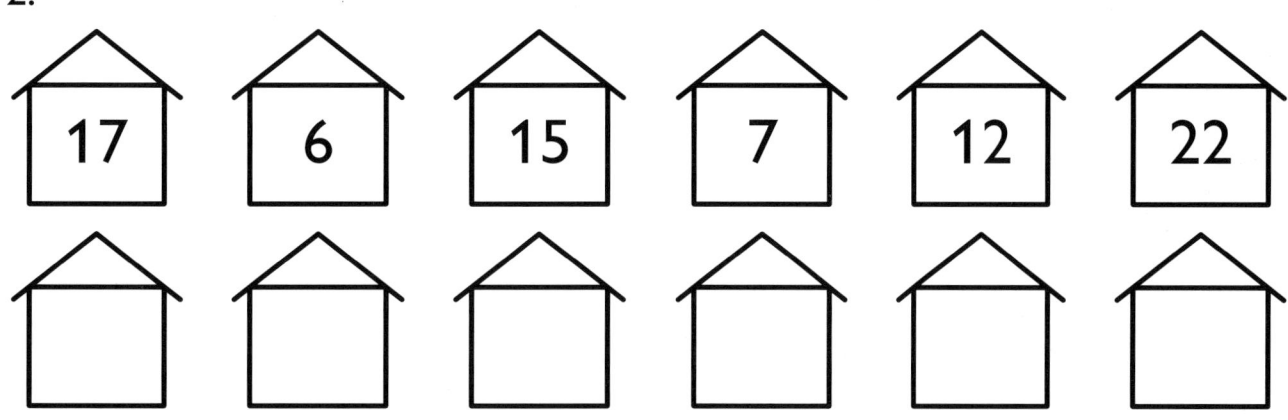

3.

4.

5.

Copymaster 43

Missing numbers

1. ⬡ ◯ ☐ = △
2. ⬡ ◯ ☐ = △
3. ⬡ ◯ ☐ = △
4. ⬡ ◯ ☐ = △
5. ⬡ ◯ ☐ = △
6. ⬡ ◯ ☐ = △
7. ⬡ ◯ ☐ = △
8. ⬡ ◯ ☐ = △
9. ⬡ ◯ ☐ = △
10. ⬡ ◯ ☐ = △

Using facts

Fill in the answers.

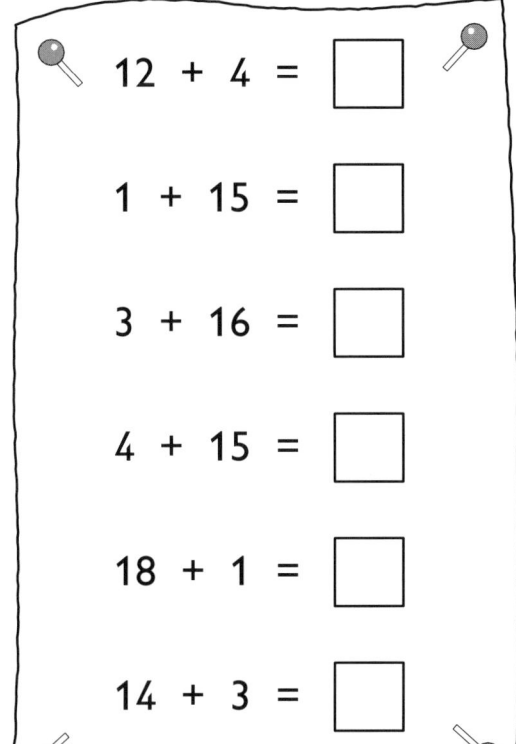

12 + 4 = ☐

1 + 15 = ☐

3 + 16 = ☐

4 + 15 = ☐

18 + 1 = ☐

14 + 3 = ☐

16 − 2 = ☐

15 − 4 = ☐

18 − 6 = ☐

12 − 1 = ☐

19 − 5 = ☐

18 − 7 = ☐

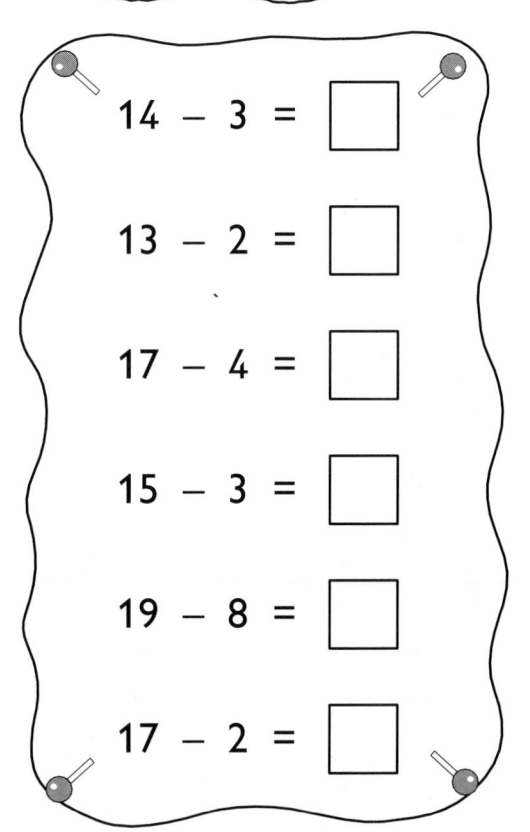

7 + 12 = ☐

0 + 16 = ☐

3 + 15 = ☐

13 + 5 = ☐

5 + 14 = ☐

11 + 8 = ☐

14 − 3 = ☐

13 − 2 = ☐

17 − 4 = ☐

15 − 3 = ☐

19 − 8 = ☐

17 − 2 = ☐

Copymaster 45

Working out change

**Colour in the coins to pay for each object.
Write the change in the box.**

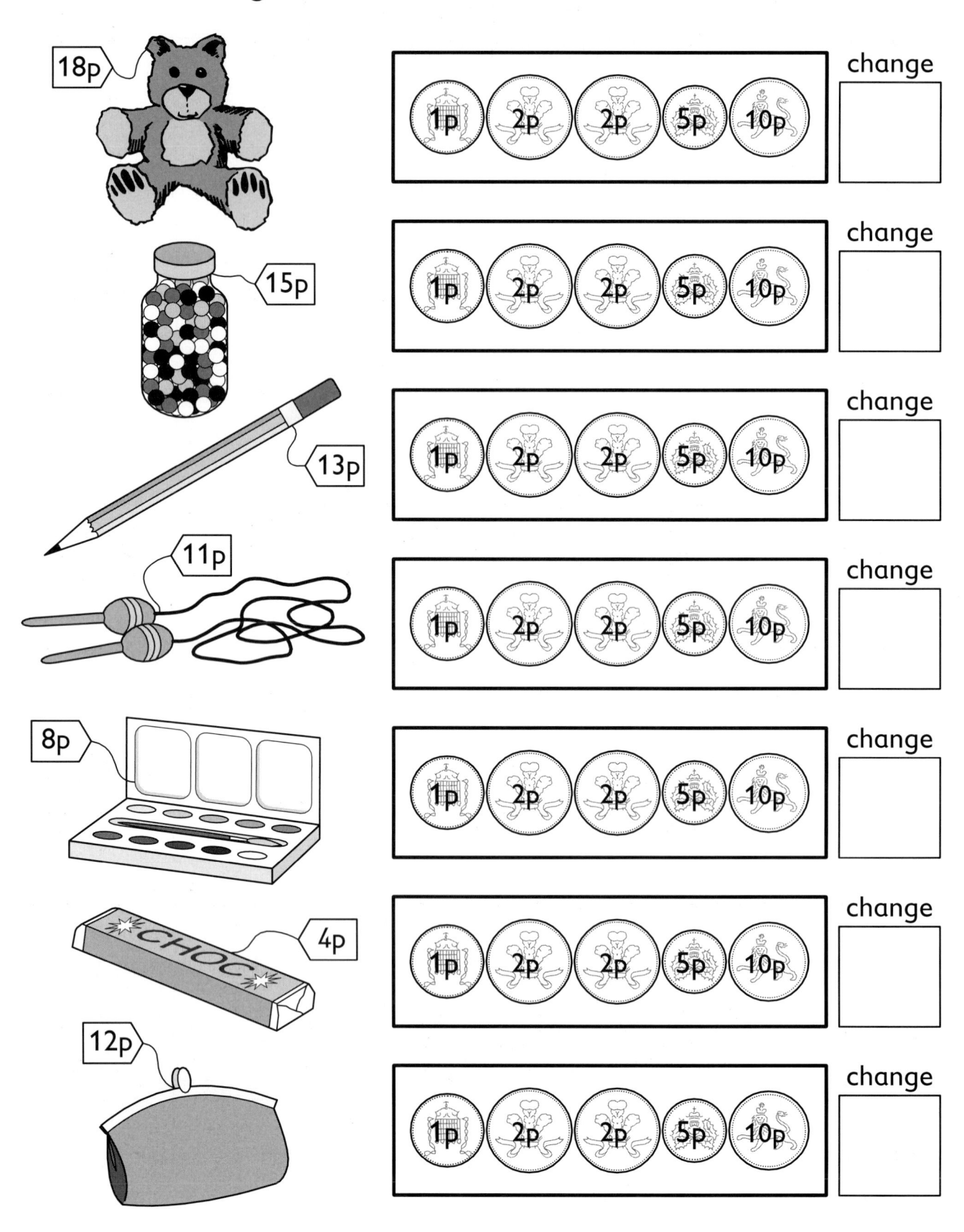

18p

| 1p | 2p | 2p | 5p | 10p | change |

15p

| 1p | 2p | 2p | 5p | 10p | change |

13p

| 1p | 2p | 2p | 5p | 10p | change |

11p

| 1p | 2p | 2p | 5p | 10p | change |

8p

| 1p | 2p | 2p | 5p | 10p | change |

4p

| 1p | 2p | 2p | 5p | 10p | change |

12p

| 1p | 2p | 2p | 5p | 10p | change |

Copymaster 46

1p	1p	1p	1p	1p
1p	1p	1p	1p	1p
2p	2p	2p	2p	2p
5p	5p	5p	5p	10p
10p	20p	50p	£1	£2

Copymaster 47

The _____ holds ☐ _____

The _____ holds ☐ _____

The _____ holds ☐ _____

The _____ holds ☐ _____

The _____ holds ☐ _____

☐ _____ fill the _____

☐ _____ fill the _____

☐ _____ fill the _____

☐ _____ fill the _____

☐ _____ fill the _____

Lots of litres

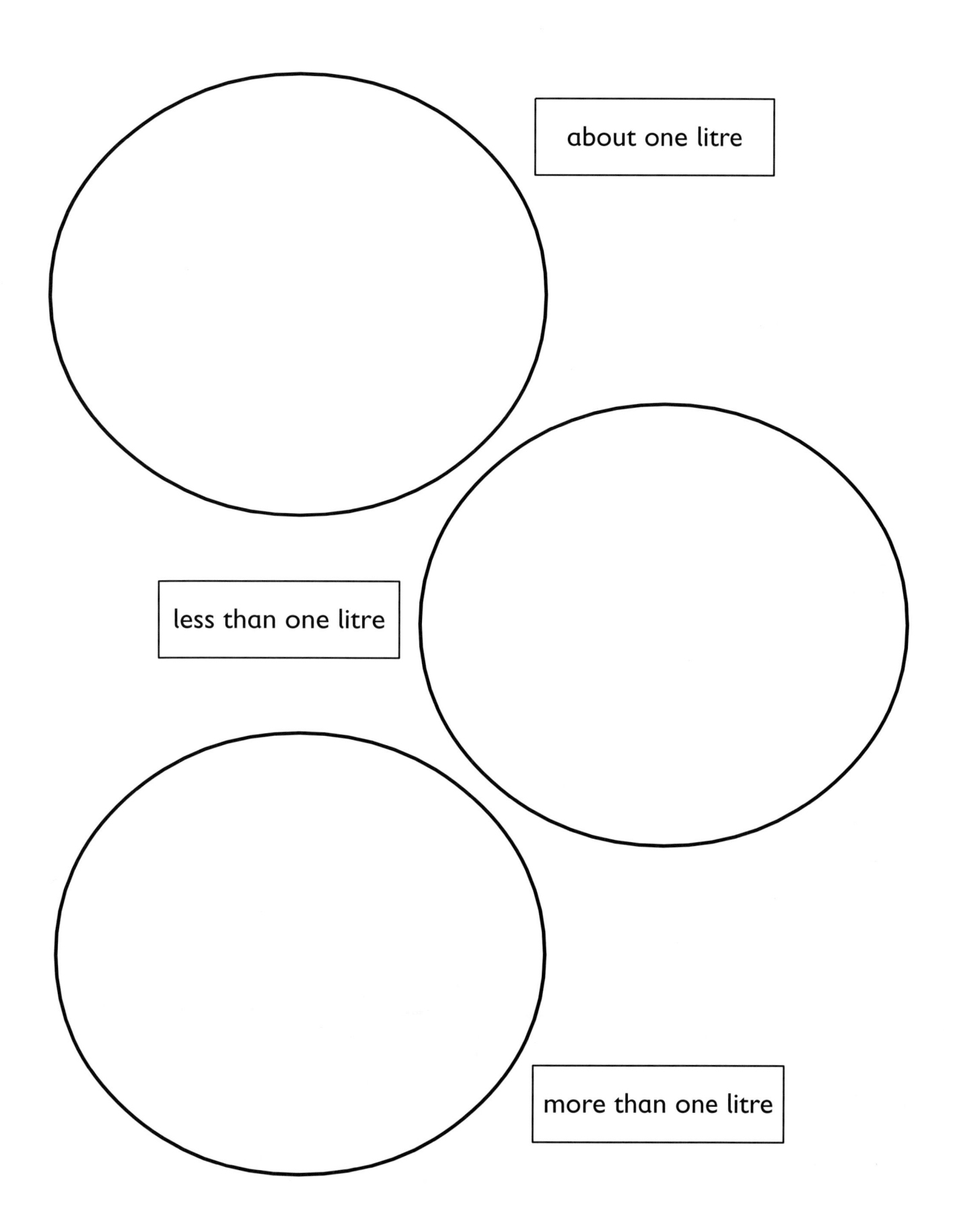

about one litre

less than one litre

more than one litre

Copymaster 49

Make these models using wooden blocks.

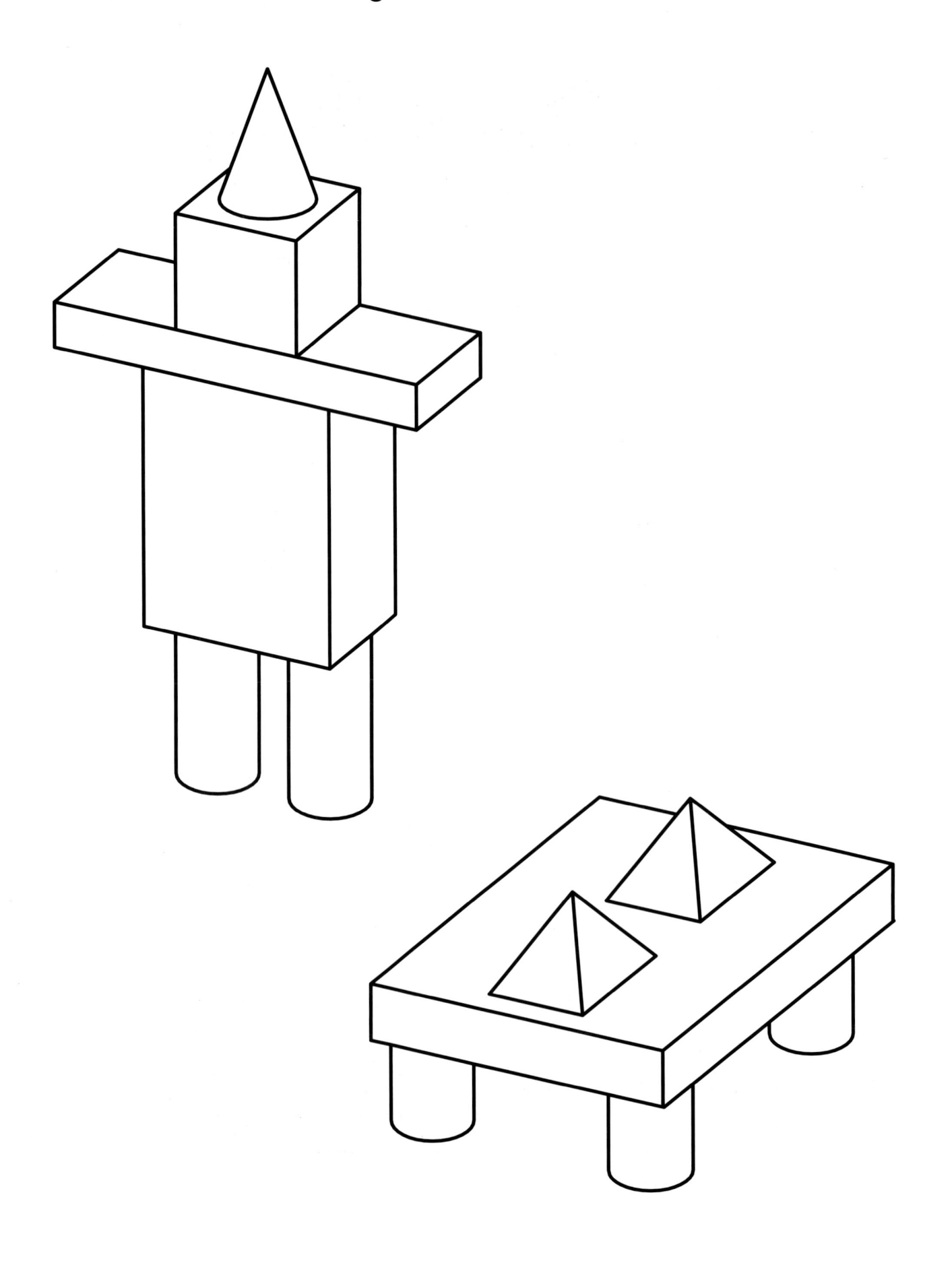

116

Make these models using wooden blocks.

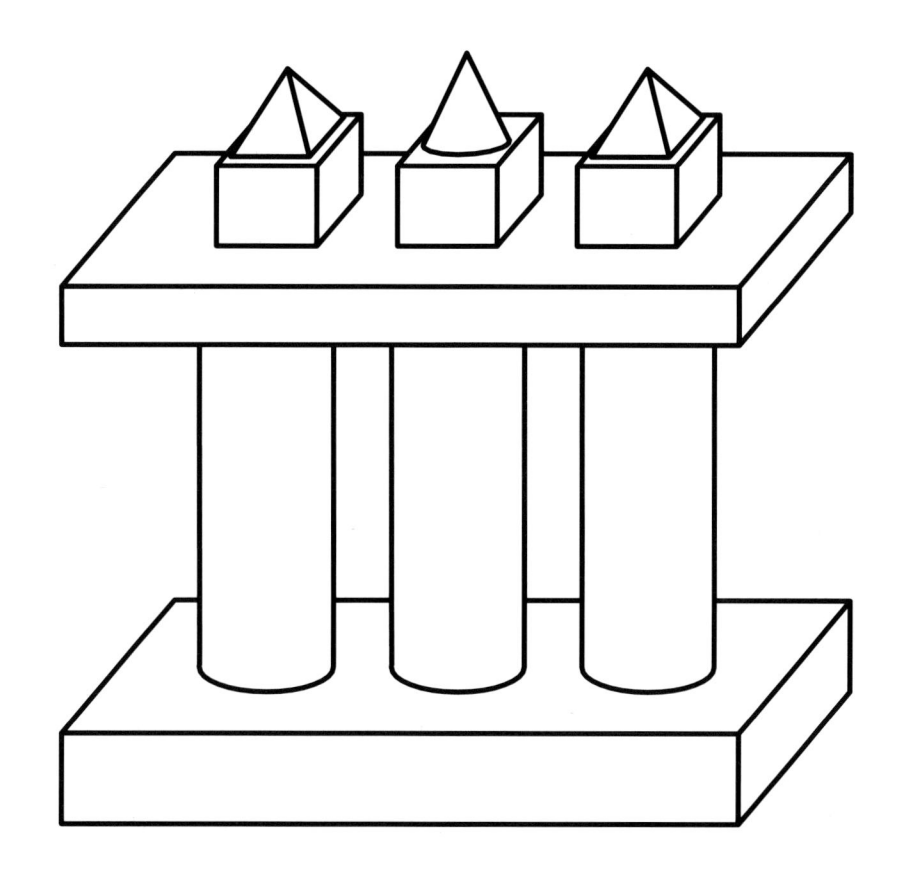

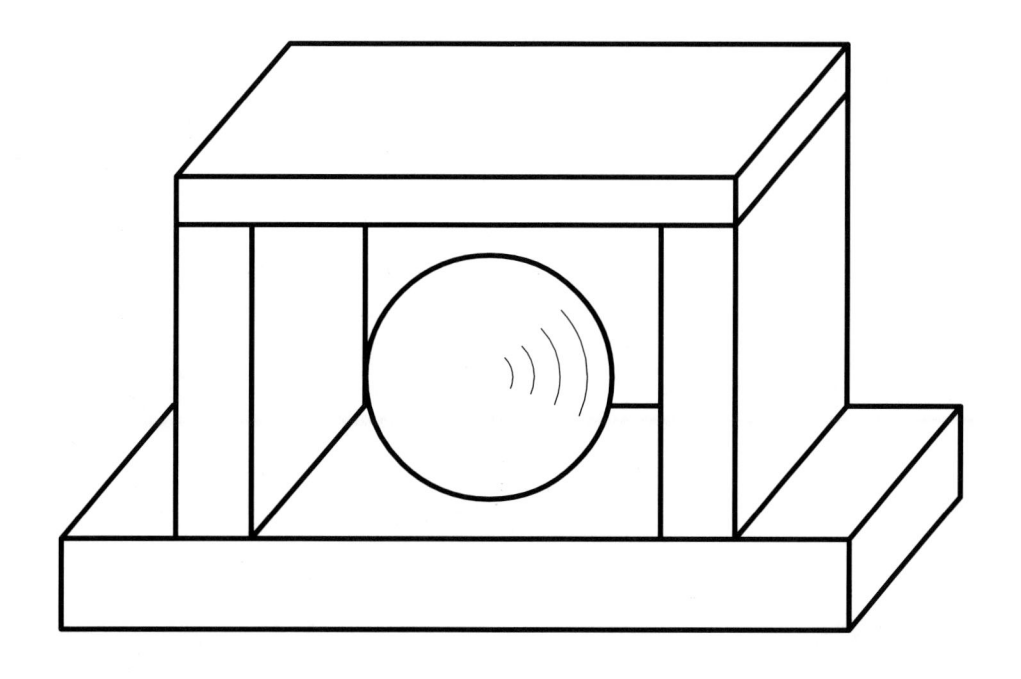

Copymaster 51

Ten more – ten less

Complete the boxes.

ten less		ten more		ten less		ten more
☐	20	☐		☐	39	☐
☐	50	☐		☐	17	☐
☐	90	☐		☐	58	☐
☐	43	☐		☐	84	☐
☐	21	☐		☐	65	☐
☐	72	☐		☐	16	☐

Making sequences

Describe the sequences.

1. 9, 10, 11, 12, 13, 14

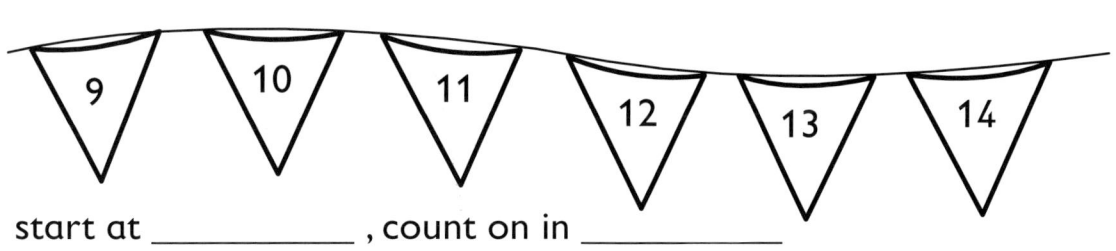

   start at _____ , count on in _____

2. 1, 3, 5, 7, 9, 11

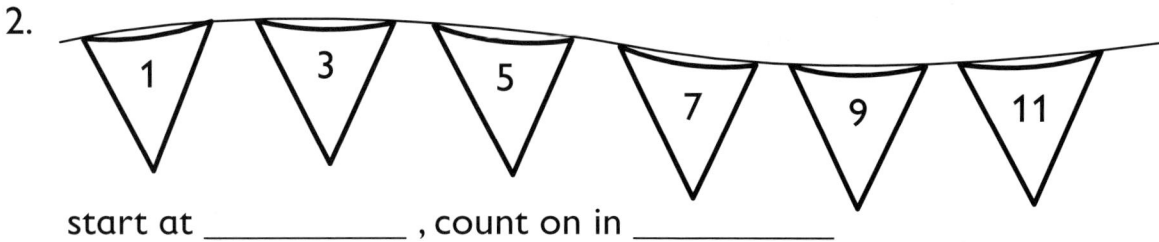

   start at _____ , count on in _____

3. 20, 15, 10, 5, 0

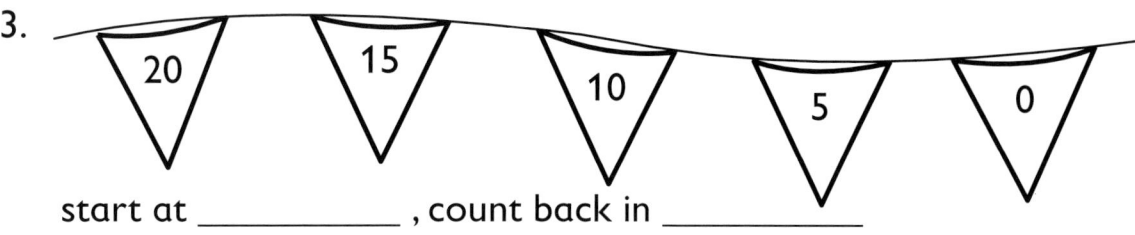

   start at _____ , count back in _____

4. 13, 23, 33, 43, 53

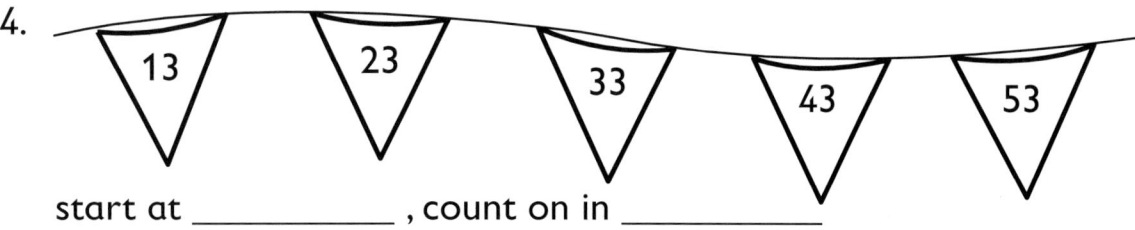

   start at _____ , count on in _____

Complete the sequences.

5. start at 8, count on in twos

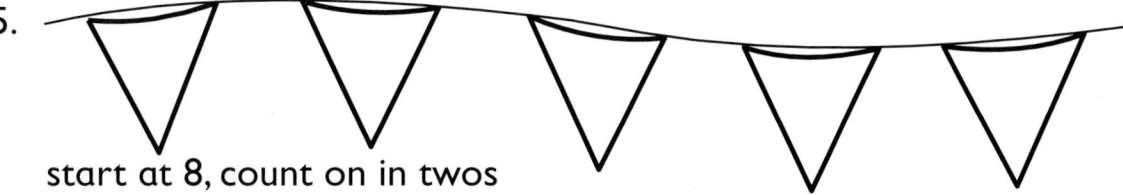

6. start at 17, count back in twos

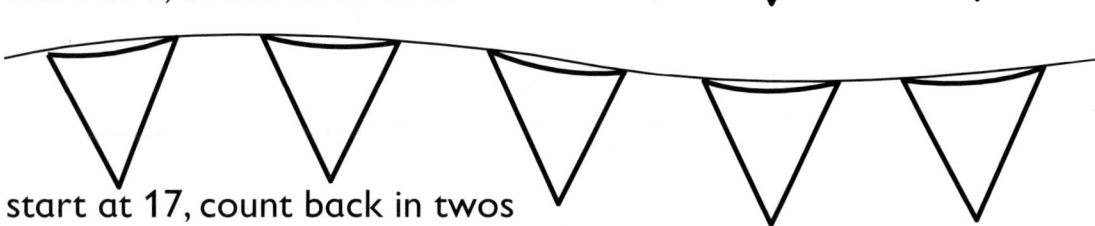

7. start at 55, count on in tens

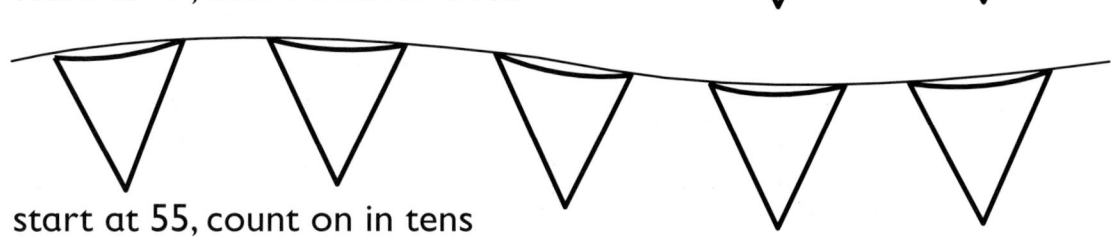

Copymaster 53

What's the missing number?

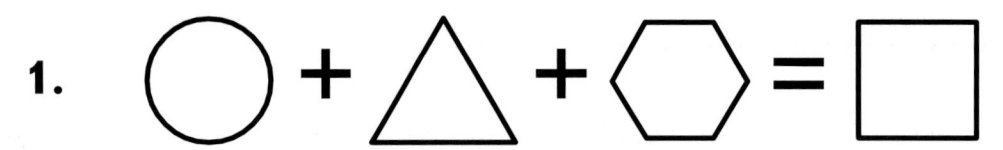

1. ◯ + △ + ⬡ = ☐
2. ◯ + △ + ⬡ = ☐
3. ◯ + △ + ⬡ = ☐
4. ◯ + △ + ⬡ = ☐
5. ◯ + △ + ⬡ = ☐
6. ◯ + △ + ⬡ = ☐
7. ◯ + △ + ⬡ = ☐
8. ◯ + △ + ⬡ = ☐
9. ◯ + △ + ⬡ = ☐
10. ◯ + △ + ⬡ = ☐
11. ◯ + △ + ⬡ = ☐
12. ◯ + △ + ⬡ = ☐

Crossing the 20 bridge

22	19	25	18
19	24	20	21
20	21	16	26
25	17	24	23

Fill in the missing numbers.

1. 17 + 8 = ☐
2. 7 + 15 = ☐
3. 6 + 15 = ☐
4. 18 + 7 = ☐
5. 6 + 16 = ☐
6. 4 + 17 = ☐

Missing numbers

Complete the number sentences.

3 + 2 = ☐

5 + 7 = ☐

7 + ☐ = 10

4 + ☐ = 12

☐ + 6 = 13

☐ + 10 = 19

6 − 3 = ☐

10 − 7 = ☐

12 − 8 = ☐

10 − ☐ = 6

11 − ☐ = 8

☐ − 6 = 4

☐ − 5 = 10

☐ − 8 = 4

☐ + 3 = 9

5 + ☐ = 10

11 + 6 = ☐

15 − 7 = ☐

8 + ☐ = 15

13 + ☐ = 15

10 − ☐ = 2

☐ + 3 = 13

Number puzzles

1. Use the digits 3 and 7 to make different 2-digit numbers.

   How many did you make? Now try with 1 and 9. How many did you make this time?

   Use the digits 2, 4 and 7 to make different 2-digit numbers.

   How many did you make?

2. How many different ways are there of scoring 7 with 2 dice?

   How many ways are there to score 5?

3. Put the numbers 1, 3, 4, 6, 7 and 9 into the circles so that each pair adds up to 10.

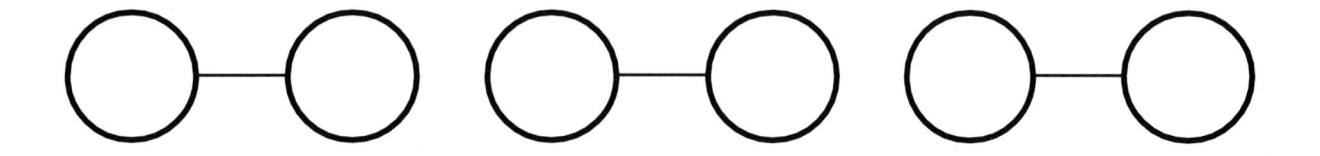

4. Put the numbers 1, 2, 3, 4, 5 and 7 into the triangles so that each set adds up to 11.

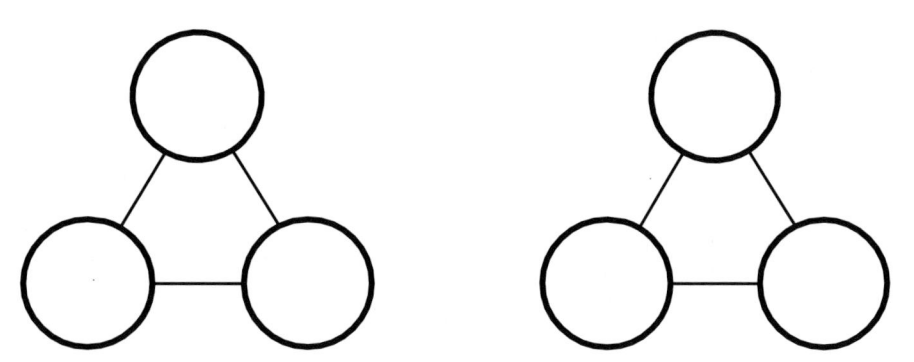

Copymaster 57

Estimating and measuring litres

Container (Draw it or write the name)	My estimate in litres	My measure in litres

- Can you find the difference between your estimate and your measure?

Capacity problems

1. A teapot holds 2 cups. How many cups do 2 teapots hold?

2. Which jug is full? ☐

   A   B   C

3. Sally's bucket holds 5 litres of water. Tom's bucket holds 3 litres of water.

   How many litres do they have altogether?

4. Match the labels to the containers.

   | empty | half full | nearly empty | full | nearly full |

5. A bottle of pop holds 6 glasses. How many bottles of pop are needed to fill 12 glasses?

6. Peter's watering can holds 10 litres.
   He has put 3 litres of water in.
   How many more litres are needed to fill it?

Copymaster 59

Earlier or later

Draw the clock hands to show times half an hour earlier and later.

half an hour earlier

The school day

Cut out the pictures and arrange them in order.

event   time

Homework 1

> This week we are learning to write the numbers from 1 to 10.

Tracing numbers

- Write a number on someone's back.
  Do it very carefully, starting at the top.
  Do they know what number you are writing?

- Ask them to write a number on your back.
  Can you guess what it is?

Homework 2

This week we are learning to understand the operations of addition and subtraction and using the appropriate vocabulary.

Number stories

- Ask someone to help you write a number story for these two sentences. Draw a picture for each one.

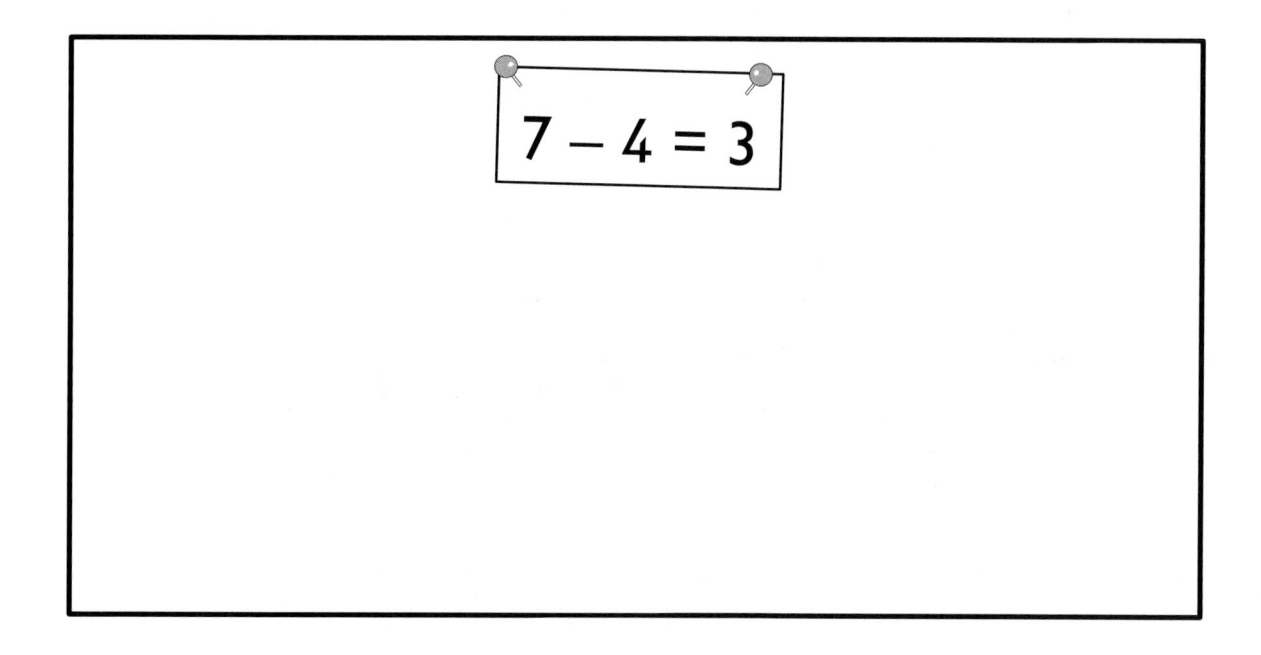

3 + 2 = 5

7 − 4 = 3

Homework 3

> This week we are finding totals up to 10p using 1p and 2p coins.

Buying fruit

Colour in the coins you would use to buy each piece of fruit.

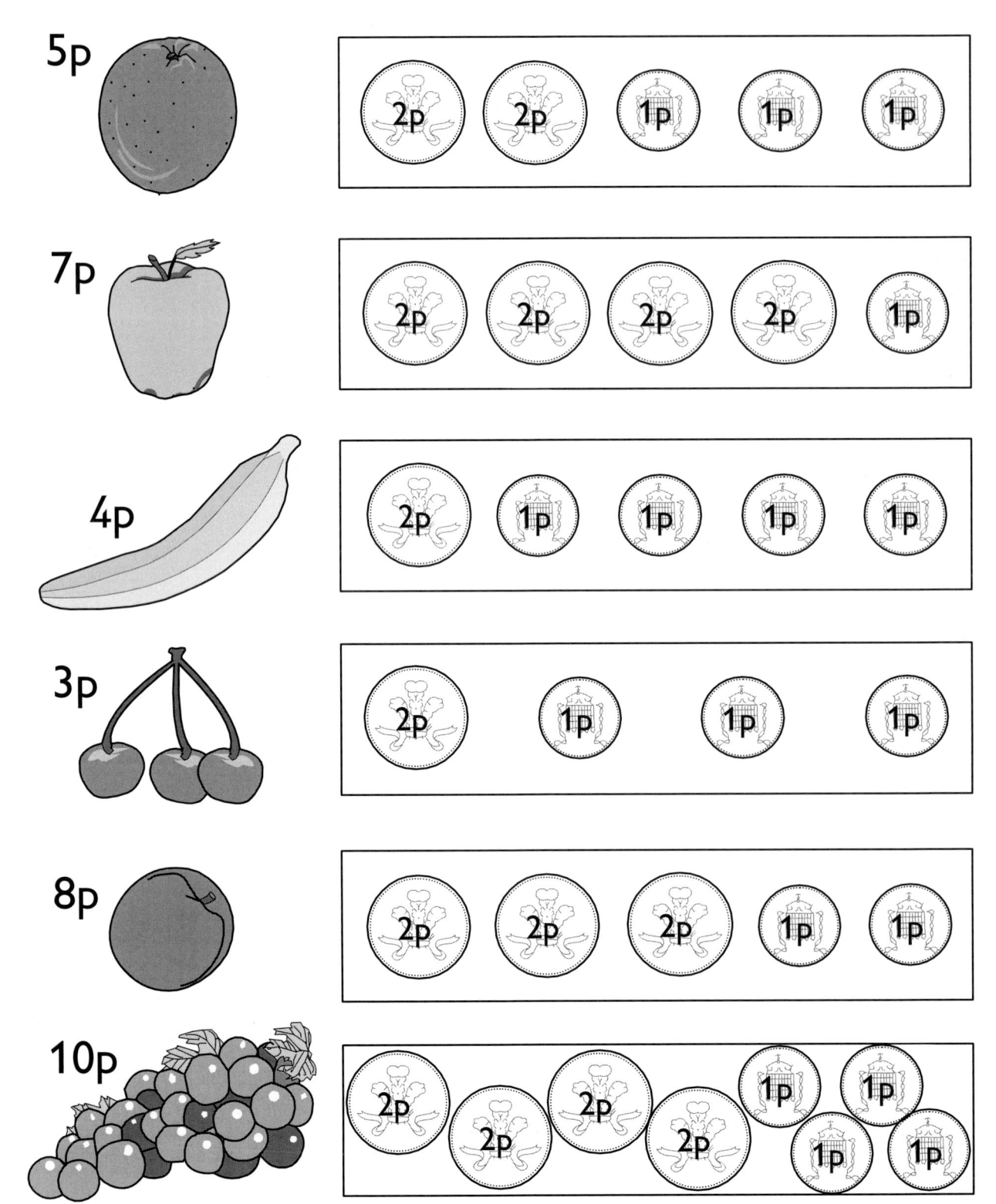

5p — 2p, 2p, 1p, 1p, 1p

7p — 2p, 2p, 2p, 2p, 1p

4p — 2p, 1p, 1p, 1p, 1p

3p — 2p, 1p, 1p, 1p

8p — 2p, 2p, 2p, 1p, 1p

10p — 2p, 2p, 2p, 2p, 1p, 1p, 1p, 1p

Homework 4

> This week we are comparing lengths of objects.

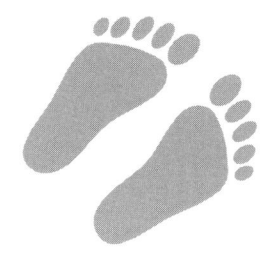

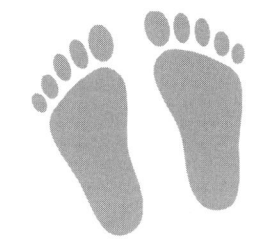

Find your feet

- Draw round your foot onto a piece of paper and carefully cut it out.

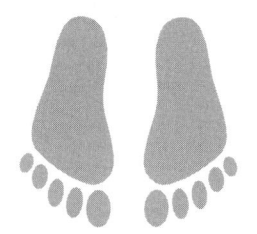

- Find two other people and ask if you can draw round their feet and cut them out.

- Put the feet in order of size, starting with the smallest.

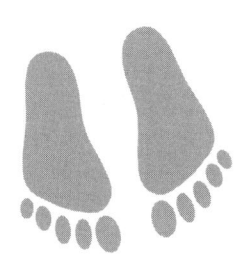

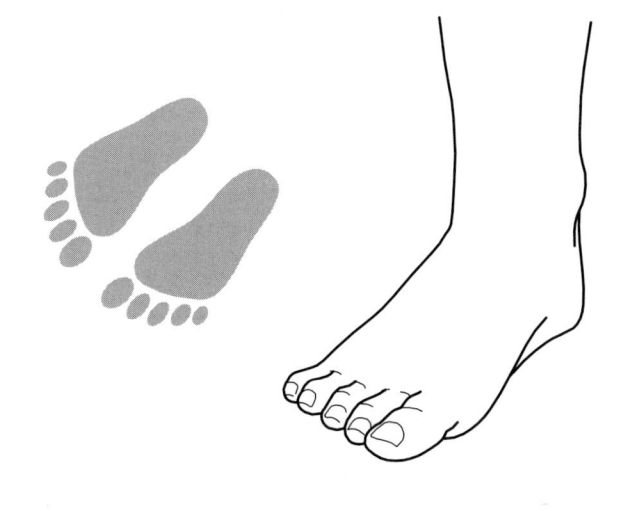

Homework 5

Sorting shapes

Draw the shapes in their correct boxes.

This week we are recognising the features of 2D shapes.

triangles

shapes with curved sides

shapes with 4 sides

Homework 6

Counting

This week we are counting up to 20.

Find some objects which are the same and count them.

Example

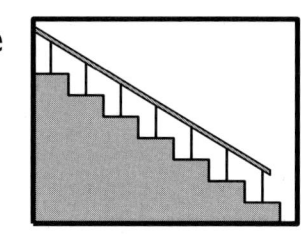

7 steps

Other objects could be books, videos, chairs, milk bottles, windows.

Picture

133

Homework 7

> This week we are learning about ordering numbers including recognising first, second, third etc. up to tenth.

Toy order

- Cut out the cards and make a row of ten toys.
- Place the cards by the toys.

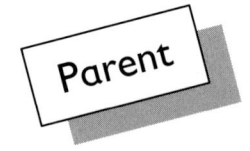

Parent

Ask your child questions about the order of the toys

e.g. Which toy is fourth? What toy is after the sixth toy? Which toy is last?

Change the order of the toys or remove one and ask 'Which toy is missing?' e.g. *the third one.*

1st	2nd	3rd	4th	5th
6th	7th	8th	9th	10th
first	second	third	fourth	fifth
sixth	seventh	eighth	ninth	tenth

134

Homework 8

> This week we have been learning about subtraction as the difference between two numbers.

Name differences

- Write down your name and count the number of letters.

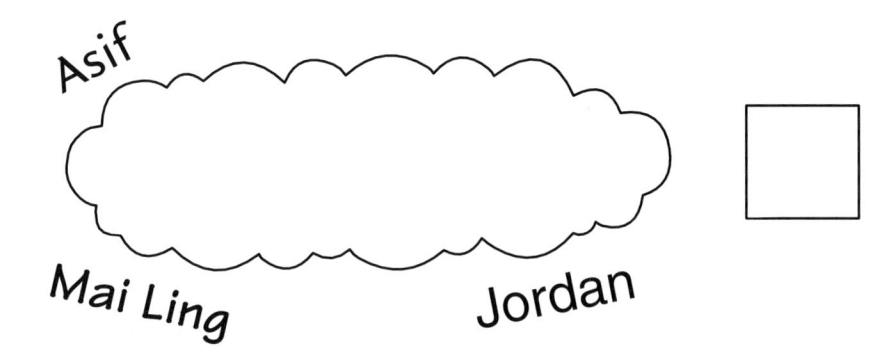

Asif *Jordan* *Mai Ling*

- Ask someone in your house to write down their name. Count the number of letters.

Tom *Joanne* *Christopher*

- Find the difference between the number of letters in your names.

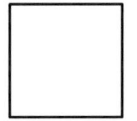

Try it using surnames as well and ask some different people.

135

Homework 9

> This week we are estimating and measuring using a one metre measure.

Family heights

- Use your metre measure to find out which people and animals are less than one metre tall,
  about one metre tall,
  more than 1 metre tall.

- Write their names or draw them in the boxes below.

| less than one metre | about one metre | more than one metre |

- Don't forget to bring your metre measure back to school.

Homework 10

> This week we are reading time to an hour on clocks.

Telling times

For each clock write the time in words.

Write down what you were doing at that time one evening.

_____ four o'clock _____

_____ o'clock _____

Homework 11

> This week we are looking at two-digit numbers and learning what each digit stands for.

On the way home

- On your way to or from school look for some two-digit numbers.
- Write some of them down and show what each digit stands for.

50　42　68　83　28　30　R84 MSC　Y36 BFD

number	where I found my number	tens	ones

Homework 12

> This week we have been identifying near doubles using doubles already known.

Know your doubles

Play this game with someone at home.

- Sit back to back and write down a number between 1 and 6. (Don't show the other person.)
- Double the number in your head and say the double to your partner.
- They halve the number and tell you the answer.
- Swap over and play a few times.
- You score one point for each correct answer.

3 + 3 = 6

6 + 6 = 12

1 + 1 = 2

4 + 4 = 8

2 + 2 = 4

5 + 5 = 10

Homework 13

This week we are finding totals using 1p, 2p, 5p and 10p coins.

Money totals

Colour in the coins to match the totals.

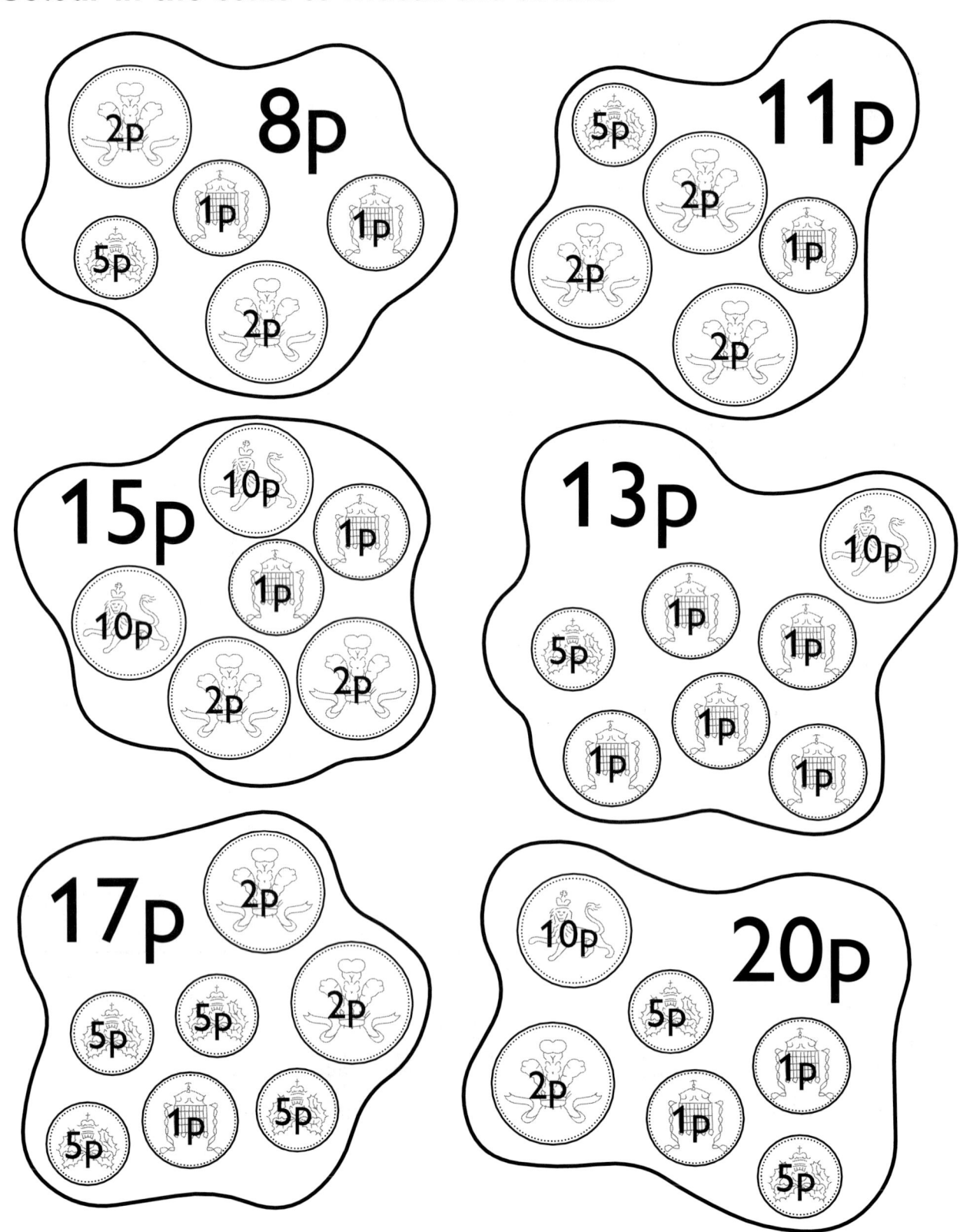

8p — 2p, 1p, 1p, 5p, 2p

11p — 5p, 2p, 2p, 1p, 2p

15p — 10p, 1p, 1p, 10p, 2p, 2p

13p — 10p, 1p, 1p, 5p, 1p, 1p

17p — 2p, 5p, 5p, 2p, 5p, 1p, 5p

20p — 10p, 5p, 2p, 1p, 1p, 5p

140

Homework 14

This week we are estimating and measuring masses of objects using non-standard units.

Same size, different mass

- Find 2 objects at home that are about the same size.
- Which one is heavier?
- Which one is lighter?

Draw them in the balance.

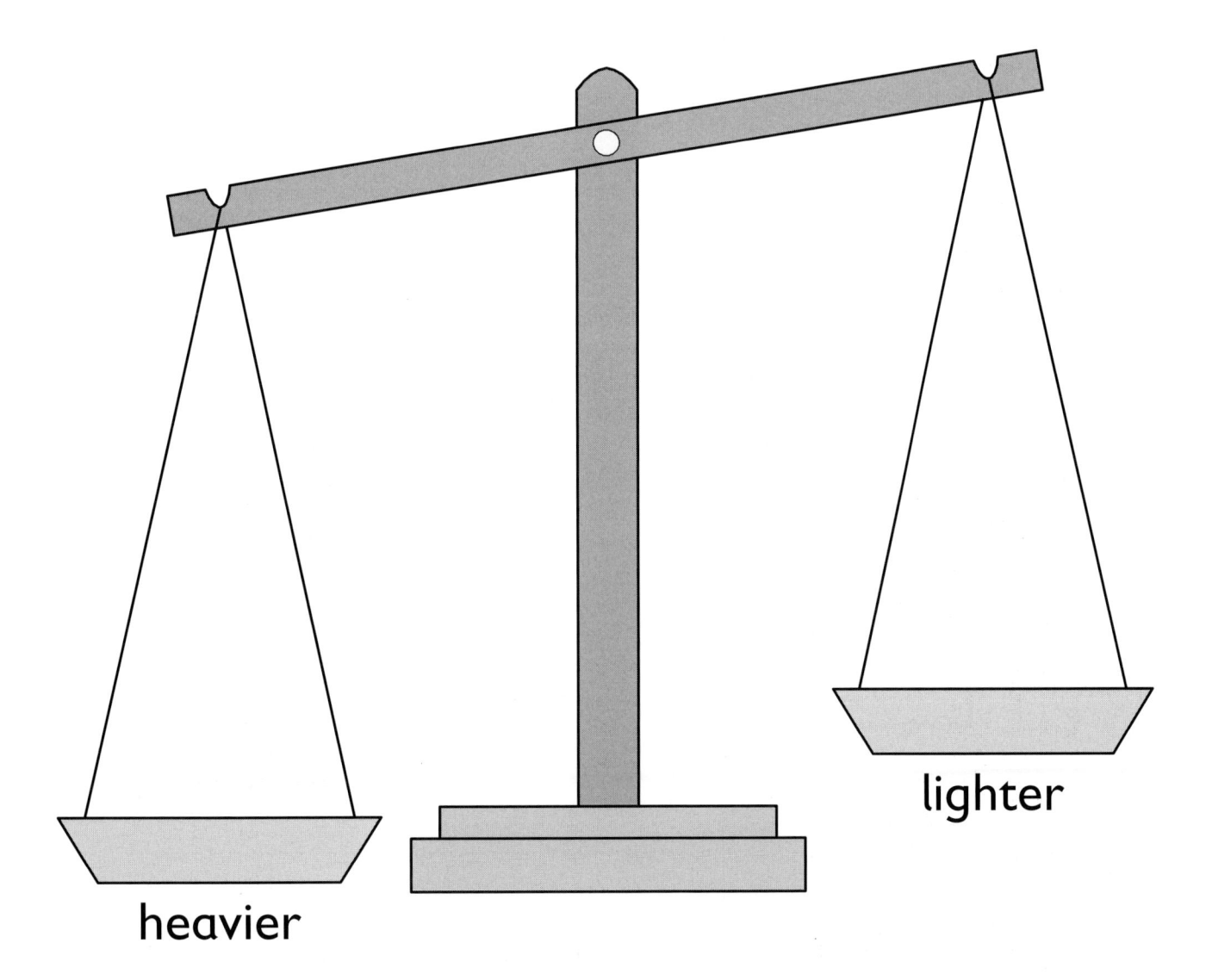

heavier

lighter

Homework 15

This week we are recognising 3D shapes.

Finding 3D shapes

Look around your home and find objects which are 3D shapes. Make a list.

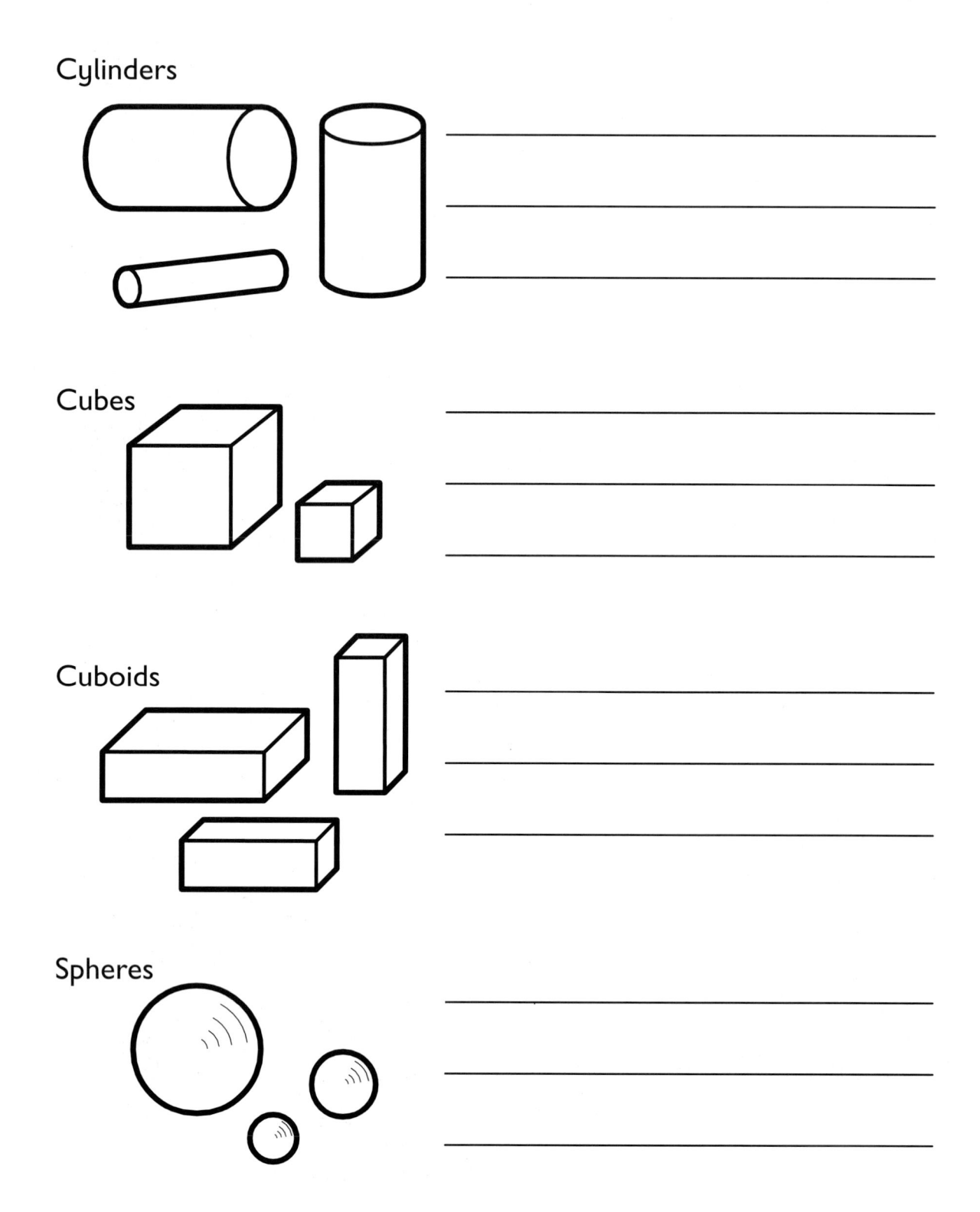

Cylinders

Cubes

Cuboids

Spheres

Homework 16

This week we are counting in different steps.

Counting in steps

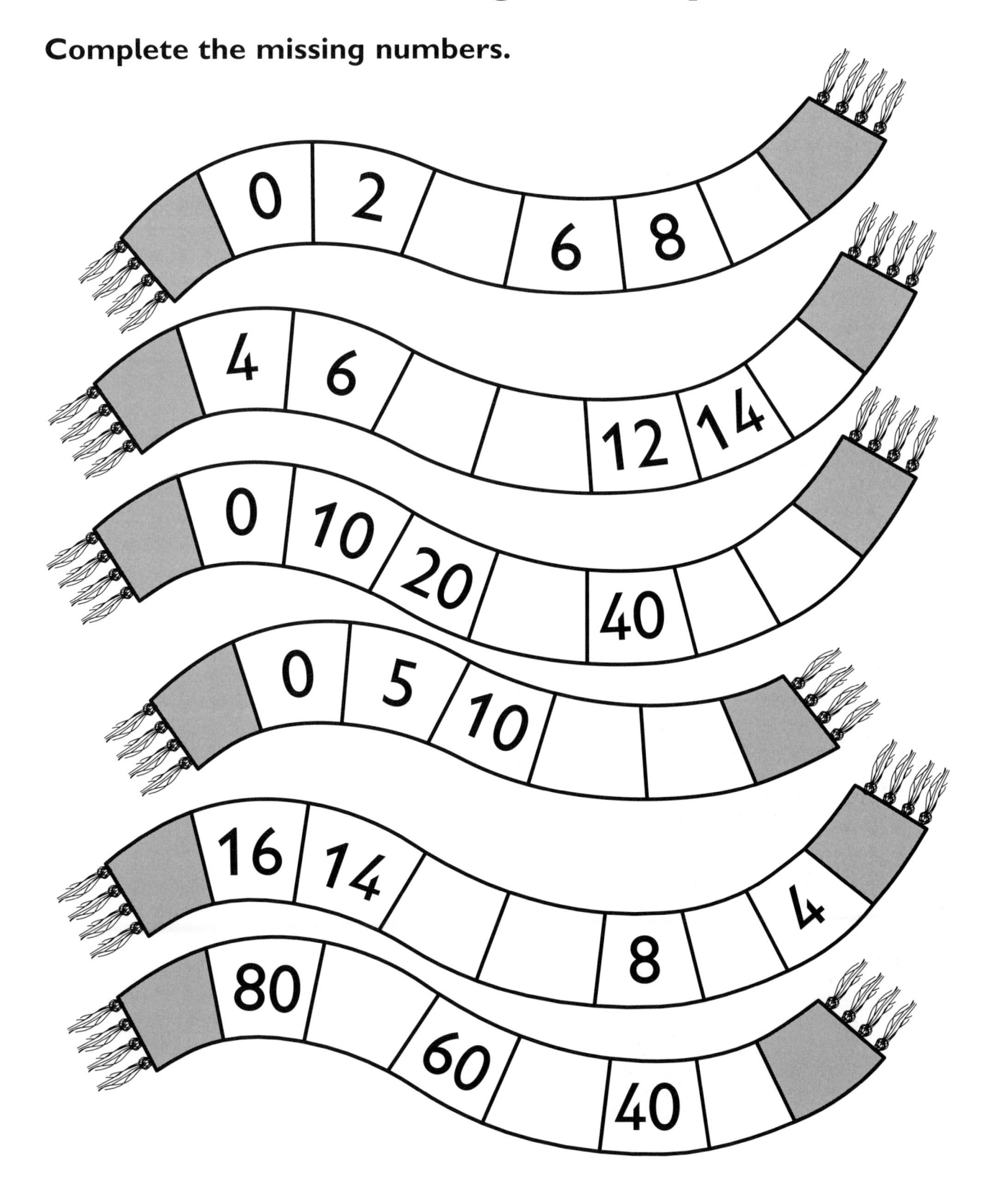

Complete the missing numbers.

0 2 __ __ 6 8 __

4 6 __ __ 12 14 __

0 10 20 __ 40 __

0 5 10 __ __

16 14 __ __ __ 8 __ 4

80 __ 60 __ 40 __

Homework 17

Estimating

This week we are estimating and counting objects up to 30.

Look at each picture for a few seconds.

Estimate the number of objects. Write it down.

Count the number of objects. Compare the two numbers.

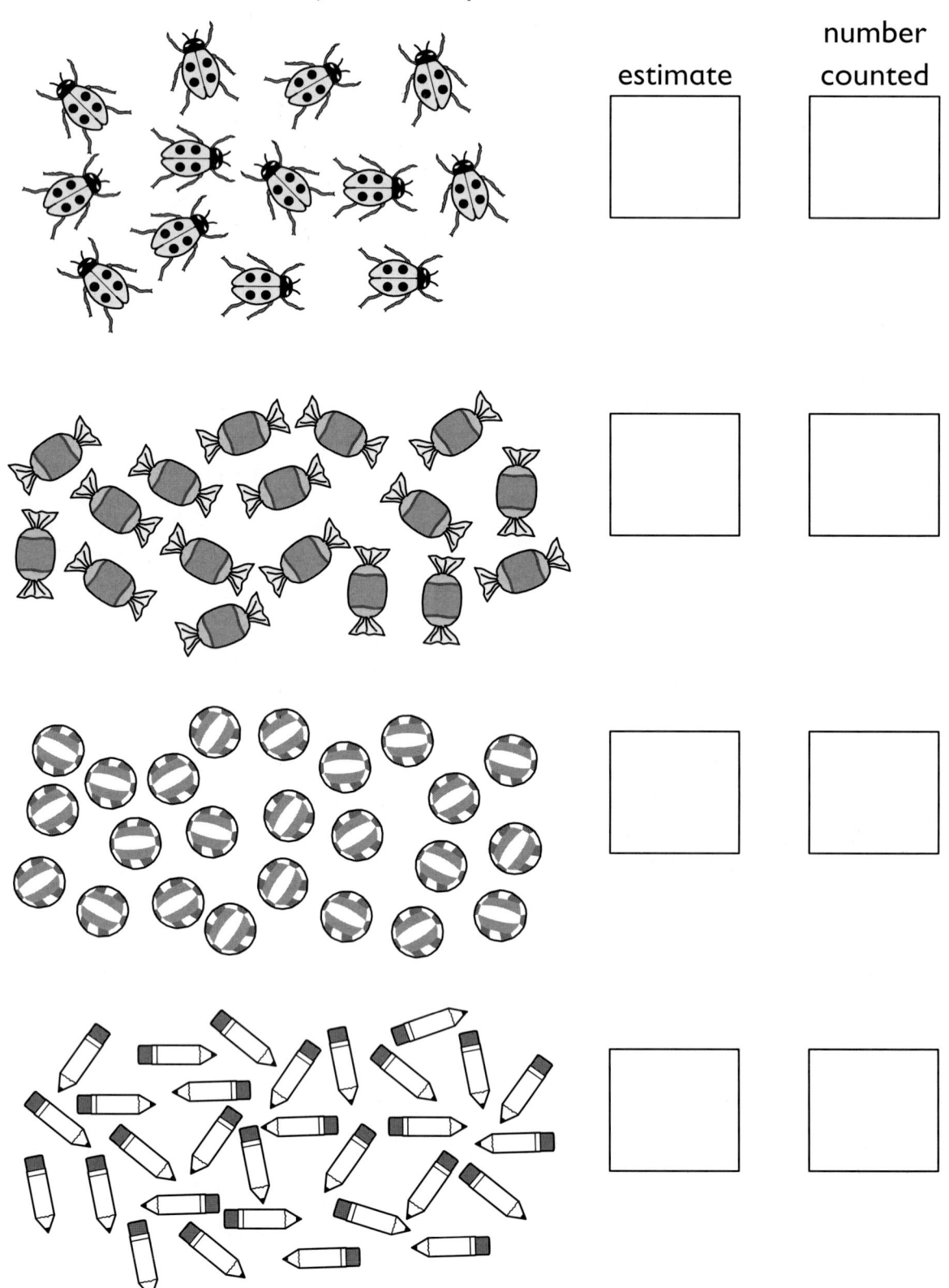

estimate | number counted

Homework 18

> This week we are finding totals and giving change.

Making 10p

- Find some coins.

- Draw round them to show different ways of making 10p.

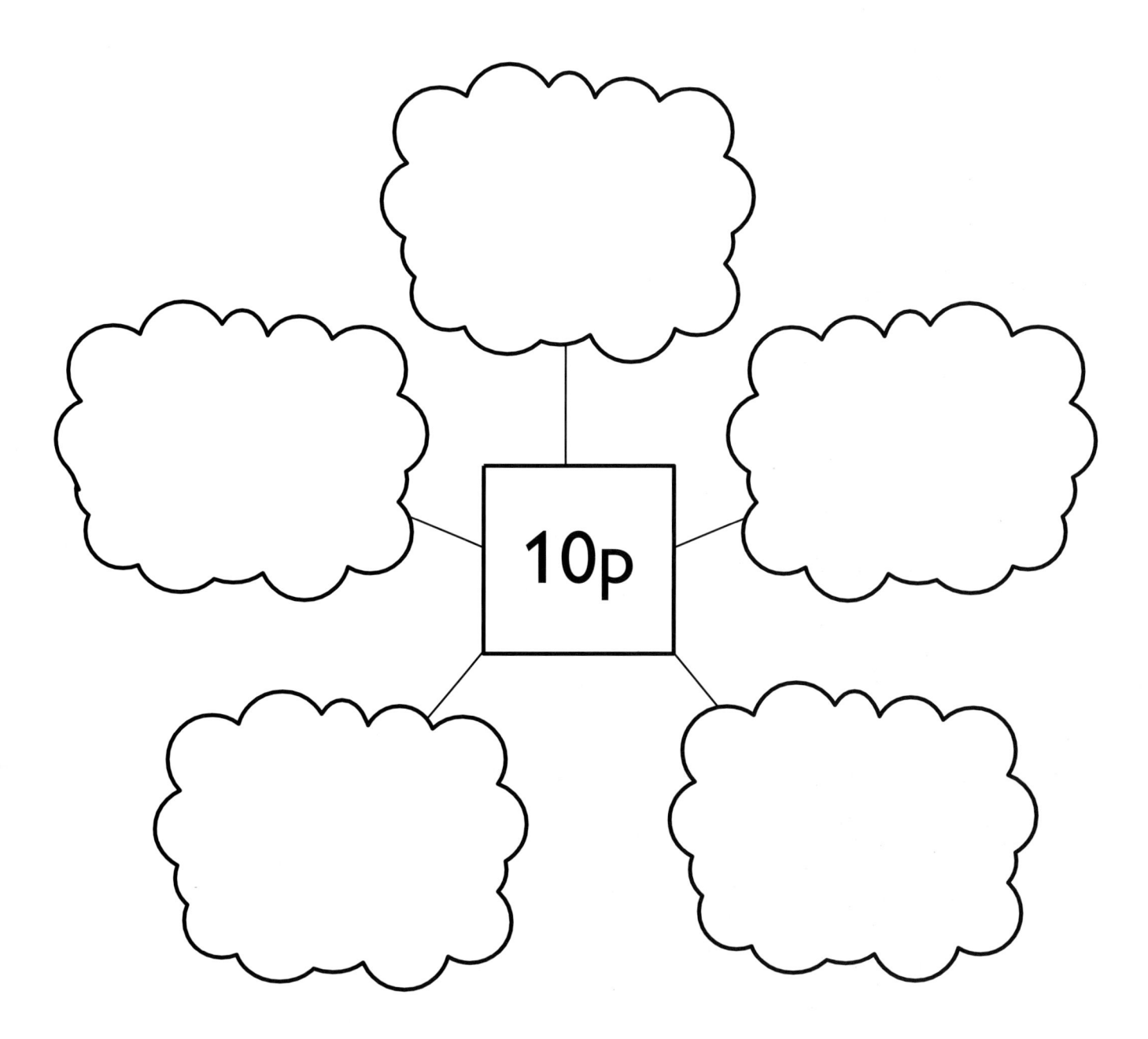

10p

Homework 19

> This week we have been measuring mass using a kilogram.

Kilogram hunt

- Look at home or in the supermarket for items that weigh one kilogram.

- It might be written as 1 kg

- Write your shopping list here.

Homework 20

This week we are sorting information into lists.

Making lists

Make a list of foods you like.

Make a list of foods you do not like.

Like	Do not like

Homework 21

> This week we are comparing the size of two numbers and identifying a number that lies between them.

Comparing numbers

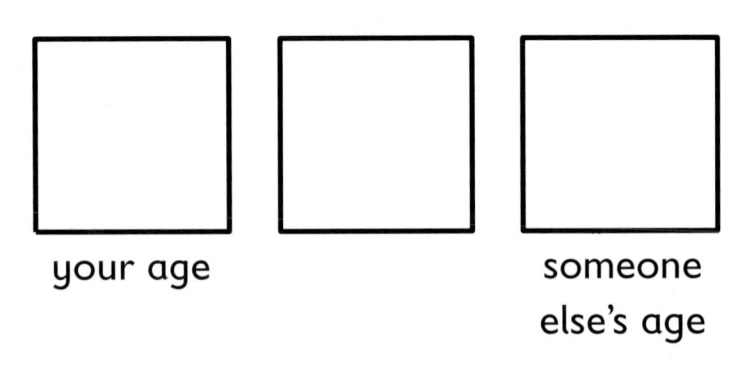

- Write down your age.
- Ask someone in your house their age and write it down.
- Now write a number that comes in between.

☐ ☐ ☐
your age   someone else's age

> Parents – ask your child to say which number in the set is the largest and smallest.

- Write down your house number.
- Write down your friend's house number.
- Now write a number that comes in between.

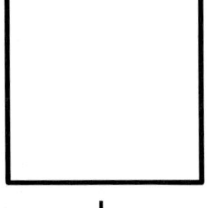

☐ ☐ ☐
your house number   your friend's house number

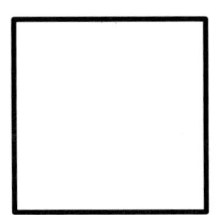

Homework 22

> This week we are using number facts to 10 to help solve other calculations.

In the bag

- Place 10 objects in a bag.

- Take out a handful and write the number.

- Count the objects left in the bag and add this number to the first number to make 10.

- Write this as a number sentence, e.g. *7 + 3 = 10*.

- Do this several times.

- Repeat the activity and write subtraction sentences.

- So 10 objects take away 6 leaves 4
  10 − 6 = 4.

Homework 23

Matching totals

Match the sets of coins to the prices.
Draw a line joining each set to the correct price.

This week we are finding totals to 20p and recognising coins of different values up to 20p.

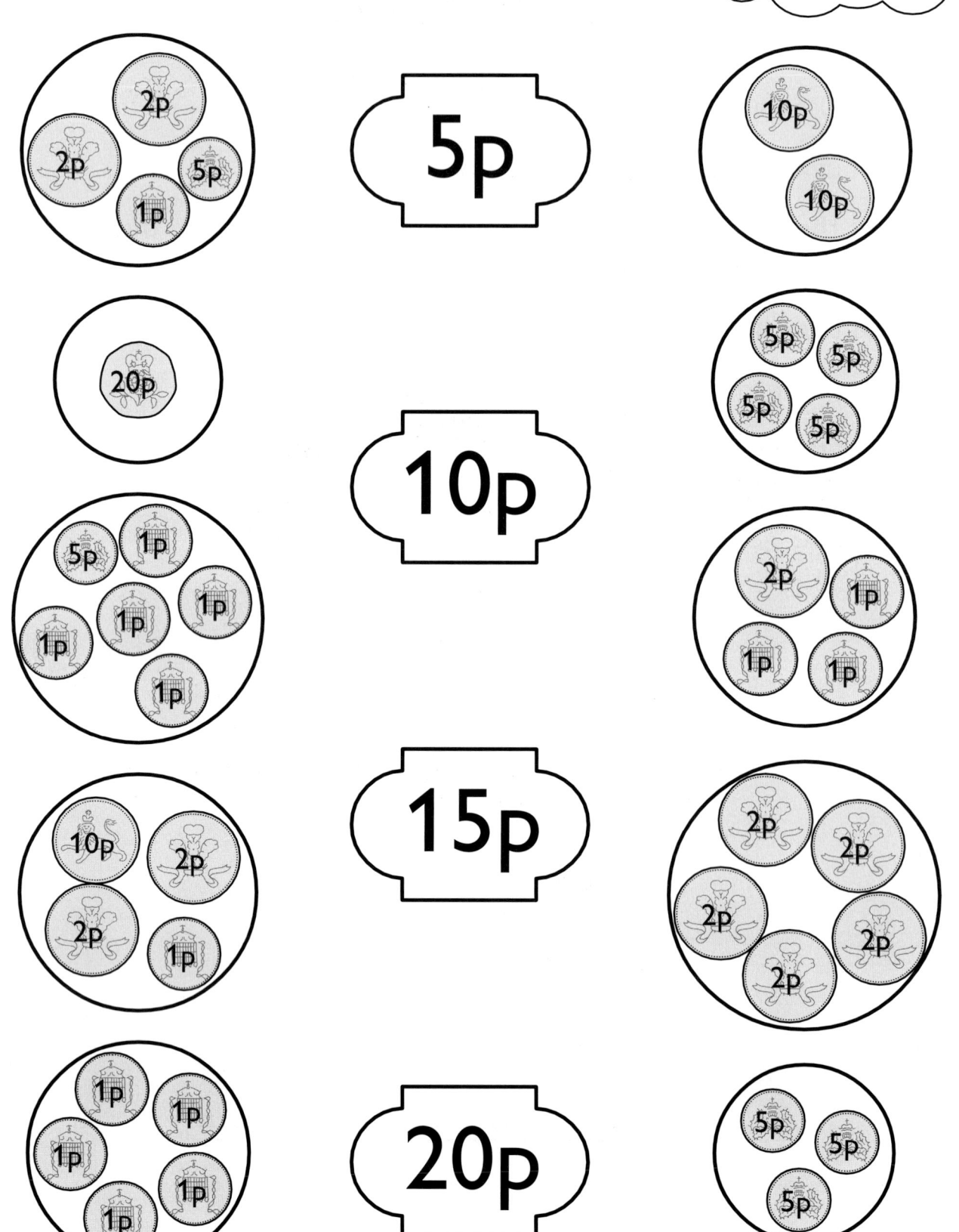

- 5p
- 10p
- 15p
- 20p

Homework 24

> This week we are comparing capacities of containers.

Cup hunt!

- Find a cup belonging to each member of your family.

- Which cup holds the most?

- Which cup holds the least?

Draw the cups in order from smallest to largest capacity.

Homework 25

This week we are looking at symmetrical shapes.

Line symmetry

Cut out the shapes below. Fold them in half. Draw a coloured line on the fold.

Homework 26

This week we are counting in patterns of odd and even numbers.

Odd and even

Join the odd or even numbers to make pictures.

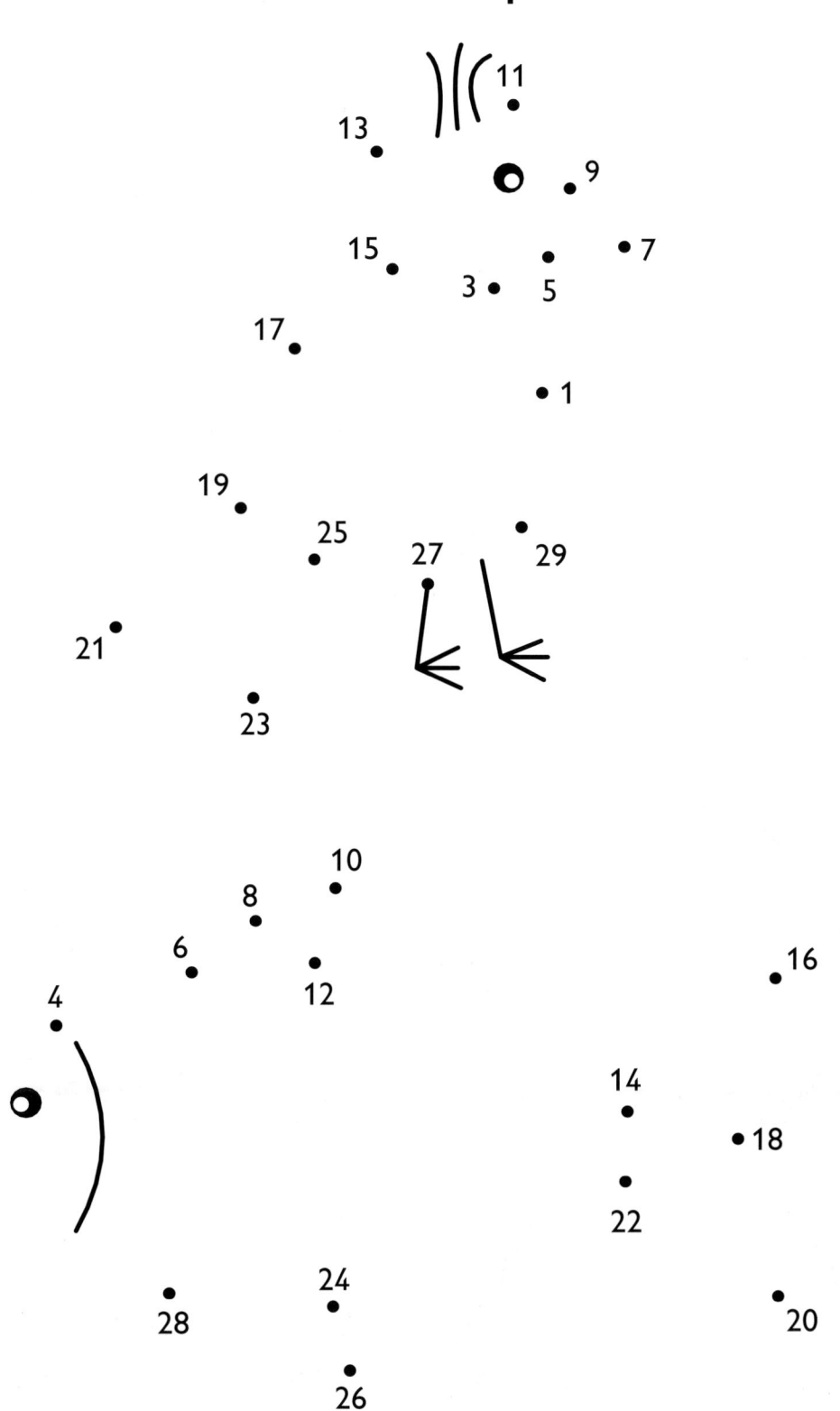

11
13
9
15
7
3   5
17
1
19
25
27   29
21
23

10
8
6
16
4
12
2
14
18
30
22
24
28
20
26

153

Homework 27

> This week we are adding 3 or more numbers.

Number plate hunt

R184 MSC

R493 FGH

- On your way home from school look for a car number plate with a 3-digit number.

C444 SDF

Y367 BFD

- Write down the three digits and add them together.

P456 SGT

A249 FHT

☐ + ☐ + ☐ = ☐

- Can you make any more number sentences using other number plates?

V663 BNM

F443 GFA

- What are the highest and lowest totals you can make?

N125 ERT

154

Homework 28

Solving problems

Use the numbers 1 to 20 and the symbols +, −, = to make number sentences with the answer 10.

Examples 13 − 3 = 10
2 + 8 = 10

This week we are choosing the appropriate number operations to solve problems.

Record your work here.

Homework 29

This week we are estimating and measuring the capacity of containers.

Look for a litre

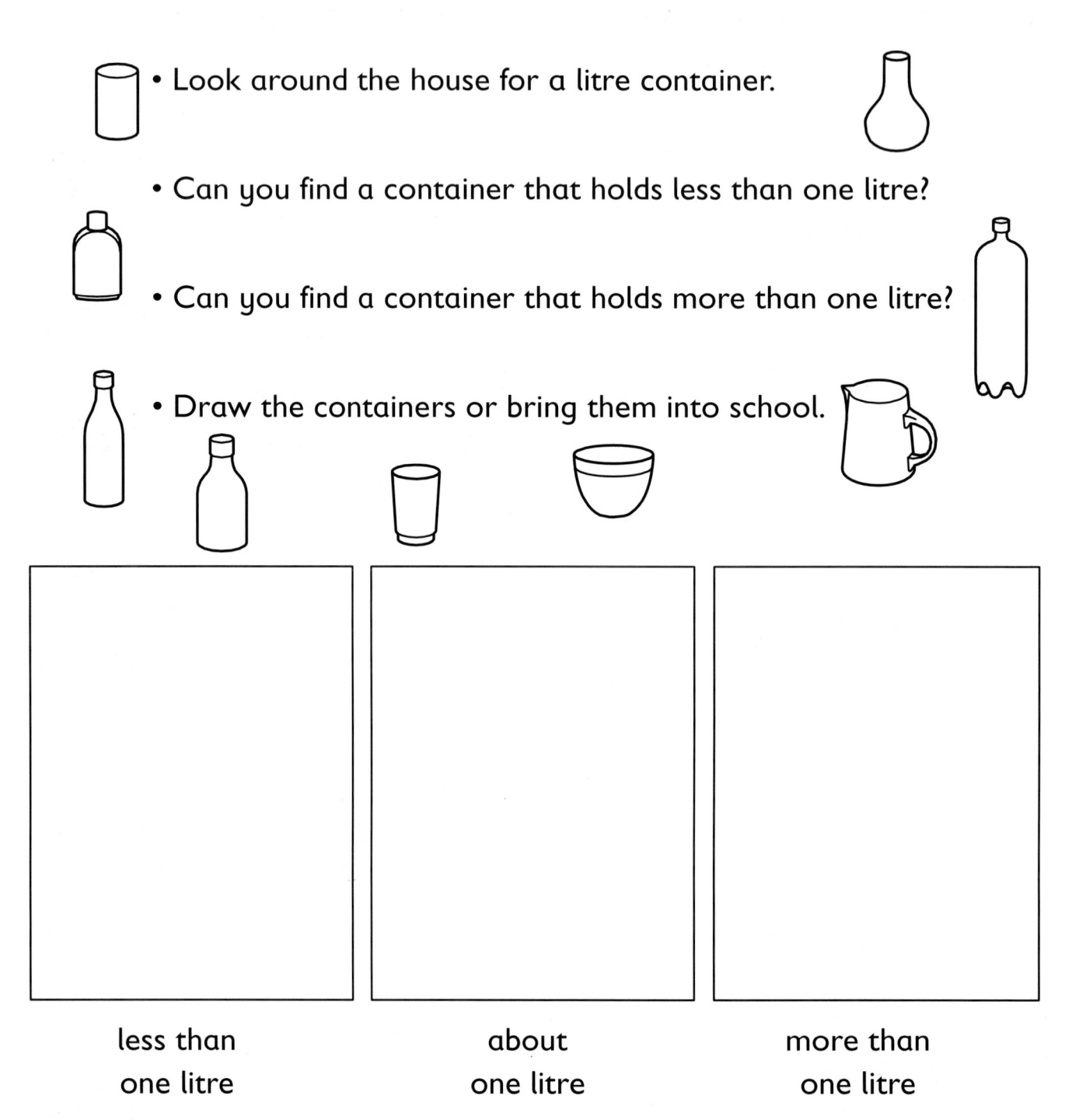

- Look around the house for a litre container.

- Can you find a container that holds less than one litre?

- Can you find a container that holds more than one litre?

- Draw the containers or bring them into school.

less than one litre	about one litre	more than one litre

Homework 30

This week we are reading time to half an hour on analogue clocks.

The time, the place

Draw a line between the event and the matching time.

Notes

Notes

Notes